T0342441

THIS

COLOSSAL

PROJECT

At the Deep Cut, south of Thorold, Ontario, 1914. A steam-powered clamshell shovel fills stoneboats pulled by mules while "navvies" ply shovels and picks on the bank of the Ship Canal channel. Modern machinery and traditional labour work alongside each other at the most difficult excavation site on the new waterway.

THIS
COLOSSAL
PROJECT

BUILDING THE
WELLAND SHIP
CANAL, 1913–1932

Roberta M. Styran and
Robert R. Taylor

McGill-Queen's University Press
Montreal & Kingston · London · Chicago

ISBN 978-0-7735-4790-2 (cloth)
ISBN 978-0-7735-4833-6 (ePDF)
ISBN 978-0-7735-4834-3 (ePUB)

Legal deposit fourth quarter 2016
Bibliothèque nationale du Québec

Printed in Canada on acid-free paper that is 100% ancient
forest free (100% post-consumer recycled), processed
chlorine free

McGill-Queen's University Press acknowledges the support
of the Canada Council for the Arts for our publishing
program. We also acknowledge the financial support of the
Government of Canada through the Canada Book Fund for
our publishing activities.

Library and Archives Canada Cataloguing in Publication

Styran, Roberta M, 1927–2015, author
This colossal project : building the Welland Ship Canal,
1913–1932 / Roberta M. Styran and Robert R. Taylor.

Successor to the authors' This great national object :
building the nineteenth-century Welland Canals, 2012.
Includes bibliographical references and index.
Issued in print and electronic formats.
ISBN 978-0-7735-4790-2 (hardback). – ISBN 978-0-7735-
4833-6 (PDF). – ISBN 978-0-7735-4834-3 (ePUB)

1. Welland Canal (Ont.) – History. 2. Canals – Ontario –
Niagara Peninsula – Design and construction – History.
I. Taylor, Robert R., 1939–, author II. Title.

HE401.W4S7938 2016   386'.470971338   C2016-903919-6
                                         C2016-903920-X

Set in 9.5/13 Baskerville 10 Pro with Aviano Slab
Book design & typesetting by Garet Markvoort, zijn digital

Contents

LIST OF ILLUSTRATIONS

ACKNOWLEDGMENTS

One of the great pleasures of research is the number of enthusiastic and helpful individuals – sometimes anonymous – whom one encounters. Here we acknowledge some of those who have assisted us over thirty years of work. But there are countless others, met casually in libraries and archives, over coffee in cafes, or on the banks of the great "ditch." Thanking the scores of individuals who have assisted us in our research would take several pages. A particular debt of gratitude, however, is owed to Donald G. Anger, Mike Bowden, John Burtniak, Liv Estrup, Alicia Ford, Dennis Gannon, Loris Gasparotto, Suzanne Hayes, the late Alun Hughes, Terry Hughes, Dana Johnson, Mike Johnson, Bridget Ker, William L. Lewis, Jane McLeod, the late Alex Ormston, Matt Onich, Stephen Otto, Robert Passfield, Carmela Patrias, Lynne Prunskus, Alfred Sagon-King, Robert Sears, Robert John Taylor, Wesley B. Turner, Edie Williams, and Sheila Wilson.

Special thanks are owed to Brian Osborne, professor emeritus at Queen's University, who earlier guided us through the pitfalls of publishing *The "Great Swivel Link": Canada's Welland Canal* (The Champlain Society, 2001) and to Arden Phair for his careful reading of our manuscript.

As well, we are indebted to the staffs of many other libraries, museums, and archives, including the James A. Gibson Library and the Niagara Collection at Brock University; the St Catharines Centennial Library (Special Collections); the St Catharines Museum; the St Lawrence Seaway Management Corporation (Niagara Region, St Catharines); the Welland Historical Museum; the Port Colborne Historical and Marine Museum; the Archives of Ontario (Toronto); and the Metropolitan Toronto Reference Library.

As will be clear from numerous references, we could not have proceeded without the aid of the staff of Library and Archives of Canada during the 1980s and '90s when we did most of the basic research. Without their guidance and cheerful help, this study could not have been completed.

Our research for this and our previous volume was supported by generous grants from the Social Sciences and Humanities Research Council. The advice and assistance of the staff of McGill-Queen's University Press, moreover, were invaluable. We are grateful to our editors, James MacNevin and Ryan Van Huijstee, and especially to our copy-editor, James Leahy, and to our indexer, Ruth Pincoe.

Every effort has been made to trace the ownership of all copyright material reprinted in the text. Any errors in this book remain our responsibility and will be corrected in subsequent editions.

A Canadian Conception:
A Canadian Achievement

When we first conceived the idea of chronicling the construction of the four Welland Canals, we planned to present the whole saga in one volume covering the years 1824 to 1973, but the men, machines, and challenges of the twentieth century burst the confines of one book, demanding a second volume. And so, in the first of our books, *This Great National Object: Building the Nineteenth-Century Welland Canals* (McGill-Queen's University Press, 2012), we described the construction of the first three Welland Canals between 1824 and 1881. The book in your hands – in effect, volume 2 of a two-volume study – tells the story of a still little appreciated chapter of twentieth-century Canadian enterprise and achievement. As in volume 1, we stress "the human element," the way in which engineers, contractors, and workers confronted manifold problems "on the ground" and created what is still one of Canada's most spectacular technological accomplishments. We stress that, more than was the case in the nineteenth-century Welland waterways, the construction expertise involved was mainly Canadian in origin.

Although not without difficulties, our research for volume 2 has been easier than was that for the first book because, with the exception of the era of the Third Canal's construction, graphic material was limited for volume 1. On the other hand, during the two decades when the Welland Ship Canal[1] was being built, the Department of Railways and Canals hired professional photographers to document the work. These talented men were: John George Williams, who worked 1912–17; James W. Jarrett, 1919–20; J.A. McDonald 1921–29; and, after 1929, J. Joy (fig. Pref.1).

Consequently, thousands of photographs recording both panoramas and details exist. These were made to assist the original construction engineers and contractors but still to help the St Lawrence Seaway en-

Pref.1 Somewhere on the Ship Canal construction site, November 1916.
Photographer John George Williams at work atop a scaffolding erected on
a flatcar of the construction railway. From such a vantage point, he and
his successors created an invaluable visual record of the building of the
great waterway.

gineers when problems arise or repairs are required. Moreover, maps,
diagrams, and plans are plentiful. These and the photographs are a
treasure trove for historians and canal buffs. We echo Richard White,
who, in describing the construction of the Grand Coulee Dam on
the Columbia River (1933–42), marvelled at the multiple perspectives
they provide:

> Each photograph is an artifact of the space between the camera
> and its object. Those taken from a distance emphasize the ab-
> stract geometric shapes of scaffolding, the linear surface of the
> cofferdam, the bulk of the great dam itself rising in the river, the
> more irregular shape of the Columbia's cliffs and bluffs. Photo-
> graphs of the middle distance reveal machines and actual con-
> struction. The machines lift and push and trundle earth and rock
> from one place and deposit it in another.

This tripartite division could apply to the precious inventory of pictures of the Ship Canal's construction. White adds, however, that "only in the close-ups do humans appear, and then they are everywhere. In these pictures men strain, lift and carry; they dangle from cliffs and from the dam itself, they perch on steel beams and climb scaffolds,"[2] but they never appear as individuals. So it is with the Department of Railways and Canals' photographic archive. Of course, the government cameramen were mandated to record the technology, problems, and progress of construction and not the travails of labourers. In our book, we have tried to provide images of the workers and devote two chapters to them, but the visual record remains limited.

For researchers working on the history of the early canals, many documents in hard copy or in microfilm exist, but transcribing mid-nineteenth-century handwriting was a constant challenge. Mercifully, by the time the Ship Canal was under construction, most records and correspondence were typewritten. Nevertheless, we found that one of our greatest "discoveries" – the diaries kept by the engineer in charge for most of the construction period, Alexander Grant, usually referred to as Alex – were in his own hand, written only as a personal record, not, of course, for the delight of historians. Deciphering his script has been a challenge, initially distressing, but ultimately rewarding, as will be obvious from the many times we have quoted him (fig. Pref.2). His daily entries tell us much – from the state of the weather and political events here and abroad to his social life and details of his travels, and always the vicissitudes of Ship Canal construction.

If the supply of documents concerning the first three Welland Canals was usually sufficient, the records of the Department of Railways and Canals in the early twentieth century are voluminous. Thousands of letters, contracts, and memoranda relating to the Ship Canal era await the historian. Both careful time management and judicious scanning are necessary. Ironically, however, the lack of a "paper trail" was still occasionally a problem, especially when verbal decisions made in meetings in Ottawa or St Catharines were inadequately recorded or when a telephone conversation was instrumental in changing practice "on the ground." For example, the only record – other than the entry in Grant's diary – of the decision to change from single-leaf to double-leaf lock gates is a pencilled note on a table of comparative estimates, indicating that the chief engineer of the Department of Railways and

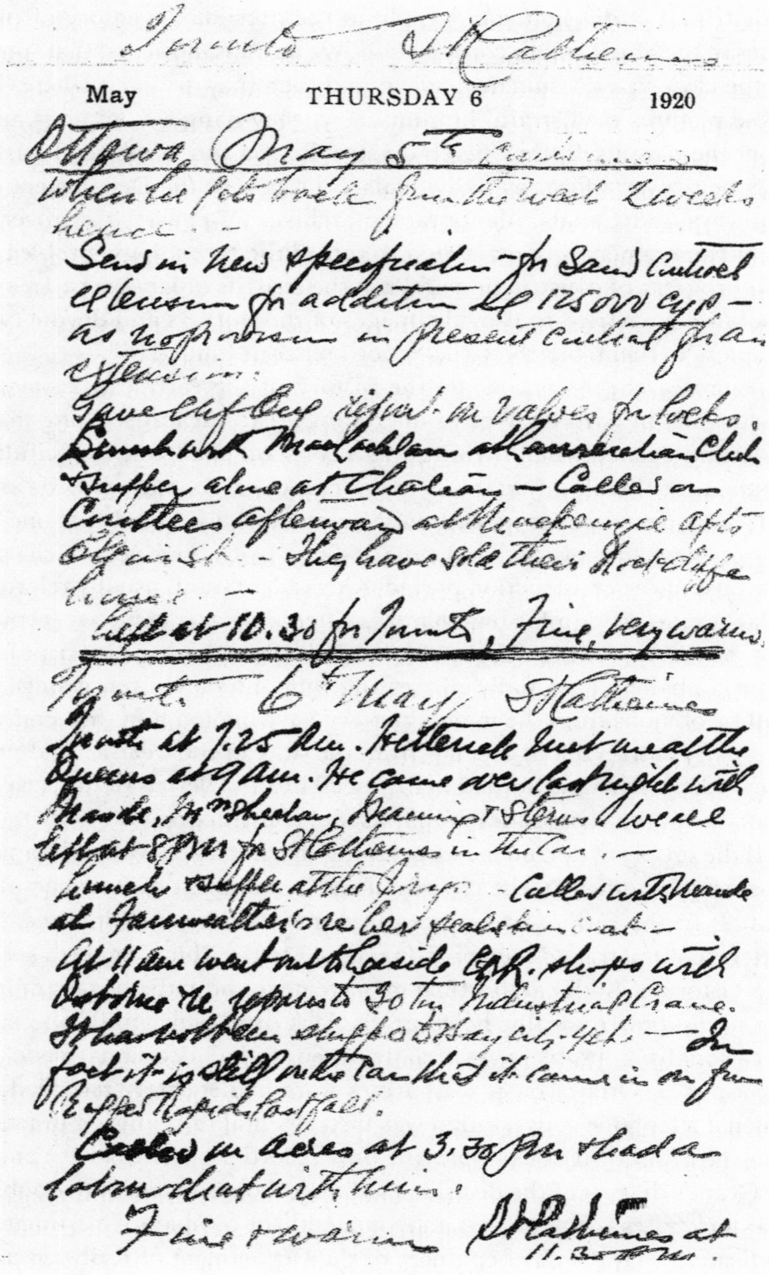

Pref.2 A page from engineer in charge Alex Grant's Diary, May 1920. A graphologist might note the firm, if impatient, hand of a perfectionist.

Canals had authorized the change orally in a meeting. Because this alteration was a major one, we are grateful for the survival of that note.

Later, we encountered another, completely unanticipated, problem. Up to 1936 the Department of Railways and Canals Records in Library and Archives Canada are an invaluable collection, well catalogued, with excellent finding aids to guide the historian, and we made good use of them. However, we were dismayed to find that, as far as the Archives is concerned, the chronicle of the Ship Canal after 1936 is a mystery. For in that year, Railways and Canals was folded into the newly created Department of Transport and, while many DOT records have been transferred to the Archives, they have not been catalogued and there are no handy finding aids. A similar situation was created when jurisdiction of the Welland Canal was assumed by the St Lawrence Seaway Authority in 1959; for the historian, the pertinent records transferred to the Archives remain impossible to locate.

Fortunately, the St Catharines office of the Seaway allowed us access to their files. From them we obtained much invaluable information for both the pre- and post-1936 periods and were able to make photocopies of many documents, now in the Niagara Collection at Brock University. Researchers should be aware of the fact, however, that many of the Seaway files have been sent off to the Archives, there to join their fellows in uncatalogued limbo. Other files have gone to the Seaway headquarters in Cornwall, Ontario.

One of the main resources for any study of the Welland Ship Canal is the magnificent work compiled by the British engineer Percy John Cowan, *The Welland Ship Canal between Lake Ontario and Lake Erie 1913–1932*. We have relied heavily on this volume, as have the engineers who have been, and are, responsible for the continued operation of the canal and for its repair and improvement. Major Cowan, MBE, had worked as an engineer for the Great Northern Railway in Britain, Egypt, and the United States. He visited the Ship Canal construction sites, consulted the engineers, and maintained a lengthy correspondence with Alex Grant, while writing a series of articles for the British journal *Engineering*. In 1935 the articles, with some additional material, were published in Cowan's book.

As in the writing of our first volume, we decided not to discuss in detail the political or financial aspects of the waterway's construction. Other historians, more knowledgeable in these fields, should step in here. To date, however, no chronicle of the construction – "on the ground" – of the Welland Ship Canal exists, a deficiency which we hope our book will help to remedy, while inspiring other historians to develop their own approaches.

When the Welland Ship Canal was inaugurated, Canadians were proudly aware of what they had achieved. The title of a booklet published by the federal Department of Railways and Canals on the occasion of the Ship Canal's official opening in 1932, *A Canadian Conception. A Canadian Achievement*,[3] encapsulates a growing self-confidence. In the 1920s, anglophone Canadians were developing a greater sense of their identity as a people and a pride in their accomplishments. Although some of this new self-awareness can be detected before the First World War, that conflict showed that Canadians could be loyal, equal allies of the Great Powers and effective warriors as in the Battle of Vimy Ridge in 1917 and in the "Hundred Days" in 1918. Canada's increased diplomatic stature was reflected in its independent role at the Paris Peace Conference of 1919, its achievement of a separate seat in the League of Nations, and later in the Statute of Westminster of 1931, through which Canada attained legislative independence from Great Britain. From 1925, moreover, construction proceeded on the Vimy Memorial to Canada's war dead. This phenomenon of growing Anglo-Canadian self-awareness and confidence was paralleled in the arts, as the Group of Seven painters sought to define and express "Canadian-ness" in their landscapes.

Equally important, the world was offered proof that Canadians were capable of great things in technological matters as well. Significantly, the formal opening of the Welland Ship Canal was postponed until it could be triumphantly displayed to the delegates to the Imperial Economic Conference in Ottawa in 1932. Although some suppliers and designers from the US and Britain had a role in the Fourth Canal's construction, the concept and the expertise came from Canadian universities, businesses, and industries, as is evident in the following chapters. Perhaps, therefore, events in technological history should take their place as indicators of Canada's development "from colony to nation." If the building of the Canadian Pacific Railway is considered a milestone in the evolution of nineteenth-century Canadian self-confidence and pride, the building of the Welland Ship Canal should take its place as further proof of growing national maturity.

One of the Very Few Great Ship Canals of the World

At least once a year, despite their distanced attitude to modern technology, a group of Amish from the United States – the men in beards and suspenders, the women in caps and long skirts – visit Lock 3 of the Welland Ship Canal, fascinated by the size of the locks and the channel and especially by the locking procedures. Like the other visitors to the Lock 3 Centre and Museum, they are impressed by the complexity of the site and the fact that the Welland Canal is a great man-made river connecting the two Great Lakes Erie and Ontario and is a vital part of the St Lawrence Seaway. They may or may not be aware that they are confronting what Robert Legget, Canada's foremost canal historian, called "one of the very few great ship canals of the world."[1]

We have already chronicled the saga of the construction of the previous three Welland Canals as the "great national object" of nineteenth-century engineers, contractors, and workers (fig. Intro.1). What may be less known is the remarkable national achievement embodied in the construction of the present waterway. We offer, therefore, this record of that two-decade saga, which resulted in a Canadian technological monument which still fascinates the public.

"AN ENORMOUS TRAFFIC IN EXISTENCE AND RAPIDLY GROWING"

As early as 1893 the talented Canadian engineer Thomas C. Keefer (1821–1915) wrote: "Notwithstanding the recent second enlargement of the Welland Canal (1871–1886), the conditions are worse now than they were in 1871."[2] The Niagara waterway, he implied, was simply too narrow and too shallow for the traffic it had to support. This situation had developed because the national economy had expanded, so

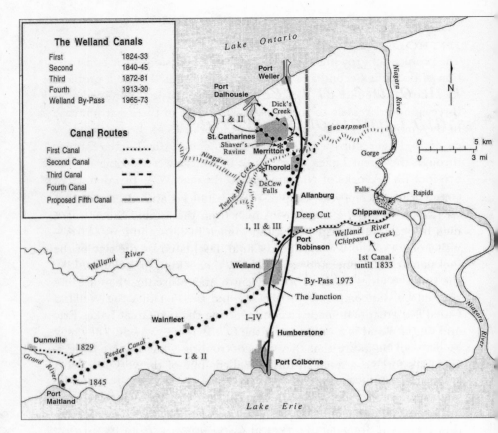

Intro.1   Map of the Welland Canals

that by 1900 Canadian production of wheat, lumber, and mineral ores was booming. In particular, due to increased immigration and settlement and the spread of cultivation on the prairies, the western grain crop had burgeoned. New railway lines – the National Transcontinental and the Canadian Northern – were constructed, supplementing the Canadian Pacific. Consequently, in one year alone, 1906–07, the amount of freight passing through the Welland from western ports nearly doubled – from 479,422 to 789,167 tons.[3] In 1912 the writer of a Department of Railways and Canals memorandum remarked on the "enormous traffic in existence and rapidly growing."[4]

"Taxed to the utmost"

The problem of growing ship size which had occasioned the construction of both the Second and Third Canals continued to be a problem (fig. Intro.2). By 1891 the Welland's narrow dimensions confined over three hundred vessels to the upper lakes.[5] Due to the great increase in the amount of grain arriving from the prairies at the lakehead by ca. 1900, larger ships were being built to convey the bigger cargoes through the Great Lakes. These bulk freighters were too big for the 270-foot (81 m) locks of Niagara's canal. In 1920 W.A. Bowden, chief engineer of the Department of Railways and Canals, estimated that 80 per cent of lake vessels could not navigate the Third Canal. Not only were the locks too small but, at the aqueduct which carried the waterway over Chippawa Creek (the Welland River), even slight fluctuations in water level caused ships' hulls to scrape bottom.[6] And so, the traditional "dialectical" relationship between growing ship sizes and the width and depth of operating locks continued to prevail in the early twentieth century.

With the mounting volume of traffic, ships' captains found that the Welland's channel was too narrow and its locks too small. The British engineer P.J. Cowan believed that such increases would ultimately create a situation in which the canal would "be taxed to the utmost."[7] Collisions of ships with lock gates and walls, or with bridge abutments, are richly documented from ca. 1900 into the late 1920s, when they increased dramatically. Typical was a 1905 note from John Laing Weller (1862–1932), superintending engineer of the Third (operating) Canal, to the Department of Railways and Canals in Ottawa, describing how the picturesquely named HIAWATHA had rammed the head gates of Lock 1 causing $1,023.56 worth of damage and delaying navigation.[8] Such problems became endemic. For example, in 1911 ships carried away three pairs of gates at Thorold and in 1912 four similar accidents occurred. Matters had not improved by 1925, when the chief engineer reported that in July the GLENCASSIE collided with one of the gates at Lock 11, causing such damage as to delay the further operation of the lock for eleven hours. In October the POPLAR BAY, laden with wheat, struck and dislodged the lower gate of Lock 10. The rush of water which ensued also carried out the upper gates and damaged the canal banks farther down the reach.[9]

Intro.2 Port Dalhousie Harbour, 1928. Overcrowding at the Third Canal's northern terminus illustrates the need for a wider, deeper waterway.

The authorities tackled the problem of the Welland's size in several ways, each being only a temporary solution. At Port Colborne ships could unload their cargoes onto lighters (smaller ships) to transit the canal or into the freight cars of the Grand Trunk Railway, formerly the Welland Railway, which ran north to Port Dalhousie. There, larger ships picked up cargoes for shipment to Lake Ontario ports or the St Lawrence system. In extreme cases vessels were cut in two so that they could pass through the canal. For example, in 1917 twenty of these long ships were partly dismantled in order to get them through the obsolete Welland.[10]

Another long-standing challenge to the canal was the problem of competition from south of the border. Because of the Welland's inadequacy, much Canadian grain was being sent to American ports on Lake Erie and thence by rail to New York City. An even worse threat

loomed, for by 1905 the Americans were planning to deepen the Erie
Barge Canal to thirty feet (9.1 m). For the next twenty years some form
of this challenge was never absent. For example, in 1919 the United
States Army Engineers, under Col. J.G. Warren, completed a report on
a projected ship canal connecting the two lakes between the Niagara
River and Lockport on the Erie Canal and Ollcott on Lake Ontario.

PRIVATE AND PUBLIC PRESSURE TO REBUILD

Various experts urged improvement of both the Welland and the St
Lawrence canals. From the 1890s various official commissions and
private associations – both Canadian and American – recommended
deepening the waterways connecting the Great Lakes and the Atlantic
(Appendix v). Eventually, Ottawa reacted. In 1903 the federal government set up a Royal Commission on Transportation to study these
problems, especially the issue of how to expedite grain shipment. The
commissioners reported in 1905, recommending improvement of the
Lake Huron ports of Midland and Depot Harbour, from which rail
lines connected to Montreal. They also urged the speedy completion
of the new grain elevator at Port Colborne and other improvements
to that harbour. Their most important suggestion, however, was the
enlargement and deepening of the Welland to the size of the Sault
Ste Marie Canal, which had been completed in 1895 with a lock depth
of 20 feet (6.1 m) and dimensions of 900 by 60 feet (274.3 by 18.3 m).
This would end the discharging and lightering of surplus cargoes at
Port Colborne.

Meanwhile, ship owners and businessmen were among the most
vigorous of those making their voices heard. Beginning in late 1906
boards of trade started to request enlargement of the Welland. From
Halifax to Vancouver petitions for reconstruction inundated the Department of Railways and Canals. Locally, in 1910 both the St Catharines and the Thorold boards of trade petitioned Minister of Railways and Canals George P. Graham (1859–1943) for enlargement. The
Dominion Marine Association and the Grain Produce Exchange of
Winnipeg also sent resolutions to Ottawa. The Great Lakes and St
Lawrence Improvement Association, formed in 1909, met with Prime
Minister Wilfrid Laurier (1841–1919), one of whose campaign promises
in 1911 was to reconstruct the Welland.

A GEORGIAN BAY CANAL?

A rival project, however, also commanded attention. The Georgian Bay Canal project, which had first emerged sixty years before, still had supporters. This waterway would have connected Georgian Bay on Lake Huron via the French River and Lake Nipissing with the Ottawa River and would have involved further canalization of the latter watercourse. The project had many supporters. In 1912 the *Ottawa Citizen*, for example, opined that "enlarging the Welland Canal will benefit only Oswego and Ogdensburg."[11] Aware of the economic benefits to the nation's capital and other communities along that route, the *Citizen* was a natural supporter of the Georgian Bay Canal.

This line, examined by engineers in the 1850s, would provide a more direct, deep waterway between Montreal and the larger Great Lakes, cutting in half the distance between the St Lawrence and Lake Huron on an entirely Canadian route, remote from the American border. The Department of Public Works favoured it and Parliament voted appropriations for several surveys which, when submitted in 1909, recommended a 22-foot (6.7 m), 440-mile (708.1 km) waterway with 27 locks, costing $100 million (over $21 billion in 2015 values). As the second decade of the twentieth century dawned, therefore, the Georgian Bay Canal seemed a real possibility and the decline of the Welland likely.

This northern line, however, would have involved much blasting through pre-Cambrian granite, ships' travel time would be lengthy, and construction was estimated to take twice as long as that for a new Welland. Remote from populated and industrial centres, the hard rock of the Canadian Shield would be expensive to excavate. The Grand Trunk Railway between Midland on Georgian Bay, Belleville on Lake Ontario, and Montreal, offered significant competition. The many locks which would have to be built and the connecting river courses following circuitous routes would make the voyage long and potentially hazardous, raising insurance rates for vessel owners. Furthermore, this route, because farther north, would have a shorter shipping season than the Welland.[12] For these reasons some businessmen were not keen on the northern line. For example, in 1914 a journalist asked shipowner Charles W. Young of Cornwall, "What about the Georgian Bay Canal?" to which Young replied that it was "not at all practical"; the route had not enough of a water supply, he said, and in addition was subject to a "dense fog which hangs on there for weeks at a time."[13]

On the other hand, the Niagara route had the advantages of drawing both American and Canadian trade into lakes Erie and Ontario and down the St Lawrence. It served Canadian ports on Lake Erie and southern Lake Huron which would face impoverishment if coal and iron ceased to pass through them. Moreover, by the early 1900s the St Lawrence system had been deepened to 14 feet (4.3 m) and improvements were being made to Port Colborne's harbour. Expert opinion estimated that rebuilding the Welland would be cheaper than a northern route and would take only five years. When Laurier, who had become more supportive of a Georgian Bay line, went down to defeat in the election of 1911, the northern scheme lost an important ally. His successor, Conservative Robert Borden (1854–1937), opted to improve the existing Welland Canal.

THE PROJECT COMMENCES

John Weller, while superintending the operation of the Third Canal, began quietly preparing for what was to be termed "the Welland Ship Canal" – the Fourth Welland Canal. Beginning in 1905, surveys were started, first to determine the right-of-way for a new canal in Niagara and then to determine the best route across the peninsula. He also prepared plans for the required locks and ancillary structures. As of 1 January 1912 he was appointed engineer in charge of the Ship Canal's construction, a position he retained until construction was halted in March 1917. Upon resumption of construction at the beginning of 1919, Alex Grant was appointed engineer in charge. When the first shovelful of earth was lifted in the fall of 1913, a start was made on what would absorb both public attention and public funds for nearly twenty years – and this despite war, depression, and massive social changes.

The sections of the new channel from Lake Ontario to Thorold were the first to be placed under contract. In spite of the outbreak of the Great War in 1914, work continued until the spring of 1917, when shortage of material and labour necessitated the suspension of work until 1919. Then, as thousands of veterans returned from Europe, Ottawa sought to find employment for them in peacetime jobs, and so construction on the canal resumed in that year. The original contractors were engaged on a cost-plus basis. This system proved untenable and was eventually abandoned in favour of the unit-price system. Meanwhile, work between Thorold and Port Colborne continued steadily.

By 1927 an army of nearly four thousand "navvies" was at work on and above the slopes of the great ditch. The waterway was opened to navigation in 1930 but the formal inauguration was postponed until 1932.

Thousands of tonnes of earth and rock had to be dredged, excavated, and blasted, but construction of the locks was the most sophisticated and demanding of the whole enterprise. They would each be over three times as long as those of the Third Canal, nearly twice as wide, and would raise ships 46½ feet (14.02 m) instead of 12 feet (3.65 m) (fig. 5.1). The Niagara Escarpment would be tackled by a remarkable set of three twin locks. Giant steel lock gates had to be manufactured and installed. These gates and the valves of the locks were to be operated by electricity, provided by a flume supplying a powerhouse at the foot of the flight locks (fig. 6.13).

Overcoming these challenges and working with this sophisticated plant was expensive. In 1912 Engineer in Charge John Weller estimated that the new canal would cost $43 million to build. His superior, Chief Engineer Bowden, soon raised that figure to $60 million. By the time of its completion in 1932, war, inflation, and economic crises had elevated the cost to $132 million ($2.25 billion in 2015 values).

Unlike the construction of the first three Welland Canals, the Fourth Canal was built largely with Canadian expertise. The previous three Wellands had been the work of engineers and contractors from Britain and the United States, as well as from Canada. By 1913, when construction began on a new Welland Canal, however, most of the engineers and contractors had been born and educated in Canada and had been professionally active here, making the Ship Canal a great Canadian achievement, perhaps the most impressive of the twentieth century.

Building the new waterway would involve challenges, innovations, accomplishments, and disasters for these Canadian builders. Accordingly, our first two chapters describe the constraints and obstacles faced by the engineers and contractors.

THIS

COLOSSAL

PROJECT

CHAPTER ONE

This Colossal Project

'Tis a mighty undertaking
Is the Welland Ship Canal ...
In this colossal project
The risks to life are great
And many brawny sons of toil
Were hurled to their fate.

These words were penned by William M. McClure, who had worked on the building of the twentieth-century Welland Canal as a blacksmith.[1] They give us a rare view of a labourer's reaction to the great scope and the sometimes-fatal dangers involved in its construction – two themes which will be prominent throughout this volume.

Between 1913 and 1932, the "colossal" reconstruction of Niagara's waterway took place in a complex modernizing country in a sophisticated but troubled civilization. On the other hand, when William Hamilton Merritt and his engineers and contractors were building the first Niagara waterway, 1824–33 (fig. Intro.1), their work was relatively isolated in a still largely forested colony, remote from bustling New England and imperial Britain. The Welland Canal Company operated in a semi-wilderness, marked by First Nations trails and villages and by a few struggling farms recently carved out of the woods by United Empire Loyalists. The complicated transportation and communication networks of the twentieth century were unimaginable to them.

Moreover, the builders of the Ship Canal worked in a context of tumultuous Canadian, North American, and world events. This waterway was constructed in the most expansive and the most crisis-ridden period of Canada's history up to that time. Its builders found themselves constrained and motivated by several forces originating beyond the construction site, beyond Niagara, and indeed hundreds and thousands of kilometres away. This chapter outlines how factors such as a European war and international economic fluctuations affected the building of the new canal. Chapter 2 deals with local, Niagara-based problems.

BOOM YEAR BEGINNINGS

In 1867, the Dominion of Canada had been created, comprising the provinces of New Brunswick, Nova Scotia, and Canada West and Canada East, which became Ontario and Quebec. In the early years of the last century, the young Dominion was expanding geographically as well as economically while a confident, exhilarating nationalism was in the air. The Ship Canal's mainly Canadian engineers and contractors began their work during this era of optimism and prosperity.

Development of the west and the stimulation of an east-west economy were now paramount in the minds of central Canadian political and business leaders. Gold had been discovered in the Yukon while northern Ontario was revealed to harbour great resources of nickel, silver, gold, and copper. The forests of British Columbia would yield timber for railways and new construction on the prairies. In the years 1875–1910, Canada entered the "Second Industrial Revolution," an era marked by technological innovation, including the mass production of cheap steel, electrification, and the development of scientific chemistry. Between 1897 and 1907, Canada's average annual industrial growth was 8.02 per cent, greater than that of the US or Britain.[2] At the same time, a torrent of immigrants poured into the country, especially to the prairie wheatlands, where they boosted the production of grain for export and provided a new domestic market for the manufacturing industries of the east. In response to this "wheat boom," the provinces of Alberta and Saskatchewan were created in 1905. (Manitoba had entered Confederation in 1870; British Columbia in 1871.) In this atmosphere of economic and technological progress the concept of a new Welland Canal was born.

These new economic and political realities demanded the expansion of transportation facilities. Ottawa subsidized the creation of branch lines for the Canadian Pacific Railway and two more transcontinental railways were envisioned. But artificial waterways also demanded consideration, for they seemed to be modern ways to facilitate efficient transportation and trade. For example, in Germany the Kiel Canal was opened in 1895 and the years 1887–94 saw the construction of the

Manchester Ship Canal in England. The completion of the Panama Canal in 1913 provided an American example of imaginative and successful waterway-building. Likewise, in Canada, man-made water channels were being developed or improved. The canal at Sault Ste Marie was refurbished in 1895. The Soulanges Canal in Quebec was opened in 1899. Seeking to expedite commerce between lakes Ontario and Huron, both the federal and the provincial governments propelled the Trent-Severn Canal connecting Trenton on Lake Ontario to Port Severn on Lake Huron to completion in 1907. At this time, moreover, both Canadian and American financial experts and businessmen were urging an improvement of the whole St Lawrence system, which eventually ensued, with the federal government's support.

THE GREAT WAR 1914–1918

In this heady atmosphere, the building of the Welland Ship Canal had got off to a healthy start in 1913. The good times, however, did not last. The Canadian economic boom subsided and in 1914 the Great War (the First World War) broke out. That conflict, which was not supposed to last more than a few months, would drag on for over four years. Construction of the Ship Canal, therefore, was constrained by Canada's involvement in a devastating foreign war. Work on the waterway stopped in 1917 and did not resume until 1919. In his *Annual Report for 1914–15*, Engineer in Charge Weller wrote that Sections 1 and 2 were already about six months behind schedule and that Section 3 was a year behind. The demands of a war economy were causing shortages of men, equipment, and materials. In that same report he noted that several timekeepers, rodmen, and instrumentmen were already "on the firing line" with the Canadian Force in France.[3] Even common labour was becoming hard to find. In 1914 as many as 2,600 men had been employed, a figure which was reduced to 2,000 by 1916.[4] In November of that year Weller was complaining about the "unprecedented labour conditions."[5] Not only men, but machines, too, left the site: in 1917 thirteen locomotives from Section 2 were sent to the battlefields of Europe.

In 1914, Prime Minister Borden had decided to maintain the country's great capital projects such as the Ship Canal during the war. However, as the conflict showed no signs of ending, as economic conditions worsened, and as a fuel shortage loomed, the Department of

Railways and Canals decided in November 1916 to close down construction of the new waterway. In January 1917 notices were sent to all contractors to cease operations by the end of March; the engineers and office staff were to be let go by 30 April. When operations were suspended, construction of several bridges was under way, the construction railway had been laid out, some watertight embankments had been installed, and the diversion of the Grand Trunk Railway at Twin Locks 4 had been built. The locks and other concrete structures were still unfinished, as was much of the excavation of the new prism, especially south of Thorold.[6] Only maintenance work, however, was to be carried on until the end of the European conflict. In Ottawa Chief Engineer William Bowden reported to the Minister of Railways and Canals that the project would survive the suspension, although "the general appearance of the work is no doubt very depressing to a casual observer."[7]

Halting a project scarcely begun deeply troubled John Weller, who was understandably concerned with its future, the fate of his office staff, and his own career. He was under considerable pressure from contractors and office employees to mitigate the effect of an abrupt and total stoppage. It was impractical for contractors simply to stop work, he knew, if only because they often shared facilities and equipment such as the construction railway. Canadian Dredging Co. Ltd, a major contractor, informed him that they would not be responsible for slides or water damage which might occur during the work's cessation. Sectional engineers declared that they could not shut down the work on such short notice and begged to retain a few men at least temporarily as a skeleton staff. E.G. Cameron, for example, told Weller that if all his men were dismissed by 30 April, the records on Section 3 would be left in "an incomplete and unsatisfactory condition."[8]

Weller wrote several pointed letters and memoranda to Chief Engineer William Bowden, outlining such problems. He recommended that certain work, such as at Lock 1, be completed in the spring of 1917 in order to avoid expensive problems when construction resumed. Never one to mince words with his superiors, Weller wrote to Bowden in March 1917: "You are no doubt aware that to leave a proper record of over $10,000,000 worth of partly finished work cannot be done properly on short notice." While he assured Bowden that the work would be suspended "in a businesslike manner," he noted the unrest among his office staff, fearing he could lose "several of those who are essential for the proper completion of the records." A month later, Weller sounded almost distraught as he again wrote to Bowden that "the Department is not justified in ruthlessly discharging all the staff, including those whose special knowledge of the work is of such extreme value to its successful completion." He feared the "disastrous" and "chaotic" consequences of a complete shutdown, envisaging with horror the prospect of being "reduced to using Italians,"[9] and begged that he be allowed to retain the engineers W.H. Sullivan (1871–1941), Cameron, and several other engineers he found valuable to the Department. Bowden, however, had his own superiors to consider and ordered Weller to dismiss the office staff by 30 April. The chief engineer did compromise on Sullivan, who eventually was put in charge of completing the records of construction. In the end, Weller was able to retain a small staff, including Cameron, until matters could be effectively wrapped up. As for the engineer in charge himself, he was laid off with six months' salary on 30 April 1917.[10]

The fact that the war caused shortages of labour and materials is clear. What is less obvious is the consequence of allowing the works to remain idle for nearly two years. Watchmen and caretakers were employed during the shutdown but they could not prevent deterioration of the work sites. For example, much of the new harbour at Port Weller on Lake Ontario silted up during the break and had to be redredged when construction started again (figs 6.11 and 6.12). Equipment deteriorated and the rock-crushing plant north of Twin Locks 4 had to be virtually rebuilt when construction started again (fig. 5.11). Stone which had been exposed to the elements during excavation deteriorated. When construction began again in 1919, about 10 miles (16.1 km) of the nearly abandoned construction railway had to be relaid, the wooden ties having rotted away. Some contractors had dismantled and/or sold their equipment but the bulk of their plant had been taken over by the Department, which sold most of it to the Canadian National Railway.

FINANCIAL CONSTRAINTS

The fiscal policies of the Ottawa government also influenced the Ship Canal's construction. Lack of funds for the Department of Railways and Canals was to be a particular problem during the war years and the Great Depression of the 1930s. Although the federal government approved resumption of construction on 24 December 1918, Ottawa felt no pressing commitment to an improved Niagara waterway at this time but simply wanted to provide employment for the thousands of "returned men" (war veterans). Consequently in the years 1919–22, Parliament appropriated annually only enough funding to keep the project alive and men working.

The new engineer in charge, Alex Grant, begged Bowden to arrange for greater parliamentary appropriations. In early August 1919 he wrote to his superior:

> We are now in a first class position, if labour conditions become normal, to carry on the work until December 31st 1919. To do so, however, will require an additional appropriation of $1,500,000.00 [$18,885,000 in 2015 dollars] and unless the Government decides to ask Parliament at the September session for such further appropriation for the Canal, Messrs. Doheny, Quinlan & Robertson, Contractors for Section No. 3, should be notified under Section No. 34 of their Contract to stop work at once.

In early November 1919 Grant told Bowden that he had no funds to carry on the work that month and that his office "will have small payrolls after the 31st of October, which will have to remain unpaid until further money is voted by Parliament."[11] However, both Grant and Bowden, and the latter's successor, Col. A.E. Dubuc,[12] were unsuccessful in extracting a higher degree of funding from Ottawa.

Not surprisingly, a rumour arose that the new waterway would be built only between the new Port Weller and Thorold. Protests from southern Niagara influenced Minister of Railways and Canals John D. Reid (1881–1929) to refute this rumour and to declare in 1920 that "the work will be proceeded with as fast as the money can be provided."[13]

When the work was again shut down in September 1919, Grant pointed not only to labour troubles but also to "the practical exhaustion of the Parliamentary Appropriation."[14] From time to time interim supply bills had been passed but for only a fraction of the amount requested. And so the engineers limited overtime for their workers and allowed no Sunday work. Although by 1923 the economy had stabilized, Parliament's attitude to the Welland still seemed indifferent. Describing the tabling of estimates for the work in February 1923,

Bowden told Grant that "there was quite a fight to prevent cutting down the amount, and we have been forced to point out the dire results which would follow any material reduction."[15] Over time little changed, although the appropriation was somewhat increased after 1922. For 1922–23 it was $8 million; 1923–24, $11,800,000; 1924–25, $11,800,000; 1925–26, $15,000,000; and 1926–27, $11,863,209. But even occasional increases were rarely sufficient. "The parliamentary Appropriation for 1926–27 is so small," declared Grant in March 1926, "that I am of the opinion that Department will not be in a position to make any payments to Contractors ... during the fiscal year 1926–27."[16] Typical was the situation he described to a St Catharines bank manager later that year. Expenditure for the fiscal year 1 April to 30 September 1926, he said, had been $8,244,399.72. Parliament had been asked for $14 million for the fiscal year to 31 March 1927, but the project had received only a quarter of this when Parliament dissolved. Consequently expenditures in excess of this amount had to be authorized by governor general's warrant.[17]

When construction recommenced in early 1919, the Ship Canal's engineers faced competition from the Queenston-Chippawa Hydro-Electric Canal project, being constructed between these two Niagara River towns, circumventing Niagara Falls. Many of the Welland's contractors and engineers believed that hiring and funding priorities on this project controlled what they could achieve on the Ship Canal work. Admittedly, Queenston required ready supplies of draglines and steam shovels as well as labour, all of which resulted in higher costs for the Welland project because the Hydro site paid workers more. The fact that expert opinion believed the production of hydroelectricity to be more important than the quick completion of the Welland complicated matters. Grant believed that contractors, too, preferred to tender for the Hydro project because of the higher rates they could claim there.[18]

The relative stability and prosperity of the late twenties ended when in 1930 the Great Depression set in. Regular appropriations from Ottawa again became harder to acquire and corners again had to be cut. Luckily, by then the waterway was largely completed and functional. The work on a dam for the large pondage between Twin Locks 6 and Lock 7, however, had to be suspended several times in 1930–31 because the appropriation was exhausted. Bills went unpaid: the

Department's account with Industrial Brownhoist of Cleveland, for example, was overdue even by May 1930.[19] In December of that year the Department sent a form letter to all the contractors on the Welland stating that parliamentary funds were exhausted but asking them to continue work because more funding would be voted by Parliament in the next sessions. Fortunately, although they knew that they would not be paid immediately, all the contractors agreed to continue working.

Meanwhile, cost-cutting was the order of the day. In March 1931, complying with Dubuc's request, Grant reduced his appropriation estimates by stopping all work not absolutely necessary to achieve a twenty-foot (6.096 m) depth for the 1931 navigation season. Other expedients were tried. For example, because the Canadian Bridge Company was demanding remuneration for their work but complete payment was impossible, their contract was extended until August 1932. In 1931 the Forestry Branch's work was suspended and the installation of the powerhouse's equipment below the Niagara Escarpment was reduced to a minimum. Ironically, the unemployment problem created by the Great Depression compelled Ottawa to provide additional amounts for construction, specifically about 355,000 man-hours of employment over and above that provided by the original appropriation in November 1931. Grant used this money to hire as many men as possible to work as hand labourers on trimming, sodding, and stone protection. No increases in salaries for office staff or engineers, however, were permitted.

Financial constraints imposed by the federal government influenced construction in other ways, too. Limitations on the federal government's budgets in the difficult immediate postwar years led to a lack of funds to offer Ship Canal employees salaries commensurate with those in the private sector. From 1 January 1919 to 1 July 1920 twenty-six salaried employees, including instrumentmen, rodmen, and draughtsmen, resigned. One left the Ship Canal office because he was offered an annual salary of $3,000 ($32,843.48 [2015]) and expenses from the Air Force in Ottawa, a much more attractive income than the $1,920 ($13,137.39 [2015]) he was earning on the Ship Canal. The departure of such men was bad enough but their leaving meant that others who would accept the low salary would also have less experience and knowledge for the job. Of course, a higher salary elsewhere was not the only motive here: with construction paralyzed by strikes and parliamentary appropriations meagre, the future of the entire project seemed dubious. Three years later when the Ship Canal bridges were being planned, Grant had to go to several bridge companies asking for the services of their designers. He simply did not have enough staff to carry on the work. The Civil Service Commission approved of this procedure but Grant must have felt that he was "working for the King of Prussia" – i.e., for an extremely stingy employer.

POWER PROBLEMS AND LABOUR MILITANCY

Weller and especially Grant were affected by a constraint closer to the construction site. In a telling memorandum on a "Programme of Work" for the 1920 season, Grant suggested a reduced scale of construction because his superiors had not yet decided on the source of electrical power. The choice was between the Ontario Hydro-Electric Power Commission at Niagara Falls or Lincoln Electric in St Catharines. Meanwhile, power from the Falls was unreliable, causing energy shortages on Section 3 in December 1919. In September 1920, although 1,600 horsepower was required, only 500 was received. The Ship Canal's power allotment was again reduced in October of that year. On one occasion, the engineers were reduced to obtaining electrical power for the Ship Canal shops and drills from the Pilkington Glassworks south of Thorold.

The Russian Revolutions of 1917 and the collapse of the old order in Europe in 1918, coupled with real local working-class grievances and a more sophisticated proletariat led to labour strife in Canada. For much of May and June 1919, thirty thousand Winnipeg workers struck for better wages and working conditions, as well as recognition of unions and collective bargaining. On 21 June, in attempting to clear downtown Winnipeg of strikers, the police injured thirty people and killed one man. Vancouver and Toronto experienced sympathetic strikes.

Niagara felt the reverberations of this social earthquake. In late 1919 many workers expressed support for a general strike on the Ship Canal construction site. This event distressed Grant and his engineers, annoyed the contractors, and brought construction to a virtual halt for several months. The labourers themselves were plagued with internecine squabbles complicated, among their own ranks, by ethnic prejudice.

CRITICS AND NAY-SAYERS

While faced with these constraints on their work, the Ship Canal build-ers knew that, beyond Niagara, public opinion was not entirely behind the enterprise. "The canal project has many enemies at Ottawa," one labour leader pointed out in 1919.[20] These critics fastened upon the con-trast between prices for work done around 1914 and those of the post-war era. Given the current economic uncertainty, asked an MP in April 1920, were the country's leaders concerned about the expenditure in-volved in restarting the Ship Canal's construction? W.V. Cope in the Department of Railways and Canals, sent the complaint on to Grant, who promptly replied with a reasoned defence. Private citizens also weighed in with their opinions. In 1920 M.J. Haney, a Montreal civil engineer, wrote to Prime Minister Arthur Meighen (1874–1960), who referred it to John D. Reid, Minister of Railways and Canals. Haney thought the project was too expensive and recommended a Ship Canal of smaller dimensions. He wrote that it was a "useless expenditure ... to provide for ocean going vessels which will not pass through it, for practical transportation purposes, in many generations."[21] Reid defended the waterway's cost and dimensions, noting that the Ship Canal plans were not designed for ocean-going vessels but for Great Lakes ships. Nevertheless, he added, "it would seem to be a matter of ordinary prudence to provide" for "salties" in the future.[22]

Such carping did not cease in more stable times. A headline in the *Montreal Star* in September 1929 exclaimed "The Welland Canal Wants More," below which the editorial waxed highly critical of the moneys spent on the Ship Canal. "The Canadian taxpayer," said the writer, "will be pardoned if he is a little startled at the news" that more funds for the Ship Canal were to be voted for in the next parliamentary ses-sion. The problem was the difference between the original estimate of the waterway's cost – $50 million – now dwarfed by the current estimate of $114,500,000.[23] Even in the Niagara District as late as 1928, a well-known Port Colborne ship captain, Dewitt Carter (1849–1933), lamented (inaccurately) "how the millions have melted like butter in an August sun."[24]

Members of the House of Commons, of course, were sensitive to the pressures of constituencies where other harbours and waterways were important. Much of both the support and the criticism of a new Welland, therefore, was inspired by local loyalties. Especially in Montreal, Ottawa, and northern Ontario, hostility to the Welland may also have been due to lingering affection for a canal connecting the Ottawa River to Georgian Bay. In 1911 J.A. Currie (Conservative MP for Simcoe North) declared that the Liberal government's Niagara surveys were "a big bluff, hung up on the people of the Welland District to make them believe that there is going to be a new canal." A larger Welland was not urgent, he maintained; the survey work was a sinecure for Liberals and a new Welland would serve only foreign vessels.[25] In 1921 an Ottawa newspaper editorial slammed the whole project as a Liberal electioneering gimmick designed to dupe the public by using terms such as "enlargement" or "deepening" when in fact an entirely new canal was being built. Parliament, said the journalist, should vote to suspend construction as too expensive at the present time. "Why rush the new Welland Canal?" he asked.[26] Similar discontent was voiced by the *Montreal Star* as late as 1929. E.A. Lancaster, MP for Lincoln-Niagara, supported the planned Niagara waterway, while G. Gordon, MP for Nipissing, in the north, favoured the Georgian Bay route. Party loyalties complicated these matters but in 1923, despite the opposition of prairie conservatives, the Conservative opposition, led by Arthur Meighen, approved of the annual expenditure for the Welland.

Clearly, by the late 1920s there was no denying that the original estimate of $50 million had been surpassed by one of almost $15 million. Some observers believed that the whole undertaking had been a mistake. In the budget debate of 1927 John Millar, MP for Qu'Appelle in Saskatchewan, declared, "I think a gigantic blunder was made when the Welland canal was started."[27] In 1929 others believed its construction was "premature" and an "unsound national policy." The enormous expenditure involved would necessitate tax increases while the traffic did not justify it, especially given the need to support the railways.[28] Many of these critics ignored the effects of inflation and rising post-war prices as well as the fact that the project had been underfunded from the start.[29]

THE CIVIL SERVICE COMMISSION

European war, financial constraints, power failures, labour problems, and critics of the Ship Canal project were only part of the context in which the engineers carried on their work. Another constraint which came from beyond the canal construction site was Ottawa's well-meant effort to expedite government procedures in an honest and legal fashion. Because many regarded Canada's federal bureaucracy to be inefficient – largely due to the patronage system – Prime Minister Wilfrid Laurier created the Civil Service Commission in 1908. Reformed in 1912 and 1918, its powers were strengthened as it was made the sole agency certifying all civil service personnel, including Third and Ship Canal employees. Accordingly, political patronage was to be abolished. Competitive examinations were introduced for some positions. Local people were to receive local jobs, while existing employees and war veterans were to be given preference. A new system of classifying jobs was also introduced. Unfortunately the increased complexity of the reforms and the morally righteous tone of the reformers created much hostility without improving efficiency to any great degree.[30]

All appointments to the Ship Canal staff were now to be made by the commission, although the engineer in charge would make the recommendations. In February 1919, moreover, Bowden warned Grant that these would have to be sent to Ottawa considerably in advance of the resumption of construction. When certain positions were being reclassified in December 1919, Bowden, appreciating Grant's position, managed to have a member of the commission visit the construction site, rather than have Grant go to Ottawa, "as we imagine it would be well for the Commission's representative to obtain some idea of the magnitude and extent of the Ship Canal work on the ground while dealing with the reclassification."[31]

Despite Bowden's sympathies, not only Grant, but also L.D. Hara, superintending engineer of the operating canal, were regularly irritated both by the detail and the time required by the commission before appointments could be made and by the sense that the bureaucrats in remote Ottawa knew nothing about the problems the engineers faced "on the ground." Later, in the Forestry Branch work, F.C. Jewett and W.H. Waddell would also endure much "red tape."

Grant's annoyance is clear in comments to Bowden when the latter, on the commission's request, asked him in 1920 to provide an inventory of plant and materials on each section:

In order to give you an idea of the amount of work involved in making these inventories, I am sending you by express today, the inventory of Sec. #1 ... The inventory for Sec #2 is twice as bulky as that for Sec #1 and that for Sec #3 is three times that of Sec #1.

Mr. Franklin [the auditor] is aware that we have made these inventories and now demands a statement of the recoverable value of the plant and material under fifty-seven headings ... I cannot see the necessity or the value of revising the inventory under any such headings ... I am accordingly not going to supply Franklin with a summary of the inventory as he wants it ... To supply him with a copy of the inventory, as it now stands, would take a good typist weeks to accomplish.[32]

Grant also objected to the unannounced visits of commission representatives and demanded one week's notice of such inspections. He complained about the commission's refusal to allow salary increases to loyal and efficient office workers and protested the arbitrary "temporary/permanent" classification of employees. By the mid-twenties, however, these problems seem to have been worked out – or the engineers grudgingly accepted the new situation.

CANADIAN NATIONALISM

The fact that the Welland Ship Canal was a great Canadian achievement was partly a result of deliberate public policy in response to a new country-wide patriotism. The work of Weller and Grant and their colleagues, however, was sometimes hampered by this growing Canadian nationalism. By the early twentieth century most contracts for canal or harbour works specified that only Canadian-owned dredges could be used and that all materials provided by contractors must be of Canadian origin. This attitude was not simply a federal policy but was a grass-roots phenomenon, exemplified in a 1920 address to the Canadian Engineering Institute by Lt. Col. R.W. Leonard, who called on members to use their positions to buy only Canadian-made machinery and supplies.

Although well-intentioned, such requirements occasionally inhibited the smooth reconstruction of the Welland. When the timber for the canal's unwatering gates was needed, for example, only Canadian producers were to be canvassed. In March 1924, therefore, Grant and the Department's agent, Hugh W. Ross, discussed "the probability of obtaining timber in B.C. & Pacific coast for unwatering gates 4 and 8." Ross was sent to British Columbia with Grant's note, to "make every possible effort to ascertain to the fullest extent what the B.C. mills can supply before you go to Oregon and Washington as we would like to obtain the timber in B.C. if at all possible." This proved difficult for Ross because, he wrote to Grant, the BC mills that could handle the order had not sufficient timber "on their own limits."[33] Ultimately, Ross obtained Douglas fir for the gates from the Ostrander Railway and Timber Company in Washington state.

Such were the external constraints or challenges that influenced the work on "this colossal project," causing delays and confusion and frustrating the builders. But "on the ground" – in Niagara itself – local issues also complicated the engineers' and contractors' efforts.

CHAPTER TWO

Challenges Facing the Ship Canal's Builders "on the Ground"

T he Welland Ship Canal was a huge Canadian technological achievement but, despite its modernity and size, its builders faced many of the same challenges in the Niagara area that had confronted William Hamilton Merritt and the Welland Canal Company. These difficulties often presented themselves in the form of questions: Where should the new channel be built? What was the best way of surmounting the 326.5 feet (99.5 m) of the Niagara Escarpment? How could the passage of ships be made faster? How could a reliable supply of water be guaranteed? How could the danger of flooding due to lock breakdown be met? How could the safety of ships and crews be assured? Some of the answers to these questions were unique; some, traditional. At the same time, new problems emerged which demanded imaginative solutions.

CHOOSING THE ROUTE

The first challenge confronting the canal builders is not one that is obvious to us today: where to build the great ditch (fig. 2.2)? Driving along the Welland Canals Parkway, which parallels the Ship Canal from Thorold atop the Niagara Escarpment to Port Weller on Lake Ontario, the tourist today might think that the waterway has always been here, so solidly does it blend with the natural and man-made landscape. Yet in 1910 and 1911 it was possible that the Ship Canal might have followed a completely different route – in fact, it might not ever have been built. For a while it seemed possible that the operating Niagara canal would become secondary to the longer Georgian Bay route, which had emerged again as rival to any Niagara connection between the Great Lakes and the St Lawrence River. But the authorities opted for a rebuilt Niagara canal.

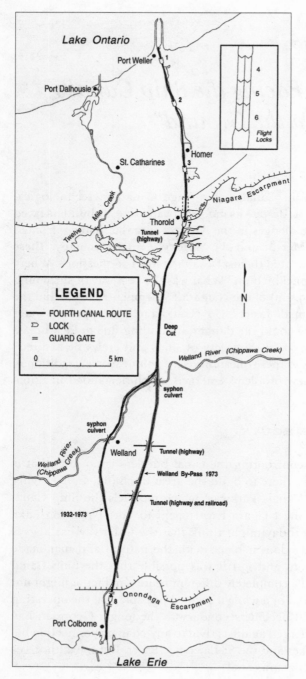

2.1 Map of the Welland Ship Canal, ca. 1973

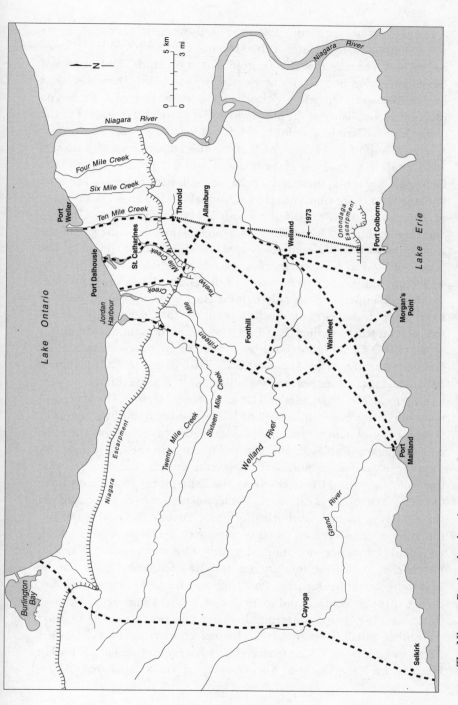

2.2   The Niagara Peninsula, showing approximate proposed routes for the new Welland Ship Canal.

Local interests certainly favoured improvement of the Niagara route. Popular lore maintains that Thomas Conlon (1844–1923), ship-owner and a member of the Thorold Board of Trade, first proposed the construction of a totally new canal in 1909.[1] D.B. Detweiler, who helped to inspire Ontario's hydroelectric system, and W.B. Burgoyne (1855–1921), publisher of the *St Catharines Standard* and president of the city's Board of Trade, also lobbied Ottawa for a new Welland.

If local supporters helped to buttress the Department of Railways and Canals in its backing of the Welland against Public Works and the Georgian Bay route, these influential men still had to fight to keep the Welland on a route similar to the traditional one. Interests in the town of Selkirk on Lake Erie, directly south of Hamilton on Lake Ontario, and Cayuga on the Grand River presented claims to be the site of the southern terminus of a completely new lake-to-lake canal (fig. 2.2). The height of land to be traversed, however, was a disadvantage here. As well, Port Maitland, at the mouth of the Grand River on Lake Erie, still had defenders as "the only natural Harbor on the North shore of Lake Erie."[2] Lobbyists continued to point out that its harbour was ice-free several weeks earlier than Port Colborne, the southern terminus of the Third Canal, and could be connected by a new channel to a northern harbour at Jordan, west of St Catharines on Lake Ontario. As late as 1924, its supporters, including the MP for Haldimand, were writing to Minister Graham and Chief Engineer Dubuc. The latter and his predecessor Bowden, as well as Weller, however, did not favour it.

As for the dynamic Weller, he had already started preparation for a new Niagara route with surveys and borings in the fall of 1905. By 1909 these were well under way on several sites, including a possible line following Ten Mile Creek from the Escarpment to a site on Lake Ontario, east of St Catharines. Weller seems to have embarked on these surveys without authorization from anyone in Ottawa but, on the other hand, no record exists of anyone in the Department of Railways and Canals questioning the legality of his endeavours.[3] When, in 1910, Weller made a preliminary report to Bowden, he believed that the best route would be one from Port Colborne on Lake Erie to Welland, thence through Fonthill and to Twelve Mile Creek and westward over to Fifteen Mile Creek, and from there to a new port on Lake Ontario.[4]

Another possible route was a channel connecting Port Colborne north to Chippawa Creek (the Welland River) and thence to Jordan Harbour on Lake Ontario. Also considered was a canal from Allanburg (near the halfway point of the Third Canal) to the flats south of St Catharines, then using Twelve Mile Creek to Port Dalhousie on Lake Ontario. This "Grenville Route," first discussed in the 1870s, was rendered "a practical impossibility" because borings revealed a lack of proper stone foundations for locks.[5] A canal here might have been good for the towns on the route but, in the St Catharines area, Welland Vale Manufacturing, the Kinleith Paper Mill, and the Taylor and Bate Brewery would be flooded out. A route farther west, using Fifteen Mile Creek, was found by borings to be unsuitable because of quicksand in the area where some locks would have to be built.

The route which Weller first favoured would have its northern terminus at Jordan Harbour at the mouth of Twenty Mile Creek on Lake Ontario, connecting to the south with the Grand River and with its Lake Erie harbour at Port Maitland or passing through Wainfleet on the old Feeder Canal and terminating at Morgan's Point on Lake Erie. Although expensive to construct, this canal would have only two locks. In February 1911 Weller's assistant reported to Bowden that surveys and borings suggested that "this route is meeting anticipations," and in July of that year Weller wrote that it "looks to me as if the Jordan route will have to be selected."[6]

Ironically, the route eventually chosen for the canal's channel north of the Escarpment – the Ten Mile Creek line, east of St Catharines – had seemed at first to be the least promising. On this route a new canal would have to intersect the operating waterway and would require bridges which would potentially interfere with navigation. It would also cross the Grand Trunk Railway line, necessitating possible realignment of the tracks or a costly tunnel or bridge. However, by March 1912 Weller had decided that the Ten Mile Creek route was the best, especially because all the locks could be founded on solid rock. As for the other routes surveyed, such as the Jordan line, they presented problems. The Jordan route, said the Minister of Railways and Canals, showed "a quantity of quicksand which has almost frightened them [the engineers] from it."[7]

The choice of the Ten Mile Creek route for the northern section of the waterway to Lake Ontario did not solve the matter of where to build the new canal south from the Escarpment to Lake Erie. Suggestions for Port Maitland as the southern terminus would have involved excavating a channel in a southwesterly direction from Thorold on the Escarpment. For this section a total of four alternative locations were considered, including one which would dam Chippawa Creek, a plan which was "abandoned as too costly because of the very heavy flood damages involved."[8] A route along the west side of Chippawa Creek and still running through the city of Welland was eventually chosen, with Port Colborne remaining as the southern terminus (fig. 2.1).

Even after work on the new canal had begun in 1913, this southern solution was not a foregone conclusion. The expense of channelling a deeper, wider prism through urban Welland was daunting, and in fact the precise route of the canal south of Thorold was not determined until a decade later. In 1922 Alex Grant, Weller's successor, discussed with D.W. MacLachlan (1881–1962), engineer in charge of the St Lawrence canals, the possibility of a route south from the Escarpment through the western outskirts of Welland, along Chippawa Creek for two miles (3.2 km), thence across the Cranberry Marsh to Lake Erie at a point about four miles (6.4 km) west of Port Colborne. He thought this would be much cheaper to build than a deepening of the Third Canal line because there was little solid rock on the route and the disposing of spoil would be easier.

MacLachlan's position reflected concern over the spiralling cost of the Ship Canal, already well under way. "I find myself asked by everybody I meet, what the cost of the Welland Canal is going to be," he wrote to Grant, "and I do not see how we are going to avoid giving it sooner or later."[9] A year later their correspondence concerned "Plan 1" with the canal constructed west of the Third Canal, terminating at Port Colborne and "Plan 2," a route east of the operating Canal, still using Port Colborne as terminus. This line would be cheaper to build and its construction would not interfere with navigation. Moreover, said Grant, it would "not cut up the town [of Welland]."[10] F.E. Sterns, designing engineer for the canal's lock gates, also weighed in with his views on the matter but it was Bowden himself who selected the line of the Ship Canal as it was built; i.e., expanding the existing canal through the city of Welland to Port Colborne. With this decision the civic authorities of Welland were delighted but would come to regret the choice.

Other than the Niagara Escarpment, few obstacles stood in the way of the new route. Given the use of modern construction equipment, the Onondaga Escarpment north of Port Colborne was much less of a geological barrier and, in the event, certain other geological features, such as "Hunt's Hollow" and the gorge of Ten Mile Creek at the Niagara Escarpment were actually useful to the builders. At Port Colborne, East Street and its buildings, including the local post office and railway station (fig. 10.3), would have to be removed, as would the Grand Trunk Railway Station at Thorold. Some rail lines had to be redirected, but only temporarily. The chosen route, therefore, seemed to offer a minimum of difficulties.[11]

FACILITATING THE NAVIGATION

Once the route was decided upon, the engineers had to consider a quasi-legal matter. Ship Canal contracts always included a clause to the effect that contractors must avoid "interruption of the navigation," a valid injunction because the new waterway would cross or closely parallel the Third Canal in several places. Consequently, construction was occasionally delayed in order to keep ships plying the older waterway. For example, the final configuration of Lock 3, located just north of the junction of the two canals, had to wait until nearly the end of construction (fig. 5.16).

Moreover, the intake monolith of Lock 7 could not be finished until late in the contractor's schedule because it would project into the Third Canal's Lock 24, which lay alongside. Similarly, the lower wing walls of Lock 7's guard gates would extend into the Third Canal channel and thus could not be finished until 1930. Meanwhile, the lower parts of the lock's south entrance walls were built through the older waterway during the winter of 1925–26 but in such a way as not to interfere with its later safe operation.

A particular problem developed at the brow of the Escarpment where the two channels lay side by side and from Thorold southwards where the routes of both the old and the new canals were often identical. Especially at the reach between Twin Locks 6 and Lock 7 atop the cliff, the danger to ships posed by construction activity was acute (fig. 6.1). Here, a difference of 51.2 feet (15.6 m) between the Third and the Ship canals and only 50 feet (15.2 m) between the channels led to seepage occurring. Steel sheet-piling had to be driven into the reach of the older canal. Still, the possibility that the earthen barrier between the two prisms might collapse was always on the engineers' and contractors' minds.

At Welland the syphon culvert construction site projected into the channel of the operating canal, which was consequently contorted into an S-curve, requiring constant dredging (fig. 6.3). This bend, as well as the dredging operations, created a danger of collisions. Elsewhere, blasting operations often forced vessels in the Third Canal to moor until the danger of flying debris had passed, a situation which also slowed navigation.

Thinking of the future and always mindful of the needs of ship captains, the new canal's planners incorporated a number of changes to make shipping more efficient. One of the most important was a more direct route for the northern section with Port Weller as the new northern terminus (fig. Intro.1). From the foot of the Escarpment an entirely new path to Lake Ontario was laid out, following the line of Ten Mile Creek and cutting more or less directly to Lake Ontario. Here, at a spot about three miles (4.8 km) east of Port Dalhousie, a man-made harbour (Port Weller) was created and two long breakwaters made of earth and rock were extended out into the lake, protecting ships from lake gales (figs 4.2 and 6.11).

At Port Colborne, where improvements had recently been made, the canal's mouth was further widened, although the old west harbour wall was retained. The system of sheltering breakwaters was made more complex. Two breakwaters already existed here, the western one extending west and east, at right angles to the old approach channel and parallel with the shore. Now an extension would branch off from the old western structure (fig. 6.9). New docks were erected for businesses and industries here as well as at St Catharines, Thorold, the Ontario Paper Company (south of Thorold), and Welland.

Another major change designed to speed the transit of ships was the fact that the Ship Canal would have only seven lift locks, much fewer than the Third Canal, which had twenty-six, and they were to be long, wide, and deep, in order "not to repeat the mistakes of earlier engineers," as J.D. Reid, Minister of Railways and Canals, said in 1920.[12] Of these seven locks, the twinned "flight" locks (numbered 4 to 6) were a unique feature in the history of the Welland and – not only by Canadian standards – a great engineering accomplishment. Earlier canals had followed the contours of the land but here the engineers eliminated the "loop" of the Third Canal and tackled the Escarpment at a right angle or, in effect, head-on. In Locks 4 to 6 the upper gates of the downstream chambers would function as the lower gates of the uppermost locks. Upbound ships could use one set of locks while downbound ships used the other, thus expediting "the navigation." The flight locks constituted one massive concrete structure 4,100 feet (1249.7 m) in length. On the brow of the cliff the single Lock 7 brought navigation up to the Lake Erie level. The phenomenon of the flight locks caused local people to describe the town of Thorold as "where ships climb the mountain."

With the safety of ships in mind, the engineers designed the upper gates of each lock to be smaller than the lower gates and to rest on a high breast wall, preventing the gate from being struck by ships moving in the lock towards them – a feature which actually repeated that of some of the locks of the First Canal. Crucially located at the Escarpment, Locks 4, 5, and 6 would have double sets of gates at both ends. A set of guard gates and a safety weir would be constructed above Lock 7, at the Ontario Paper plant (fig. 6.8). By the time Locks 4 to 7 were being built, Alex Grant and others believed that their guard gates and service gates did not provide enough protection against flooding for the flight locks and the locks northwards to Lake Ontario, and so they installed the aforementioned fixtures. To house the control mechanism of these guard gates, a four-storey concrete tower, the largest lock-side structure on the Ship Canal, would stand on its east side. The Thorold-Allanburg Road would cross here on a jackknife bridge. The designing engineers hoped that these new features would make transitting the canal safer and faster.

PREVENTING COLLISIONS AND FLOODING

Aware of the potential danger of ships colliding with lock gates, the engineers installed safety devices, "Gowan safety horns," which functioned like interlocking teeth, on all the Ship Canal gates. These had first been used on some Third Canal lock gates. If struck by a ship, one gate could open four feet (1.2 m) from its partner without completely losing contact with it.[13] On 5 January 1922, Nassau W. Gowan, their inventor, and James Battle a contractor, met with Grant to discuss these devices, which were installed on all the new gates.

In addition, lock gate fenders consisting of thick wire cables 3.5 inches (9 cm) thick were set up at each lock to restrain ships which might not stop in time from crashing into the gates. Such "ship arresters" were in use on the Panama and had been studied there by Ship

Canal engineers. The fenders justified their installation when they protected the gates in three accidents which occurred in one year alone,
1932. Few HIAWATHA incidents would occur on the new Welland.

The safety of the waterway was also a consideration when unwatering gates were designed and installed. These fixtures were to be used
once a year, when repairs might be necessary on the regular lock gates.
At Lock 1 they would close off Lake Ontario. They were installed at
Locks 2 and 3, and at Twin Locks 4 where they divide the long reach
between this point and Lock 3. They were also used at Lock 8 to separate Lake Erie from the summit level. Whereas the operating lock
gates had fenders of white oak, Douglas fir was used for the unwatering gates. Wood was preferred to steel for these gates because they
would always be immersed in water, whereas steel (as in the operating
gates) had to be periodically inspected and painted. Steel guard gates
were constructed at Locks 6, 7, and 8, as well as at the summit level.

Another concern was the safety of personnel. Hence the lock gates
were equipped with footwalks and handrails (fig. 3.5). Locktenders on
this version of the Welland would not be in danger of plunging off icy
gates into the freezing water below, a not uncommon event on the first
three Welland Canals. With the exception of the bend through Welland, the new waterway's 25-mile (40.2 km) length eliminated the sharp
and dangerous curves of the Third Canal and shortened the overall
distance between the lakes by 1.25 miles (2.4 km). South of the flight
locks the new channel followed approximately the same route as the
first three canals. Here, the channel of the Third Canal was dredged
and widened. Between Welland and Humberstone the original west
bank was set back to provide the extra channel width required. At
the request of local residents, the curving route through Welland was
retained – something they would come to regret (fig. 10.6). The shorter
length and fewer locks halved the time a vessel took in transit. When
finished, the Ship Canal had a navigable depth of 25 feet (7.6 m) but an
extra 5 feet (1.5 m) could be added inexpensively when the navigation
needed it in the future.

With the Humberstone weir, the regulating function of Lock 8,
the summit level guard gates, and the Thorold guard gate and weir,
the complex of locks at the Escarpment was secure if a high head of
water from Lake Erie threatened to flood the main channel. In addition to weather conditions, however, the authorities also had in mind

the several attempts to blow up locks and disrupt shipping which had occurred in the canal's history, most recently in April 1900. Such nervousness seemed extreme in the late twentieth century and so the Thorold guard gates were removed during the construction of the By-Pass (1967–73). On the other hand, in the twenty-first century – particularly after the events of 11 September 2001 – the reinstallation of such fixtures might well be considered a wise move. The addition of protective fencing has been a step in this direction.

GUARANTEEING A WATER SUPPLY

The locks of the first three canals were supplied with water through valves built into the lock gates but the Ship Canal's locks, which would hold much heavier volumes of water, required a more sophisticated system. The solution was a system of culverts built into the lock walls: large arched tunnels were set back 18 feet (5.4 m) from the face of each wall, running parallel to it. Each was 14 feet (4.2 m) wide and 16.5 feet (4.9 m) high, large enough to handle the great amounts of water needed to fill each lock. They were connected to the lock chamber by ports in the walls. Each culvert would receive water from the adjacent weir at the upper end of the lock and, to empty the lock, would discharge it out into the channel below the lower gate. At the Escarpment locks, however, water intake would be more difficult because there were no raceways or weir ponds on the east side of each lock. Therefore, at Twin Locks 6 the intake would be on the east wall, taking water from the large pondage near the Escarpment's summit and a long cross culvert would supply both the east and west locks. To take water directly from the Lock 6 chambers, Twin Locks 4 and 5 would be supplied by culverts or conduits in the upper ends of their centre walls (fig. 5.6).

At Port Colborne, Lock 8 served to regulate the supply of water to the Ship Canal. It was not a typical lift lock, for its average lift was only about 3 feet (1 m). At the time of its construction, however, it was one of the longest canal locks in the world – 1,380 feet (414 m). Because the authorities planned to duplicate it at a later date it was built just to the east of the canal's centre line (fig. 5.8).

The source of water remained Lake Erie, but near Lock 8 a part of the Third Canal was "recycled." Although time and enterprise had provided the engineers with new machinery and materials, Lake Erie had not changed at all. Storms at Gravelly Bay could still raise the water level there as much as 12 feet (3.6 m). Therefore, at Humberstone a regulating weir, which also served as a bridge for the town's Main Street, was built across the Third Canal as an additional control. On the northern stretch of the new waterway, the Third Canal below the Escarpment is used as an overflow channel between Twin Lock 6 and Lock 3.

Between Thorold and Port Dalhousie the channel of the Third Canal had been flanked by a series of ponds which were to guarantee a steady supply of water for each lock. To function effectively the Ship Canal required even larger amounts of water than had the Third Canal, so large pondage areas were established at most locks, such as at the twin locks. At Lock 2 another large pond stretches up the channel about 8,000 feet (2438.4 m), reaching almost as far as Bridge 4 at Homer. An even more extensive pond serves Lock 3. At Locks 1, 2, and 3, waste weirs and channels, with spillways closely flanking them to the east, reflect the Third Canal's arrangement. Lock 7 is supplied from a large regulating basin formed by flooding the upper valley of Ten Mile Creek above the Escarpment.

Hydroelectric power, which had already been introduced to the Third Canal, would run the Ship Canal's locks and bridges. For example, the steel wire ropes which opened and closed the lock gates were operated by electrically powered winches. For this purpose and for general illumination, heating the lockside buildings, and operating its self-contained telephone system, the new waterway created its own hydroelectricity. A powerhouse was built at the foot of Twin Locks 4 using water drawn from above Lock 7 (fig. 6.13). In effect, the powerhouse used the drop of the Escarpment to produce energy for the canal's operation. The entire canal was to be lit electrically from end to end.

The new locks were constructed, not of the traditional stone, but of concrete, a relatively new construction material. Concrete was also used in weirs, breakwaters, spillways, and bridge abutments, as well at certain other sites such as at a stretch from the north end of Lock 8 to where the canals diverge. Here the sides of the new canal were of concrete-faced rock. Some of stone masonry of the Second and Third Canals has survived well over a century, while parts of this concrete work on the Ship Canal have already deteriorated.

"END OF WELLAND CANAL"

Despite all the delays, Lock 8 at Port Colborne was opened in the fall of 1929. "We put the tug John Manley through the lock no. 8 & the canal on section no. 8 as far as Ramey's Bend," wrote Grant in his diary on 9 September. "This is the first boat through the Guard Lock of the Ship Canal." Then on 16 September, Lock 8 was placed in commission and four boats were locked through, including the MEA-FORD of the Canada Steamship Lines. Grant noted that this passage marked the beginning of the end of the construction of the Welland Ship Canal.

With the start of navigation in spring of 1930, the authorities decided to transfer traffic from the Third to the Ship Canal on the stretch between Lock 3 and Port Weller. By June 1930 all of the Ship Canal summit level was in use, as well as Locks 4 to 7, but only a 14-foot (4.26 m) draft was available. For the last month of the navigation season in that year, however, a depth of 18 feet (5.5 m) was provided at certain spots on the waterway for vessels of St Lawrence size and the flight locks were in operation.

An engineer's memo of 22 November 1930 read, "Last boat passed up the [Third] Welland Canal Locks 11 to 24. From this time to end of season both upbound and downbound traffic taken care of by the Ship Canal route." This file is annotated "End of Welland Canal," an ominous title which of course referred only to the last operation of the Third Welland Canal and the inauguration of the Welland Ship Canal.[14] Although the Department of Railways and Canals had hoped for a formal opening in 1931, this did not occur until August 1932, when delegates to the Imperial Economic Conference of that year were invited to attend a ceremony of international pomp and circumstance and to admire the Canadian accomplishment.

With the largest ships on the Great Lakes passing through it, the Ship Canal immediately justified its existence for, despite the Great Depression which meant that traffic on the St Lawrence and Sault Ste Marie canals declined in the 1931 season, tonnage passing through the new Welland actually increased.[15] By 1934 the depth had been increased to 25 feet (7.6 m) between Port Robinson (about midway between Thorold and Port Colborne) northward to Port Weller, and to 27.5 feet (8.4 m) between Port Robinson southward to Port Colborne. Both harbours had been dredged to 28 feet (8.5 m) below lake level. In

1959 the Welland Ship Canal became part of the St Lawrence Seaway, with a draft of 27 feet (8.2 m) throughout.

In 1967 construction began on the "By-Pass," a new channel which would involve construction of a route to the east of Welland, eliminating the large curve in the Ship Canal and freeing up railway and road traffic through that city. A new syphon culvert and new tunnels would be required here but no new locks. The By-Pass was finished in 1973 (Appendix IV).

The statistics were – and remain – impressive. But what is perhaps most remarkable about the Fourth (or Ship) Canal is the fact that the locks operate by the force of gravity on water, virtually the same principle employed by Alfred Barrett and his fellow engineers on the First Canal a century earlier. They would probably have agreed with a twentieth-century Canadian poet who called the canal "inspiring, grand, [and] impressive."[16] Nevertheless, they might have been daunted by the prospect of excavating such a huge "ditch," an undertaking which John Weller, his team of engineers, and small army of contractors and subcontractors began in 1913.

CHAPTER THREE

Vision, Skill, and Courage

W ho were the men who, for nearly two decades, designed and supervised the construction of the Ship Canal through the Niagara Peninsula, men who were, ideally in the words of one of them, "prepared to get up at five o'clock every morning and stay on the job until late at night every night"?

Such dynamos, of course, were the civil engineers and contractors. The proliferation of Canadian railway and canal construction in the latter half of the nineteenth century resulted in the expansion of the profession of civil engineering. Since its inception, the federal Department of Public Works had always employed a cadre of engineers and a roster of competent contractors. With the creation of the Department of Railways and Canals in 1879, however, the need for men capable of designing and overseeing the increasing number of large public works projects became urgent, and McGill University in Montreal, the University of Toronto, Queen's University and the Royal Military College, both in Kingston, as well as the École Polytechnique in Montreal began to offer programs in civil engineering. In fact, by 1900, writes J. Rodney Millard, Canada had produced "a corps of capable and experienced engineers that was already building spectacular new works that were attracting world-wide attention." Of necessity, the number of contractors able to carry out the engineers' plans also expanded to meet the growing demand.[1] At least some of the heads of contracting firms were themselves trained as engineers (fig. 3.3).

The close collaboration between the canal planners and the builders evident on the Welland Ship Canal project began on previous "jobs" such as the Intercolonial Railway in the Maritimes and the Soulanges and Trent-Severn Waterways, and extended into the post–First World War days of construction of the Ship Canal. Although the engineering cadre in Canada was still a small one in 1913, it was a close-knit group.

The extent and, to some degree, the nature of the friendships which could develop among the engineers and contractors whose work they supervised must have expedited construction of the new waterway. These relationships are amply revealed in the diaries of Alexander Grant, the engineer in charge of construction of the Ship Canal from 1919 until his retirement in 1934.

While excavation of the ever-larger "ditches" of the first three Welland Canals had become increasingly complex, that of the prism of the Fourth Canal involved removing even more tonnes of earth and rock and directing greater volumes of Lake Erie water into a channel connecting to Lake Ontario. The undertaking demanded strength of character from engineers whose training and talents were often taxed to the extreme and who were often placed under great psychological pressure. Timetables had to be met and machinery of various types had to be coordinated and serviced. Difficulties, foreseen and unpredictable, both technological and non-technological, were encountered and had to be overcome. At times a sense of the absurd was also necessary.

"NO GREAT ENGINEER CAN BE A NARROW MAN"

So spoke Prime Minister R.B. Bennett when he addressed the Engineering Institute of Canada at their forty-eighth annual meeting in Montreal on 8 February 1934. "Engineering had contributed more to Canadian material progress than any other institution," he was reported to have said. "No other professions had ever offered more opportunities for wide vision."[2] This raises the question: do large, expensive engineering projects naturally attract vivid, idiosyncratic personalities? Given the evidence provided in our first volume, *This Great National Object: Building the Nineteenth-Century Welland Canals*, the answer must be "yes." In that book, we met such men as William Hamilton Merritt, H.H. Killaly, the Keefers, and John Page. If we consider the engineers in charge of the Ship Canal's construction, John L. Weller (1862–1932) and, later, Alex Grant (1863–1955), not to mention some of the sectional engineers, the history of the Fourth Welland's construction supports the point. We shall see several examples of how, typically, Weller and Grant were both ready, on occasion, to disagree with, to reprimand, and even to disobey their Ottawa superiors.

As with the nineteenth-century Welland Canals, much of an engineer's time was spent in consulting with and supervising the work of the

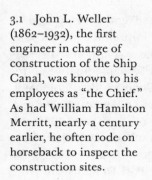

3.1 John L. Weller (1862–1932), the first engineer in charge of construction of the Ship Canal, was known to his employees as "the Chief." As had William Hamilton Merritt, nearly a century earlier, he often rode on horseback to inspect the construction sites.

contractors who were responsible for the actual work and who were occasionally fractious or inefficient. Nevertheless, the Department of Railways and Canals was fortunate indeed to have had the talented men it was able to attract to the project.

"AN ENGINEER OF WELL-ESTABLISHED COMPETENCY AND REPUTATION"

John ("Jack") Laing Weller was intelligent, creative, hard-working, ambitious, and feisty[3] (fig. 3.1). Born in Cobourg, Ontario, he graduated from Royal Military College in 1883 with a First Class Certificate. He then took a position with the civil service, at first on the Trent River system. In 1885 he served as a lieutenant in the 57th (Midland) Battalion, assisting in the suppression of the North-West Rebellion. Having served as staff adjutant under General John M. Laurie, Weller then rejoined the Department of Railways and Canals. He was promoted first to assistant engineer on the Cornwall Canal Enlargement in June 1887 and to resident engineer before long. By 1894 he had an assistant, W.H. Sullivan, who would follow him to the Welland.

While working on the Cornwall Canal, Weller continued to be active in the militia, joining the 59th Stormont and Glengarry Battalion of infantry, rising to major by June 1897. In 1886 a Rifle Association had been formed in Cornwall and Weller took to the sport and became so adept that he was one of two members of the Canadian Bisley team, travelling to England in 1896, where he placed in the prize list on eight occasions.

In May 1900, having already worked on the Trent, Murray, and St Lawrence canals, he was put in charge of the Port Colborne harbour improvements; on 28 November of that year he was appointed superintending engineer of the Third Welland Canal. An imaginative entrepreneur as well as an engineer, he owned the Concrete Pole Company, which pioneered the use of reinforced concrete poles for power and streetcar companies As well, in Thorold, several houses of concrete, another of his company's experiments, are extant. He encouraged his assistant, W.H. Sullivan, to proceed with his innovative design for concrete scows: the PIONEER was launched at Port Dalhousie in November 1910.

By this time Weller was already deeply involved in planning for the further enlargement of the Welland. As far back as 1905 he had ordered surveys for a new canal. This work he carried out along with his regular duties until Christmas Day 1911, when he wrote to W.A. Bowden, the chief engineer of the Department, asking that he be moved from his position as superintending engineer of the operating Welland and put in charge of the surveys and design of the planned Ship Canal. Bowden supported this suggestion and Weller was appointed to the new position in April 1912. F.C. Cochrane (1852–1919), Minister of Railways and Canals, approved of the appointment, noting that Weller had already, "for some time past, been engaged in making surveys for the proposed ship canal and is an engineer of well-established competency and reputation."[4]

Upon assuming his new position, Weller rented space for an office in St Catharines and gathered a staff together. In the summer of 1912 he had a building erected behind the Third Canal office at the corner of Yates and St Paul Streets, into which he and his men moved in January 1913. "The new office is fully equipped," he wrote, "and enables good work to be turned out with dispatch."[5]

Weller's tenure as engineer in charge was a lively one. An energetic and intellectually curious engineer, he was confident of his own abil-

3.2 Kingston, Ontario. Wall of Honour, Royal Military College. In 2013, this plaque bearing John L. Weller's name was installed.

ities. For eight days in March 1913 he and Chief Engineer Bowden inspected the Panama Canal. This visit "completely satisfied me," he reported, "that my designs, while differing radically from the Panama canal, are fully equal if not superior to them or the conditions to be met with in the proposed Welland ship canal."[6]

Not long after his return from the Panama, his work was temporarily interrupted when he had one eye removed as a result of a diseased optic nerve.[7] Apparently this had been bothering him for years but does not appear to have affected his competence, although it may have made him more irascible. According to his son-in-law, Eric Muntz, he was "as diplomatic as a hedgehog."[8] From Ottawa's point of view, he seemed to carry on the Ship Canal construction independently of any direction from the Department. When he did not report to Bowden on flooding problems in Thorold South in 1916, for example, the latter admonished him: "This is not the only instance which has recently come to my attention of your failure to fully report on phases of the construction works under your jurisdiction which should be reported upon by you."[9]

When difficulties resulting from the First World War halted construction in May 1917, he was retired from the project but was taken on as a consulting engineer when work resumed in 1919, serving in this capacity until 1926.[10] During his tenure as engineer in charge of construction, his testy personality did not alienate his underlings, for he surrounded himself with a group of talented and dedicated young engineers who would supervise the work and who were invariably loyal to the engineer they called "the Chief." As for the man himself, he died in 1932, having lived to see Port Weller named for him. In 2013, his name was added to the Wall of Honour at Royal Military College, Kingston (fig. 3.2).

"A FINE LOT OF YOUNG MEN"

Weller took pride in his sectional engineers, describing them as a "fine lot of young men who have taken great interest in the work."[11] After Alex Grant took over in 1919, he might have said the same thing. Names such as Jewett, Sterns, or Lazier will appear frequently in the story of the canal's construction. The vast majority were Canadian-born and -educated, with degrees from McGill, Toronto, Queen's, and Royal Military College. Even though occasionally sorely pressed with problems and crises, they seem to have been conscious of the significance of the Ship Canal project for Canada's economy and history. After the canal was completed in 1932, some went on to illustrious careers.

These men were not sedentary, either mentally or physically. As was true of their nineteenth-century counterparts, they usually had to be prepared to leave their offices to slog through the mud of the deepening canal prism, inhale the concrete dust of the lock sites, negotiate with wayward contractors, and face disgruntled labourers. Indeed, they were peripatetic, following the work from place to place on site or abroad. Their commitment to the Ship Canal took them from time to time to various parts of North America, inspecting vertical lift bridges and other canal features. In 1913 Weller toured the Panama, and in 1919 Grant wrote to the Isthmian (Panama) Canal Commission about their lock gates and sluices. In November 1925 Sterns was in

3.3 At the Flight Locks, 1932. Ship Canal engineering staff gather for the official opening, with Alex Grant in the centre of the front row. To his right is his wife Maude, with engineer Frank Sterns and his wife (with the long necklace) to Mrs Grant's right.

contact with the Panama Canal Zone authorities on the same subject, and he and Grant visited Panama in 1926. When Grant was in Great Britain and Europe in 1928, "the first real holiday that I have had in my life & the first trip back to bonnie Scotland & home since I came out with Father Mother & brothers in 1872,"[12] he visited contractors in Alloa, Scotland, and London, England, as well as the Manchester Ship Canal, the North Sea and Kiel canals, and the harbour works at Amsterdam and London.

We know the Ship Canal engineers mainly from their monthly reports and occasional memoranda and letters to Weller and Grant. Their writing reveals scientifically trained minds with a total grasp

3.4 (*left*)   Weller's son-in-law, Eric Percival Muntz, one of the several young engineers working on the construction of the Ship Canal in 1915.

3.5 (*right*)   At a giant Ship Canal lock, ca. 1930. A construction engineer proudly shows off his creation to his family, standing safely on a new lock gate equipped with railings (a feature unknown on earlier locks).

of the technological challenges they faced. They usually wrote in a sober, objective style, omitting the personal. But now and then flashes of humanity and its foibles appear in these cool typewritten accounts of a month's work. Engineer E.P. Murphy occasionally wrote almost purple prose, giving a good sense of the pride and perils of a conscientious engineer. Some, like F.S. Lazier and F.C. Jewett, peppered their missives with colourful complaints about workers and contractors. As well, Jewett seems to have regarded Grant as a kind of father confessor, expressing fully to him the stresses and tensions of supervising part of such a large, complex project. The outspoken Jewett could also be abrasive when he believed that the highest standards were not being met. For example, in 1921 he wrote to a contractor:

> Why not organize your work at Lock #2? Quit squabbling over trifles. Get things going right ... I was forced to report to the Engineer-in-Charge at the end of September that your Lock #2 work was the worst organized and handled piece of concrete work that I had ever seen. I don't like the idea of having to say so again. I think your troubles 99% of your own making. You can't bull a concrete job like you can a shovel cut.[13]

Lively prose, but not calculated to improve relations between the Department and its contractors. Grant reprimanded him for his language.

Jewett's memorandum was intemperate but accurately reflects the continual stress felt by Ship Canal engineers. By 1929 the authorities intended that the Ship Canal would be officially opened on Dominion Day, 1 July 1930. As early as May of that year the pressure of the looming opening date was evident in part of Jewett's monthly report to Grant:

> WARNING
> Our time is short this season ... In another week we will be started on the south end centre wall of Lock 6. I haven't seen the intake building plans yet. How about materials? Our Humberstone force should be at the Guard Gate by May 31st. How about the big building there and materials for it? Are we going to be held up? And Lyall! [the contractor] Can he have the safety weir concreted out to Pier #8 by Aug. 1st – just three months to do the job ... Something else to worry about. By June 10th. We will be back to Lock #7. We want to do everything on the east side – intake valve house, lower control and the three small machinery houses. The backfilling must be completed ahead of us. Will it be completed?

Three months later Jewett still felt under pressure. In August 1929 he lamented to Grant, "September is likely to be a hectic month. For once I wish it had 60 days in it instead of only 30."[14]

Jewett was speaking for many of his colleagues who, from week to week over the years, experienced hundreds of unpredictable incidents which taxed their forbearance. For example, in June 1915 a spark from a passing locomotive caused a fire, destroying an old stone building in Allanburg which had served as engineers' offices. Because the blaze occurred in the daytime, all the records and papers of the Department were saved and the old office was rebuilt. Another fire in November 1919 destroyed the office of Baldry, Yerburgh, and Hutchinson, contractors on Section 2, consuming the annual inventory, pricing books, stock cards, receiving books, and stores allocation records. Such an event was probably accidental – and how could the following be anticipated? In May 1919 a locomotive, which had been ordered for the Construction Railway from the United States, arrived with all its fittings gone.

For these sectional engineers and their staff, new structures were built to serve as offices, or older structures, such as at Allanburg, were requisitioned. For Section 2 a new two-storey building was erected at Homer, near St Catharines, close to the new prism. This would serve as both office and accommodation for the operating personnel. Other such buildings were older structures, adapted for use by the staff. For example, the engineer's office for Section 3 was an older home above Lock 7 in Thorold. (This is now The Inn at Lock Seven.) What later became the Welland Club in that city served as offices and rooms for single staff. Most of the engineers found suitable accommodation in homes in the area but they had to help search for residences for their married staff, a task for which degrees in civil engineering did not prepare them.

"THE SHIP CANAL HAS BEEN MR. GRANT'S HOBBY"

These words of a St Catharines journalist[15] might suggest that Alex Grant's work on the Welland was akin to a leisure-time pursuit. On the contrary, like his predecessor Weller, he was concerned with the Ship Canal night and day. Grant's own description of the ideal qualities of a contractor could easily apply to himself: "Still in early middle life, very active, and prepared to get up at five o'clock every morning and stay on the job until late at night every night, and at the same time employ lots of driving force, good judgement and horse sense."[16]

Alexander James Grant was born in Dufftown, Banffshire, Scotland, whence his father Peter, emigrated to Canada in 1869, bringing his wife and family over in 1872 (figs 3.6 and 3.7).[17] He attended St Mary's

3.6 Alexander (Alex) Grant
(1863–1955), Weller's successor,
enjoyed golf and "card parties"
and was not above "doing
a highland fling" (*Diary*, 17
September 1920) but his work
ethic was formidable.

College, Montreal, and the University of Ottawa, beginning his career
as an engineer on a survey for the Canadian Pacific Railway. In 1885
he joined the Department of Railways and Canals on the Cape Breton
Railway (1887–91), after which he worked on the building of the Soulanges Canal (1891–1903) under Thomas Monro, with whom he maintained close ties until the latter's death in 1903.

In mid-December 1902 he was told to report to Port Colborne,
to take charge of the improvements there. At that time he was, said
George Graham, Minister of Railways and Canals, on the way to
becoming "one of the most efficient engineers in the whole department."[18] Barely settled in the new post, he was recalled to the Soulanges because of Monro's heart attack. Later that year he married
Monro's nurse, Maude Kerr.

At the beginning of April 1906 Grant was appointed superintending
engineer of the Trent Canal, where he worked until 1919. He later recalled that when he left the Welland in 1906, he "never again expected
to have anything to do with the Canal, but old Dame Fortune willed
it otherwise."[19] On 1 January 1919 he assumed the duties of engineer in
charge of the Welland Ship Canal project.

3.7   St Catharines, 2012. A street sign in a new suburb, the first permanent public recognition of the role of Alex Grant in the construction of the Ship Canal. (Port Weller was named after the first engineer in charge.)

That Grant was already a "man of ripe experience and mature judgement,"[20] as *The Engineering Journal* said, is without doubt. Also beyond question is the fact that he was every bit as dynamic and feisty a character as his predecessor, John Weller. He was the sort of man about whom stories accumulate, many of them probably apocryphal. A Ship Canal office worker, for example, described Grant's "whiskers and a white wig. When he got mad, it would go crooked and he'd look rather strange, with his hair off to one side. He had a policy of bawling somebody out every day."[21]

If we question the accuracy of this colourful view, we cannot doubt that Grant was a more-than-conscientious administrator and a perfectionist engineer. His diaries indicate that, while he was not averse to praising a good job, he did not suffer fools gladly. Moreover, he was always aware that "the devil is in the details." Early in 1922, for example, following a discussion on labour rates on Sections 1 and 2 with the contractor J.P. Porter, when the latter quoted letters from possible subcontractors, Grant wrote: "Are these letters schemes of Porter to build up claims years hence on acct [*sic*] of alleged high schedule rates. He claims he tendered on the work on the prospect of common [labour] being 24¢ per hour early in the contract. The rate for common labour on the work today is 37½¢."[22] Over the next four years Grant frequently complained of Porter's slow progress on the work – to Porter himself, to Porter's sons Fred and Richard, and to the chief engineer in Ottawa. For example, later in 1922, he wrote to Bowden concerning the necessity of "proceeding much more energetically" with Porter's work.[24] As late as 1928, he was still complaining about this contractor's practices either in his diary or to the chief engineer.

At the same time, Grant did not allow professional dissatisfaction to interfere with long-standing friendships, for he was a very sociable man. Many are the examples of his hobnobbing with fellow engineers. Rather more surprising are the convivial times he spent with contractors, some of whose work he occasionally condemned. The Grants frequently had dinner, or played golf or cards, with the contractor J.P. Porter and his wife. For example, on 31 December 1922, they saw the New Year in at the Porters' home. Typical of Grant's friendships was a small dinner party following the funeral of W.A. Bowden on 5 February 1924. Hosted by David Dick of Welland, president of the National Sand and Gravel Company (a supplier for the Ship Canal), the guests included contractors Lyall, Porter, and Robertson, and engineers from Ottawa, the Trent, and the Ship Canal. "We had a pleasant time & drank a silent toast to the memory of our departed friend, W.A. Bowden."[24]

He had a gift for friendship. His diary reveals his distress over the death in 1927 of his longtime friend, the contractor Hugh Quinlan of Montreal. The firm of Quinlan & Robertson had worked on the Lachine and Soulanges canals, and on a number of dams in Quebec, Ontario, and New York, and elsewhere. They had built ships in Quebec during the First World War and were involved in paving work in Quebec, Ontario, and southern England. After his death Grant noted "I have known Hugh since 1896."[25] It was Quinlan who had driven the Grants about Montreal for temporary distraction during the last illness of Grant's brother John and who placed his car at their disposal on the day following the funeral, to help them with the necessary business affairs. Quinlan's partner, Angus W. Robertson, was also a close friend with whom Grant often spent time when he was in

Montreal, when they both happened to be in Ottawa or Toronto at the same time, or on Robertson's frequent visits to construction sites on the Ship Canal. Robertson also often chauffeured Grant about Montreal when the latter had a number of professional appointments. They would visit mutual friends together and were frequent companions on the golf course, at lunch or dinner, and at the card table. Although Grant could be irascible, his basic amiability must have helped smooth over many a crisis during the canal's construction.

William Hamilton Merritt rode on horseback up and down the First Canal site personally inspecting the locks and prism of "his" canal and indicated to contractors and engineers alike that he understood what was going on and demanded efficiency. The same concern drove Grant, whose diary records that, in his late sixties, he often would be driven to one site, then would walk, sometimes for several miles, usually accompanied by one or more of his engineers and a contractor, from one area to another, even in bitter winter weather. On Saturday afternoons, even occasionally on a Sunday, his son Alex Jr would be his companion. One such Saturday resulted in the following note to Porter: "I was out at Lock 3 on Saturday and note that no excavation has yet been done by you behind monoliths 12 & 13 at Elevation 330"[26] – a typical admonition to a contractor. He urged an immediate start on the work.

Also characteristic was his memorandum to Atlas Construction Company in June 1926, which indicated that, when he was "over Section 6," he noticed a break in the embankment at Atlas's spoil area north of Chippawa Creek, near Port Robinson. A large amount of excavated material had fallen into the creek on 3 June, partially blocking it and threatening to cause a flood. On the 7th Grant discussed the matter with E.O. Leahey, associated with Atlas, and visited the site on the following day. On the 15th he demanded that Atlas clean up the mess and at their own expense.[27] In 1933 a similar missive went out to E.C. Shurley, the canal's structural steel inspector. As if describing his personal property, Grant wrote: "Last evening I walked up the west bank of the Canal from Bridge No. 4 to Lock No. 3," where he found a bulge of rock fill which needed attention. "I do not want any large masses of rock along here projecting above the bottom elevation of the Canal prism."[28]

Not only was Grant regularly present and active on all the Ship Canal construction sites, but he also toured other canals. Apart from his visits to Panama and to European canals, he visited many areas in Canada and the eastern United States, including both the American and Canadian Sault canals, the Erie Canal at Black Rock, New York, as well as canals in Quebec and the Maritimes. Through such visits he kept up to date on canal engineering and did on-the-spot research into questions about bridges, locks, and water control.

According to his diary, he often took the overnight train to Ottawa, a journey that in the 1920s could take over nine hours. (Presumably he took a berth.) Arriving in Ottawa well before 8 a.m., he would have breakfast, spend the day at the Department of Railways and Canals with the chief engineer, and, as often as not, after dinner with friends, return to St Catharines on the night train, heading straight for his office the next morning. From 1919 to 1921 he averaged six trips a year to see the chief engineer, a maximum of nine trips in 1919 and 1924, down to three in 1929 and 1932. In addition to these meetings at headquarters, he met with Bowden eight times at the Ship Canal and with Dubuc, thirteen. On these occasions, as well as in numerous telephone conversations, important decisions were sometimes made, with no "paper trail" for historians to follow. For example, on 12 May 1922, Grant recorded that "Mr Bowden called me on the phone at 4 pm & told me secs 3 & 4 were to be advertised for re-letting immediately, tenders returnable 9th June & and to begin closing down work immediately."[29]

Grant maintained much more cordial relations with the chief engineers in Ottawa than had Weller. In fact, he considered that Bowden had been "a real friend to me."[30] They met on a number of occasions, both in Ottawa and on the construction sites. For example, on 8 and 9 May 1919, Grant was in Ottawa, consulting with Bowden. On the 13th Bowden joined him in St Catharines, whence they motored straight out to Lock 2,

> round which we spent an hour. Lunch at Sec 2 camp where we met Russell [of Baldry, Yerburgh & Hutchinson, contractors, Section 2] ... & Jewett. After lunch we went to Port Weller & looked over lock 1, & the sand bins. We then went by rail to Queenston Road & lock 3 where we looked over the slides etc. Continued our journey to Thorold where we met Doheny & Quinlan [contractors, Section 3]. Looked over watertight bank of Lock 6 pondage & excavation at south end of section. Supper at the

contractors house Thorold & then motored back to St Catherines [*sic*]. Lazier [Division Engineer, Section 3] with us.[31]

Such expeditions were typical. His energy, stamina, and dedication were remarkable. It was not unusual for him to work in his office until 11 p.m.[32] His Roman Catholic faith took him to Mass most Sunday mornings, but by afternoon he was often in his office or touring one site or another. Even when on holiday, Grant was always "on call." From the Britannia Hotel on the Lake of Bays in Muskoka in August 1927, for example, he communicated with Niagara by telegram, keeping informed on the canal's progress.[33]

Although he loved his work, his diary occasionally suggests on-the-job stress. On 2 September 1921, for example, he recorded: "This past month was the hardest & most strenuous work that I have ever experienced in the 35 years of my connection with the Dept Rlys & Canals. Everyone in the office, engineers & draughtsmen have been working 3 hours every evening on the plans & specifications for secs 3 & 4 Welland Ship Canal, and also several men in the Thorold office on the quantities."[34] In October 1924, after a morning meeting with Civil Service Commission representatives, he took Bowden over the north end of the canal, then "returned to St. C. after a fatiguing & disagreeable afternoon." It had rained all forenoon and a high east wind blew "cold & very raw."[35] Most telling is his lament in 1925 that modern life was filled with "too much telegraph, telephone and worry generally." This was after an hour spent at Mount Vernon, in Virginia, "with the memories of George Washington ... The generation of Washington's time knew how to live & take life leisurely & probably got more out of it in one year than we would in 10 today."[36]

Despite such occasional darker moments, Grant was not without a sense of fun. During an engineers' conference held in Niagara Falls 16–17 September 1920, he played first base in a baseball game. His team was the "Giants." While he does not mention this feat in his diary, he does say that, at the dance that wound up the meeting, "Jack [Horgan] & I made an exhibition of ourselves dancing a highland fling & marching around the ballroom with the pipers."[37] (No doubt after some liquid refreshment.) His diary reveals that his favourite recreations included playing cards, golfing, and curling, both with professional friends – engineers, contractors, Dr John McCombe, head of the canal's Medical Service – and with visiting dignitaries and members of what he described as "St Catharines 400," the social elite of the city.

Grant's impatience with some of the contracting firms may say more about his perfectionism than about any particular contractor's dilatoriness. In fact, many of these men had wide and varied experience. J.P. Porter, for example, was described by a local newspaper in 1921 as "one of the best known contractors in the Dominion," having done "some very big work for the government," including the Halifax harbour terminals.[38] In 1922, Grant himself described Porter as "a man of considerable ability" who "always carried on the work energetically and in a manner satisfactory to us."[39] Nevertheless in that same year Grant condemned Porter's "very slow progress" on Section 3.[40]

Grant's good relations with the chief engineers in Ottawa did not prevent him from gently rebuking a superior on occasion. In November 1926 he reminded Dubuc about the latter's lack of response to a letter he had sent two weeks earlier concerning a bridge's power requirements. "[I] now beg you," he wrote, "not to let the matter get pigeonholed in the Department."[41] In the privacy of his diary, he recorded strong and penetrating observations regarding his important contemporaries. For example, when the problem of getting enough hydroelectric power for the canal arose in 1920, he opined that Adam Beck, founder of Ontario's Hydro-Electric Power Commission, "is hoodwinking & playing rag tag with the Dominion Gov't."[42]

With underlings Grant could be, to say the least, brusque. When lumber was not delivered by a Grimsby firm as ordered, he exploded (in print) to a departmental purchasing agent, "what kind of a one-horse outfit is the above concern?" When shipments of British Columbia fir were slow to arrive, he told Knox Bros. Ltd of Montreal that their lack of action was a "damned poor showing for your firm."[43]

When it was not mildly profane, his vocabulary was vivid. In May 1924 he told Jewett: "When the Contractor's agent begins operations this season between Lock 1 and Bridge 2, cleaning up the bottom of the Canal prism and its slopes, do not permit him to jump about all over the place, like a jack-in-the-box, as he did last year, but make him clean up the bottom and the slopes of the prism as he moves forward."[44]

On the other hand, Grant was not blind to accomplishment and provided praise when he evidently felt it was earned. In 1924 he told J.P. Porter that his work on Sections 1 and 2 had been "carried on with considerable energy, with the result that about 65% of the work has been executed in an experienced and workmanlike manner to our entire satisfaction."[45]

He also had a strong sense of the importance of public relations and of how a canal should look to users and passersby. To Jewett he wrote in October 1923, "Have Porter right away clean off the mud that the teams deposited on the roadway approaching the east end of Br. no. 1 from east and north … Now is the time to do it before the heavy rains come on. After it gets wet, the approaches to the bridge will be in a horrible mess."[46]

Grant loved gardens and horticulture, even suggesting that the canal's Forestry Branch plant seeds which he had himself collected while in Scotland in 1928. He exhibited great interest in the branch's development, constantly encouraging its director, W.H. Waddell. In his correspondence – otherwise devoted to technical engineering matters – he wrote with enthusiasm about the beautification of the canal. To Dubuc in 1930, for example, he described his plans to make "a small park" at the corner of Chapel and Peter Streets in Thorold, near Lock 7."[47]

His considerable talent did not go unrecognized. In Ottawa in 1924 to attend the funeral of chief engineer Bowden, Grant was offered the latter's position by the Deputy Minister of Railways and Canals. His diary noted: "I told him that I would not consider it at $8000." After the funeral, on the following day, the offer was repeated by the departmental office engineer and again refused. Grant remained in Ottawa over the weekend and on the Tuesday was informed by the Deputy Minister that the minister himself wanted to see him. For the third time Grant refused, on the grounds that an additional $800 a year (he was getting $7,200) would not be sufficient compensation for the added responsibilities. Later that day Grant was informed that the position had been offered to Colonel A.E. Dubuc, then superintending engineer of the Quebec Canals, and accepted.[48]

Further testimony to his reputation among his peers came in 1930 when he was elected president of the Engineering Institute of Canada. While he was not always comfortable in the chair, perhaps because he was a "hands-on" engineer, he fulfilled his responsibilities to general satisfaction. His greatest professional reward came in 1934 when, at the forty-eighth annual meeting of the Engineering Institute of Canada, he was awarded the Sir John Kennedy gold medal, the highest award given by the institute.

This occasion was a fitting conclusion to the professional career of a dynamic, hard-working, occasionally complex individual who retired on 31 March 1934 in his seventy-first year. His diary entry for that date reads: "At midnight tonight I ended my active life with the Dept of Railways & Canals Canada after 48 yrs service in the Dept. ... I have no regrets leaving active life. I am tired mentally & physically & glad to rest & very thankful to Almighty God that I have good health & strength to enjoy the evening of my life in peace & contentment with my family."[49]

The Welland Ship Canal remains a monument to both John Weller[50] and Alex Grant. Following his last official day in office in 1934, the latter generously acknowledged the contribution of his colleagues: "My last day in the office as Engineer [in] Charge of the Welland Ship Canal since the 1st January 1919. A long time in which God has blessed me with good health & strength & also gave me good assistants without whom we could not have carried the work through to a successful issue. Deo Gratias."[51] Presumably these "colleagues" included the sectional engineers and possibly the many contractors.

THE PROCESS OF CONTRACTING ON THE SHIP CANAL

Despite Weller's and Grant's intense commitment to the building of the Ship Canal, their work depended on that of contractors who carried out the actual construction of the prism and the locks. Despite disagreements, they had to work daily with these men, who in turn were subject to procedures, regulations, and frustrations (figs 3.8 and 3.9).

When the first three versions of the Welland Canal were built over the nineteenth century, the basic process of contracting for public works projects changed little. Engineers drew up plans and specifications for each section of the work, tenders were called for, and contracts awarded, usually to the lowest bidder. Legal agreements were then made for a certain task to be done for a certain sum, according to the specifications, usually within an agreed time. Sureties were required to guarantee that the work would be performed as agreed and contractors were responsible for hiring, supervising, and paying labour crews and for supplying the equipment necessary for the excavation, dredging, and other work required. Provision was made for a "drawback" (withholding of a fixed percentage of the estimated value

3.8   On 14 August 1916, at Section 2, the contractor Henry Osborne Baldry (representing the firm of Baldry, Yerburgh & Hutchinson) confers with Hector Frederik Jansen Estrup, engineer in charge of that section. Despite disagreements, mistakes, and misunderstandings, Ship Canal engineers and contractors often conferred and usually worked together well. (They both had an interest in building a superior waterway.)

of the work) of usually 10 to 15 per cent, a reserve which might be drawn upon by the contractor if unusual expenses occurred but which would then be subtracted from a future payment. Monthly "progress estimates" were made by the sectional engineer and the contractor paid accordingly.

The Great War ended in November 1918 and by early December the Department of Railways and Canals was considering resumption of work on the Ship Canal. The pre-1917 contractors were approached but refused to take up the job again under the old agreements, citing problems with uncertain supplies of labour and equipment. They did agree, however, to work on a cost-plus basis rather than the more usual estimated fixed-cost tenders. The former sort of agreement meant that the

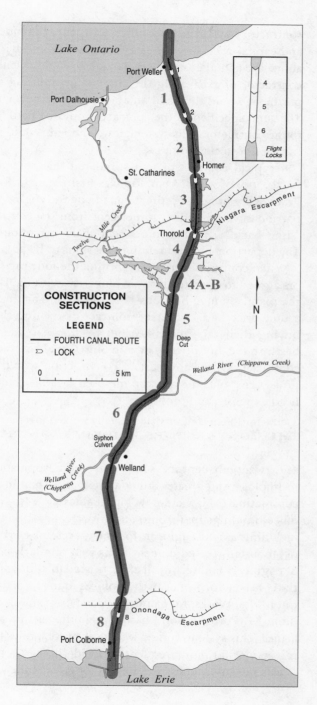

3.9 Construction
Sections on the
Welland Ship Canal

Lake Ontario

Port Weller

Port Dalhousie

1

St. Catharines

2

Homer

3

Niagara Escarpment

Twelve Mile Creek

Thorold

4

4A-B

N

5

Deep Cut

Welland River (Chippawa Creek)

6

Syphon Culvert

Welland River Creek (Chippawa)

Welland

7

Onondaga Escarpment

8

Port Colborne

Lake Erie

4

5

6

Flight Locks

CONSTRUCTION
SECTIONS

LEGEND

FOURTH CANAL ROUTE

LOCK

0   5 km

contractors would supply office staff, superintendents, bookkeepers, and capital necessary for carrying on work and be allowed 8 per cent above the actual cost. The department would calculate the cost to the contractor of excavating the channel or building the locks. The Department would then add an amount to reflect the contractor's profit. The sum, specified in the contract, would be paid by the Department to the contractor. This system, it was hoped, would encourage the contractor not to cut corners.

A typical contract of 1921 stipulated that a tenderer must deposit $1,150,000, of which $350,000 was first payment for plant and stores. From every progress estimate, made by the engineer monthly, the Department would deduct 10 per cent from the contractor's earnings as "draw-back" as well as 10 per cent of the net amount of that estimate. The department would retain these sums to be paid later.

When contracts were re-let in 1919, the four pre-shutdown contractors agreed to operate on a cost-plus basis with the Department owning the plant. By 1922 Sections 1, 2, and 5 were again re-let, this time on a unit price basis, with the contractors owning their own plant and buying their own machines but Section 3 remained on a cost-plus basis. In the unit price system in Ship Canal contracting after 1921, the contract price for any part of construction would include the direct project cost plus the markup imposed by contractors for general overhead expenses and profit.

THE CONTRACTORS WORKING "ON THE GROUND"

The twentieth century saw vastly more sophisticated construction technology and greater attendant expense than in the past. Canadian contracting firms were now big businesses, with head offices in posh office buildings in Toronto and Montreal and their own on-site staffs including a civil engineer, foremen, account clerks, as well as gangs of labourers. The equipment firms were similarly complex, with teams of engineers and technical experts available for consultation either on the construction site or in their offices or manufacturing shops. Hamilton Bridge Works, for example, had shops in both east and west Hamilton; J.P. Porter & Sons, based in Halifax, set up an office in St Catharines. This system worked well, with automobiles for short trips and a rail service far more frequent and widespread than is available today. It was not unusual for the contractor A.W. Robertson to take a night train from his home in Montreal, spend the day visiting Grant and/or a construction site, then take the late afternoon train to Toronto, then back to Montreal.

The new canal was divided into eight (originally nine) sections, with each major contractor taking up one or sometimes two. (Appendix II and fig. 3.9.) The engineers of the Department of Railways and Canals planned the construction of the Ship Canal, detailed plans and specifications were published, and then, as was mandatory, contracts for the work were awarded by public tender to contractors from the private sector. It was then the responsibility of the engineers to supervise those contractors and ensure their proper execution of the work.

While many more of the Ship Canal engineers and contractors were Canadian than on the past reconstructions, some of the contractors were still British or American. For example, the Scherzer Rolling Lift Bridge Co. of Chicago designed Bridge 4 at Homer, while Harrington, Howard & Ash of Kansas City were consulted as designers of the remaining bridges. Wellman-Seaver-Morgan and the American Shipbuilding Co., both of Cleveland, designed the pontoon gate lifter. British firms with shipbuilding experience also had subcontracts for the gate lifter's construction.[52]

Otherwise, Canadian firms predominated. J.P. Porter and Canadian Dredging received most of the work on the Ship Canal sections. Hamilton Bridge Co. built seven rolling lifts as well as two vertical lift bridges; the Canadian Bridge Co. of Walkerville, Ontario, built eight vertical lifts, while Dominion Bridge of Lachine, which had built bridges for the Lachine Canal, had a contract for one vertical lift. Canadian Westinghouse was awarded four contracts, as was Canadian General Electric, while Montreal Locomotive Co., Foster Wheeler of St Catharines, and Canadian Vickers of Montreal, had three each; Dominion Wire Rope, Dominion Foundries & Steel (DOFASCO), Anglo-Canadian Wire Rope, Horton Steel of Welland, and English Electric each had two contracts, as did the firm of Cameron & Phin of Welland.

For equipment, materials, or services, contracts were awarded to dozens of other Canadian firms, many local. Cement was supplied by Canada Cement of Port Colborne and sand by National Sand & Materials, Co., of Welland. Gurney Scale Co. and the Steel Company of Canada (STELCO), both of Hamilton, received equipment as did Canada Brass Co. and Herbert Morris Crane & Hoist Co., both of Niagara Falls, Ontario. In addition to work done on contract, many of the companies acted as subcontractors on specific jobs for other firms or supplied specific equipment on the basis of purchase orders.

One of the most complex contracts was that to Collingwood Shipyards on Georgian Bay for a mammoth gate-lifter. So complicated was its construction that Collingwood let out ten subcontracts. Chief of these was that for the main engine and generating set, which was taken by W.H. Allen & Sons of Bedford, England.

CHALLENGES FOR THE CONTRACTORS

If engineers were faced with many challenges, contractors had their own problems: disputes with workers over wages – which could stop construction —as well as difficulties with their subcontractors. Weather conditions were troublesome on many occasions, adding to the contractors' worries. In 1916, for example, construction on Sections 1, 2, 3, and 5 was retarded by heavy rains in April and May.

The Lyalls in particular may have regretted their association with the Ship Canal project, for they seemed to be beset by continual crises involving subcontractors, labour, accidents, finances, and the weather. In his annual statement to shareholders in May 1924, president William Lyall suggested some of the difficulties of the company on the Welland contract. The "past year ... was a most trying one for our company," he said, citing a strike of steam shovel men and the need to pay higher wages for shorter working hours.[53] In a memorandum to Grant, Lyall said that "during last winter [1924] we encountered the *worst* conditions of weather in the history of the district, causing us heavy expense and delay."[54] As well, Pilkington Glassworks procured an injunction against Lyall, preventing blasting near their plant. The memo to Grant points out that throughout the summer and autumn of 1922 the contractor had been urged to get on with the drilling and blasting opposite the Pilkington plant while the plant was shut down. Lyall & Co. delayed so long that bad weather made it impossible to begin the work so that, when they finally did begin, the plant had reopened, with the inevitable result: on 6 June, when nine holes had been fired in the rock excavation, the resulting vibrations caused one of Pilkington's furnaces to spill hundreds of tonnes of molten glass. The Glass Company applied for an injunction to prohibit further blasting but the Department, anxious to proceed with construction, had the injunction lifted, and before the year ended, Pilkington closed the plant.

Although Lyall's problems were especially extensive, they reflect the difficulties that could bedevil any contracting firm on the Ship Canal.

None of the new Welland's contractors, however, was as plagued by accident as was Lyall. For example, during a particularly bad winter, a high wind blew over one of the firm's 150-foot (45.7 m) concreting towers, for a financial loss of $50,000 and loss of the tower for six weeks. On 1 August 1925 the worst accident on the canal since 1913 occurred. When the company was lowering a Blaw-Knox steel form on the flight locks, a shackle broke, wrecking the form, killing three men, and injuring several others (fig. 9.1).

Unfortunately, worse was yet to come, again on the first of August, in 1928. A 500-ton gate collapsed at Lock 6, killing eight men and sending twenty-four to hospital, where two died later[55] (fig. 9.2). The following year Lyall had another locomotive crane topple over, which, said Grant, "looked like carelessness."[56]

Contractors' problems could sometimes arise from disputes not with the engineers or their subcontractors but with other contractors. In 1925, for example, J.P. Porter complained to Jewett that the unfortunate Lyall would not co-operate with him on arrangements to control Ten Mile Creek where their two sections adjoined.[57] Earlier, in May 1924, rumours circulated that Lyall might abandon his contracts for Sections 3 and 4. Despite a number of troubles, however, the firm managed to survive until September 1929 when they went into liquidation, dismaying their subcontractors and further troubling Alex Grant's sleep. On 24 September he went to Ottawa, meeting with G.S. Currie, the liquidator appointed to handle the business, and Mattice and Gardiner, Lyall's partners in the Steel Gates Company. A suggestion that excavation should be carried on by subcontractors Roger Miller & Sons did not meet with Grant's approval.[58] Arrangements were made for the work to be carried on under Currie's direction.

On Section 8 problems with rock excavation reflected contractors' challenges along the whole line. At the end of July 1924, for example, Northern Construction's shovels revealed seams in the rock that produced "1000 gallons per minute of water" and "flooded out 2 steam shovels for about ten days." In September of that year heavy rains flooded the south end of the earth excavation, submerging three shovels for a week (fig. 6.15).

Nevertheless, wrote the Sectional Engineer Kydd, "the shovels worked night and day during the whole time of work, the dump ground being electric lighted [*sic*] for this purpose."[59] In a rare example of an engineer praising a contractor, in 1930 E.P. Murphy lauded the company for the way it had recently cleaned the area of Lock 8 and made it "shipshape ... in such a manner as to reflect great credit on the Northern Construction Co. who did it."[60]

THE SUBCONTRACTORS

Over the period of construction, scores of subcontractors worked on the new Welland.[61] For example, the Steel Gates Company of Montreal, responsible for construction of the massive lock gates, subcontracted much of the work because their shops were not big enough.[62] Montreal Locomotive Works sublet the motors for the gate machines, as well as for the valve-operating machines, to Harland Engineering of Canada with the result that the motors were built by Harland's parent company at Alloa, Scotland.[63] The Cutler-Hammer Company of Milwaukee supplied some of the switches, also on a subcontract to Montreal Locomotive Works.

Subcontracting was not confined to the more complicated technical aspects of the work. The section of the Ship Canal at the Lake Erie end, Section 8, was contracted to A.W. Robertson of Montreal, who, from the outset, subdivided the work for three different contractors. In the same way, E.O. Leahey, who, with Atlas Construction Company, had been awarded Section 6, subcontracted most of the excavation work outside the syphon culvert to J.P. Porter, who was the main contractor for Sections 1 and 2.[64]

Lyall & Co., sorely tried in many ways, seem to have been unusually unfortunate with their subcontractors. In 1922, A.E. Rigby, as their subcontractor, started excavating the prism on Section 3. By 18 April 1923 he and Lyall were at loggerheads. The following year Lyall and another of his subcontractors, G.L. Campbell of Montreal, were again in a dispute. The report that reached Grant noted that an agreement had been reached dissolving contract on 16 May. J.A. Grant & Co. took it over as of 30 September, although their association with Lyall was of fairly short duration. By at least late September of 1925 he was working for E.O. Leahey on the syphon culvert on Section 6 but by June 1927 he had left and Jack Horgan had taken over his responsibilities.

In all these disputes, Alex Grant remained neutral. For the engineer in charge, subcontractors were agents of only the main contractors.

For example, when in 1928, concerned about the slowness of delivery of motors to Montreal Locomotive Works from their agent in Scotland, Harland Engineering, he wrote to Montreal: "We only recognize the Harland Engineering Company as your agents, consequently we have no control over them and, for the delivery of the motors on time, we have to look to you ... As the Harland Engineering Company are your agents, it is a matter between you and them as to how many motors you have in your shop for testing out the gate and valve machines and with this situation I have nothing to do."[65] And thus Grant distanced himself from some headaches.

CONTRACTORS' "INGENUITY AND HEARTY CO-OPERATION"?

"It is only fitting," wrote the British engineer and journalist P.J. Cowan, "to pay tribute ... to the ingenuity and hearty co-operation displayed by the engineers of the many contracting firms engaged [in building the canal]."[66] Was Cowan being tactful or was he too removed from the scene of the action to know of Grant's problems? We leave it to our readers to decide. At all events, we concur with Robert Legget when he praised the "vision, skill and courage"[67] of the men who conceived and executed this great project.

Our next chapter takes us further into the excavation of "the ditch," which presented problems for the engineers and contractors over the period of construction that can only be described as unexpected, disastrous, and occasionally ridiculous.

CHAPTER FOUR

Excavating the Prism

The Welland Ship Canal is still a dominant feature of the Niagara Region, a broad waterway attracting wildlife, tourists, and locals to its banks. In the winter months, when much of the canal is de-watered, Niagara residents are still amazed at the width and depth of the empty channel – often over 200 feet (61 m) wide at bottom, over 300 feet (91.4 m) wide at water level, and nearly 30 feet (9.1 m) deep. While excavation of the ever-larger "ditches" of the first three Welland Canals had become increasingly complex, that of the prism of the Fourth or Ship Canal involved removing even more tonnes of earth and rock and directing even more Lake Erie water into a new channel connecting to Lake Ontario.

FROM THE FIRST SOD TO THE FIRST SHIPS

When work began on the Ship Canal in 1913, canal construction machinery was still often powered by steam but now was increasingly supplemented by petroleum and hydroelectric power, developments of the Second Industrial Revolution. When Section 9, including Port Colborne harbour, was amalgamated with 8 and separate Sections 4A and 4B were spun off from 4, south of Thorold, such changes resulted not only from the growth of highly specialized Canadian contracting firms engaged in public works throughout the Dominion, but also from the much greater power and variety of equipment available.

By April 1913 the specifications for Section 1, at the northern end of the site, had been drawn up, and in May the Department asked Alfred Noble (1844–1914), a New York consulting engineer, to examine the plans for the new canal (fig. 4.2). His report, which, said Weller characteristically, "fully endorsed my plans and proposals,"[1] moved the authorities to call for excavation tenders. The initial contract was

4.1   Somewhere in Niagara, probably between 1905 and 1913. Ship Canal surveyors mapping out the line of the great ditch. Do they proudly sense the importance of their work?

signed on 1 August 1913 and soon the first shovelful of earth was removed in Section 1. Unlike the events of 1824, no public sod turning or banquet took place. The war halted construction in 1917, but from January 1919 through the rest of the year to the spring of 1920, some work resumed, beginning with the purchase and replacement of plant sold during the conflict and the job of restoration necessary before active construction could be resumed. Sections 2 and 3 saw most of the activity with the largest number of labourers employed, especially in the fall of 1919. In the early twenties, contracts were entered into for the remaining sections.

In 1926 the harbour and piers at Port Weller were completed, and by the fall of 1927 the whole project was three-quarters complete. The locks, finished by 1930, were constructed to allow 30-feet (9 m) navigation while the reaches between locks were to be excavated for only 25-feet (7.6 m) navigation. Towards 1930 pressure from shipowners to send their larger vessels through the completed part of the channel

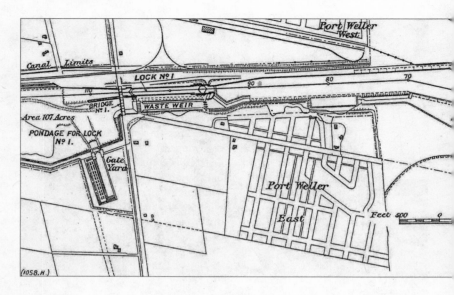

increased. Certain dredging projects, however, had yet to be completed, and even when these were finished deepening of the locks in
the future was considered likely.

Construction of new bridges began in 1925 with the last finished in
1930. The syphon culvert at Welland, also begun in 1925, was in operation by 1930. Nevertheless, these dates should not be considered mile-
stones in the perfection of such structures, for adjustment went on for
months afterwards. Although the canal began operation in late November 1930, contracts were still being executed even after the formal
opening in August 1932. In fact, improvements continued to be made
regularly. As was the case with the first three canals, the Ship Canal
was never considered "finished."

MODERN MACHINERY

Even from the vantage point of the twenty-first century, the number
and variety of plant used in Ship Canal dredging and excavation is impressive. Certainly, the nineteenth-century engineers Killaly or Page
would have been amazed – and envious.

Removing material from the bottom of the old prism or deepening
harbours was fundamental to the "ditch digging." Dredges with pic-

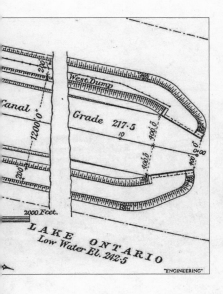

4.2 Port Weller. The gate yard, Lock 1, the harbour, and the piers. This plan, as many others reproduced in this book, has an ordered clarity that, although it aids in our understanding of the canal's construction, contrasts sharply with the apparently chaotic nature of the construction site revealed in contemporary photographs.

turesque names such as DOMINION and DRAGON ROUGE worked on the Port Weller and Port Colborne harbours or the widening and deepening of the older channel. Some were clam dredges which lowered, closed, and raised a single bucket on cables. Others, like the PRIMROSE, SHUNIAH, and STEWART were suction or hydraulic dredges, which used airtight suction piping and a centrifugal pump to raise material from the deepening prism. The DELVER, FUNDY, and EXCELSIOR were dipper dredges, equipped with a long boom on which was a bucket with digging teeth and a bottom door held by a spring latch controlled by the operator (fig. 4.3).

On the dry excavation, great steam-powered shovels and draglines snorted and clattered away. For example, at work on Section 1 in 1913 were a Brownhoist locomotive crane with a clam-shell bucket, a Bucyrus steam shovel, a Bucyrus dragline excavator, a Marion-Osgoode steam shovel, and two Western spreaders. In 1914 three such draglines and twenty shovels were employed on the whole site. By 1925 some of these were electrically powered. That year, two such "3" machines, the "largest of their type in the world," were brought in by J.P. Porter for work on Section 6.[2] Another type of excavating machine was a dragline shovel with a long boom held at an angle to the ground from which hung a bucket which was drawn toward the shovel by a

4.3   The dredge PRIMROSE, built by Matthew Beatty and Sons of Welland, typical of the dredging equipment used in Ship Canal construction.

dragline. Its teeth faced the machine, whereas on a dipper shovel the teeth faced outward. As with some dredges, a clamshell shovel had a long boom with a two-jaw bucket attached to two lines. One line was used to raise and lower the bucket while the other pulled the jaws together in a digging motion, opening by gravity when the digging line was released. Grading machines were hauled by traction engines or by teams of mules. Essentially ploughshares, five of these were at work on Section 2 in 1914, ploughing furrows, the earth from which was turned onto a belt running at a right angle to the machine and dropping the spoil into dump wagons following alongside. Such were some of the more impressive machines which chewed away at the clay, shale, and quicksand of Niagara (see this volume's frontispiece).

For drilling blast holes in rock, Keystone and Cyclone drills were run by electric motors. Dynamite was inserted into the holes, after which detonation would loosen the stone. A Sullivan channelling machine was used to cut rock, "by what is practically a large saw operated by steam."[3] Rock had to be drilled and blasted underwater, too. For this purpose, Ingersoll-Rand submarine drills on 80-foot-long

4.4 A shunter engine and cars of the construction railway, which ran along the west side of the new canal from Merritton to Port Weller.

(24.4 m) boats could be seen at Port Colborne harbour. Each had a steam plant, an air-compressing plant for clearing the drill holes, a blacksmith's shop for sharpening, and an electric light plant.

Other machinery was virtually stationary. On Section 3 the contractors O'Brien & Doheny and Quinlan & Robertson erected a rock-crushing plant, just north of the Grand Trunk Railway line. Here, near Merritton,[4] all the rock, mainly sandstone that had been blasted from the Escarpment, would be crushed and carried away by the double track construction railway on Sections 1, 2, and 3, for use in concreting or backfilling at the first three locks and in the piers of the new Port Weller harbour (fig. 5.11). A washing plant was built nearby in order to remove shale and dirt from some of the stone. Less impressive but equally necessary were the scores of barges, scows, and tugs plying the harbours and the channel.

In order to "recycle" rock excavated and later pulverized at the rock-crushing plant, the Departmental engineers designed and Departmental forces laid out the construction railway on the west side of the channel from the flight locks to Lake Ontario (fig. 4.4). The railway's hoppers and dump cars carried stone to and fresh concrete from the crusher. Seven and one-half miles (12.1 km) long, the line also carried aggregates and contractors' supplies such as steel. The storehouse and yard of the railway was at Port Weller, on the site of the present Mary Malcolmson Park. Construction of the line began in the fall of 1913 and was finished by July 1914, but not before the rails had sunk in several places, necessitating the addition of further ballast along the tracks. The construction railway had to cross the route of the Third Canal between Locks 10 and 11, so a temporary steel swing bridge was installed there in 1915, south of Lock 3, where the two channels intersected near the present site of the St Catharines Museum.[5]

This railway was essential to the efficiency and success of the whole project and was exceptionally busy in the early 1920s. In October 1920, H. Lampard, its superintendent, reported that the greatest number of trains on one day in that month was fifty-eight. In 1928 he reported that on one day in August 396 trains travelled the line and that in that month alone, twenty thousand cars were hauled.[6]

Like many features of the Ship Canal works, however, the system was not perfect. In fact, the construction railway could itself be an obstacle to the canal's construction. A timber trestle bridge carrying it over Twin Locks 5 in the mid-twenties retarded construction at that site until late in the project. Elsewhere, excavated material, heaped carelessly onto railway cars, tended to fall off when the train was under way. In 1922 George McDonald, a labourer, had a leg broken by a falling clump of rock and hard clay. Such objects could be as big as a cubic yard (0.9 m³), endangering not only men but also locomotives, speeders, and interlocking equipment. A danger to trackside communities were the sparks from construction railway locomotives which, in dry hot summers, caused grass fires.

Variants of such plant are still in use today, but were undreamed of by the Welland Canal Company in the 1820s. Even in this era of Canada's Second Industrial Revolution, however, mules were still employed on the Ship Canal's building sites. Used in teams, these long-eared beasts, usually brown in colour, with short manes, were preferred to horses, although the latter were employed when mules were unavailable. They pulled both wagons or scrapers, even grinding outfits. Several photographs show as many as thirty mules patiently (or stubbornly?) awaiting their master's commands (frontispiece and fig. 8.2). At one time on Section 6, where the channel between Port

Robinson and Welland was being excavated, over four hundred mules were used to pull graders.[7] Some experts believed that mule power was as efficient as machine power.

The new technology was undeniably an aid to efficiency but it could daunt even experienced engineers. Although electricity had been introduced to the Third Welland over twenty years earlier, the more sophisticated system installed to operate bridges on the Ship Canal disturbed the Departmental engineer, M. Brodie Atkinson, who wrote to the Hamilton Bridge Company asking that "some protection" be installed on the switchboards in bridge control rooms to prevent someone from accidentally activating the machinery. He had "found himself leaning up against the switchboard but fortunately the electric current was cut off." A Hamilton Bridge engineer replied that he was "certainly surprised that any of his engineering friends would be so careless as to lean up against a switchboard. It is not the best way of discovering whether the current is on or off."[8]

Sometimes the engineers' problems with technology were trivial but still annoying and occasioning further delays. In 1931, for example, installation of the turbines in the powerhouse at Twin Locks 4 was held up because the Departmental engineers did not have wrenches suitable to fit the nuts on the turbine governors. Their request to the manufacturers, S. Morgan Smith-Inglis Company, to remedy the deficit was met with an incredulous reply: "In all of our experience with the large number of ... governors we have furnished for various installations, we have so far met with no request for wrenches."[9]

For the most part, however, the engineers adapted well to newer demands on their ingenuity and skills and confronted trivial nuisances with a sense of humour. Jewett, in fact, collected a "museum of defective parts," such as a shaft and pinion with broken teeth removed in 1930 from Bridge 4 at Homer. Apparently all such oddities were to be "handed over to Mr. J."[10]

"A MOST INTERESTING TIME"

Niagara's geology had always presented special problems for the engineers and contractors. Whereas the builders of the First and Second Canals often had to cut their way through virgin forest, the Ship Canal engineers and contractors faced mainly meadows and fields, which rendered their job easier. Because the new waterway would be deeper and wider, however, they had to deal with rock formations which the earlier, shallower versions of the waterway never encountered. For example, the "Rock Cut" between Port Colborne and Humberstone had to be deepened and widened. Frequently, clay of the consistency of stone had to be cut through. The notorious hardpan confronted contractors such as Peter Lyall, who had to tackle it at the site of Twin Locks 4. In addition, "mudstone," another rocklike material, caused him much added expense and delay, and may have contributed to his eventual bankruptcy. Intractable stone and clay were not the only geological challenges. In the excavation of Section 6, between Port Robinson and Welland, the contractors met peatbeds which, because they provided unstable foundations for structures, had to be completely removed.·

As ever, "the treacherous blue clay" caused the sides of the developing prism to collapse, occasionally burying shovels and draglines and even killing men. Labourers operating spreaders to push excavated material at the site of fills often had "a most interesting time," said Weller, with solid lumps of clay "of the consistency of soft putty" often a metre or more wide.[11]

At Section 8, where at times the drilling and blasting of rock were carried on with continuous day and night shifts, the heavy clay curtailed operations. Whereas the early part of summer of 1925 was dry and conducive to the work, heavy rains in the fall hampered the work because all the material was that heavy clay. Oliver Phelps's nemesis in the 1820s – quicksand – was encountered in the 1920s between Lock 3 and Bridge 5. On Section 4, near Thorold, contractors struggled to excavate rock where the heavy surface strata broke up into large slabs, which required extensive redrilling and blasting. The fissures in this stone were filled with earth, making the rock unsuitable to crush for concrete.

Not surprisingly, the Deep Cut between Allanburg and Port Robinson still demanded imaginative treatment. Because this stretch of the Third Canal remained in service but was to be enlarged, the contractors could not unwater it at any time during the main construction season; that is, it was impossible to excavate it "in the dry," so most of the excavation was done by dredging. Blasting was necessary at the Deep Cut's northern end, where some rock was encountered. Again, however, the explosions had to be carefully controlled for fear that disturbed rocks would become a dangerous obstruction to the navigation. Because the construction railway did not extend south of the Escarpment, such rock had to be transported by barge to Lake Erie, to be dumped outside the eastern breakwater.

"Slips," or landslides, which had plagued the builders of the First Canal, continued to occur in the twentieth century, as on Section 7 in 1930 when the raising and lowering of the water level caused several extensive slides on both sides of the channel. Some sites were more prone to slides than others, such as the area around Bridge 12 at Port Robinson, where in 1931 the new piers showed instability, necessitating the laying of a reinforcing slab. Near the village of Homer, the banks failed repeatedly during construction – and still require attention today, as the pilings of Bridge 4 have had to be reinforced repeatedly. The problem was caused by the removal of earth from the bottom of the slopes during the deepening. The remedy was the excavation of the top of the bank to alter the slope, thus reducing the weight there and providing stability. Elsewhere, the prevention of such slips was undertaken by putting down concrete slab protection, or sometimes "stone pitching," on the banks or by removing any material which gave an indication of probable movement and dumping rock in its place.

Niagara's climate, too, continued to inhibit the digging of "the ditch." In December 1921 Section 5, although far inland from Lake Erie, suffered from a storm which caused very high water in the summit level of the operating waterway. Water flowed over the top of the canal's guard gates, flooding the previously unwatered new prism to the north and damaging the recently laid sodding on the slopes. Near Port Colborne, heavy rain flooded the Rock Cut on Section 8 in the fall of 1924. Three shovels were nearly submerged in the prism here and were immobilized for a week (fig. 6.15). On Section 6, south of Port Robinson, the unusually wet fall and spring of 1926–27 and an early "freeze-up" delayed work on the watertight embankments. Back on Section 8, heavy rains in the fall of 1925 inhibited excavation already made difficult by the ubiquitous heavy clay.

Sometimes it was human handiwork that retarded excavation. At Port Colborne in 1929–30, near the new Bridge 21, stonework of the Third Canal, although in good condition, had to be removed and was difficult to dismantle. Local industries, although they stood to benefit from the new waterway, were not always co-operative. On Section 4, in October 1924 the Department had to hire its own labour to remove tracks, pulpwood, and other materials belonging to the Ontario Paper plant, "owing to the latter Company making no attempt at their removal in spite of repeated instructions from the Department to effect their removal."[12]

For his part, Grant was not indifferent to the challenges faced by contractors. In 1930, when reporting on the rock excavation in the prism and north of the new guard gate, he acknowledged the contractor's "very efficient and vigorous programme during the past Winter months" – high praise from a demanding perfectionist.[13]

By the beginning of the fourth decade of the twentieth century, the channel of the Welland Ship Canal had been completed. Since then, however, the improvement of the great ditch has never ceased. While there is as yet no "Fifth" Canal, two major developments have occurred: the expansion of the channel during the construction of the St Lawrence Seaway and the building of the massive "Welland By-Pass" with its syphon culvert and tunnels (Appendix IV). On these projects, new technology – more complex instruments and larger, more powerful machinery – aided the builders. Yet although the present Welland is notable for its size and modernity, the process of enlarging and improving it presented engineers with many of the same problems that confronted Barrett and Keefer or Weller and Grant.

DEEPENING THE PRISM

The St Lawrence Seaway was inaugurated in 1959 but the concept was not then new. The perceived need for canals on the St Lawrence/Great Lakes system probably began when Jacques Cartier encountered the Lachine Rapids in 1535. Certainly, the foundation of the modern Seaway began with the construction of canals along the St Lawrence in the early 1700s. The idea of an Atlantic–Great Lakes waterway was still alive when in 1801 the explorer Alexander Mackenzie wrote to Lord Hobart, British Secretary for War and the Colonies, describing a Seaway-like network of waterways along the St Lawrence between Lake Ontario and Montreal. William Hamilton Merritt had also envisioned such a complex of canals, including the Welland, and had done more than anyone else to disseminate the idea in his time. "His" canal was never designed to stand alone, linking only lakes Erie and Ontario, and he would not have been surprised to see it enlarged twice after his death.

The fourth incarnation of "Mr. Merritt's Ditch" was vastly larger and more complex than Merritt could have imagined. It would, how-

ever, fulfill his vision of a link in the waterway joining the Atlantic
and the heartland of North America. Even by 1850 the Welland had
become a vital part of an international system of shipping and trade.
Both Canada and the United States had important interests invested
in its maintenance, but changes to it and to the St Lawrence system
would involve high-level diplomatic negotiations. The American concern for the Welland, therefore, continued, not so much in financial
commitment, as in Merritt's day, but in economic interdependence.

Of course, the living nexus of trade in wheat, coal, iron, and other
products did not wait on diplomacy. Soon after 1932 over 100 million bushels of wheat were passing through the Ship Canal each
season, making Canada the world's leading exporter of grain. One
serious problem remained: the St Lawrence canals were still a relative bottleneck because their locks were smaller than those on the
Welland. Moreover, the river's navigable channels were only 14 feet
(4.3 m) deep, while Niagara's "great swivel link" was deeper at 30 feet
(9.1 m) – all of which created an imbalance in the system. Meanwhile,
the phenomenon of the increasing number of ships and the growing
size of cargoes continued.

Since the late nineteenth century, international discussions had
taken place on the matter of a co-operative venture between Canada
and the United States, and especially a "deep waterway" of a uni-
fied depth from the Atlantic to the lakehead. To this end, in 1905 the
International Waterways Commission was created. In 1909 the International Joint Commission succeeded the Waterways body. Among
other things, the interested parties considered how to synchronize the
size of the St Lawrence locks and channel with those of the Welland
(Appendix v). As in the past, however, events not originating in Niagara or the river/lakes basin affected development of the Welland and
its links to the ocean. After 1914, major wars and worldwide depression intervened. Partly for these reasons, in 1932 and later in 1941, the
United States Congress balked at making a contribution to improving
what would be the American share of the St Lawrence canals.

After the Second World War, the Canadian government made plans
to build the waterway alone, and in 1951 the St Lawrence Seaway Authority, a crown corporation, was established. Agreement with the
Americans was achieved in 1954. In Canada, the crown corporation
would construct, operate, and maintain the Canadian portion of the
St Lawrence River between Montreal and Lake Erie. The St Lawrence Seaway Development Corporation was formed by the American

government to operate two locks near Massena, New York. The project also included the American locks on the St Mary's River operated by the American Corps of Engineers and the Canadian lock at "the Soo," today run by Parks Canada. Construction began, therefore, in 1954, while the volume of trade on the Welland continued to grow. Even in the five years before the enlarged waterway system's completion, the volume of traffic on the Welland doubled to over six million tons (5,443,108 tonnes) of freight annually.[14]

Reflecting the international significance of the Seaway, of which the Welland was a part, its official opening in 1959 was attended by Prime Minister John Diefenbaker, Queen Elizabeth II, and President Dwight D. Eisenhower. Unlike the 1932 festivities, however, no great ceremony was held in Niagara to inaugurate the Welland's expansion as the continuing and essential heart of the mighty waterway system.

As part of the Seaway project, the St Lawrence locks would be rebuilt on the same dimensions as the Welland's. At the same time, the channel of Niagara's canal was to be dredged to 27 feet (8.2 m) of water where the bottom was of earth. Excavation "in the dry" was to be undertaken to a depth of 30 feet (9.1 m) where it was rock. And thus "this colossal project," begun in 1913, continued to grow in size throughout the twentieth century.

The prism of the Ship Canal was merely a channel for water to pass from Lake Erie to Lake Ontario. This water was essential for the movement of ships but even more necessary were locks built into that channel at regular intervals to lift or lower the ships. Without these structures, the "ditch" would simply be another fast-moving and dangerous river. Building these lifts is the subject of our next chapter.

CHAPTER FIVE

Creating the Lifts

The widening, deepening prism of the Ship Canal was an impressive sight – if also dusty, noisy, and occasionally very wet. In the "dry" excavations, the roar and clatter of heavy steam shovels added to the loud bustle of dredges, scows, and tugs in the operating waterway. Belching white steam and black smoke, the construction railway's locomotives hauled rattling hoppers along the channel's west bank. Near Merritton, the rock crushing plant slammed and crashed its product into shape.

As the excavation of the prism developed, a major, but not insurmountable, challenge to the Welland Ship Canal builders remained: how best to get boats up and down the Niagara Escarpment? With each version of the canal, the locks had become larger, in response to the ever-increasing size of ships, and fewer, in order to speed up transit (fig. 5.1). By the early years of the twentieth century, advances in technology had led not only to construction of vessels of a size undreamt of in the 1820s but also to equipment and materials which could construct locks of mammoth dimensions.

Partly as a result of these developments, the Escarpment would be surmounted by the massive double flight locks, built at a right angle to the cliff (fig. 5.6). This abrupt rise of land has several "breaks" where the sheer wall has disintegrated into gentle inclines. The Ship Canal's builders made use of the one caused by the course of Ten Mile Creek, which tumbled over the ridge in a picturesque waterfall. But this "commonsensical" solution to getting ships up and down the cliff left open the question ...

WHAT KIND OF LOCKS?

John Weller played a pivotal role in the original design of the Ship Canal. Confident and knowledgeable, Weller had the courage to

FIRST WELLAND CANAL
STARTED 1824 —— COMPLETED 1829

TYPICAL LOCK

TYPICAL VESSEL
LENGTH 100 FT. – CARGO CAPACITY 185 TONS

LENGTH BETWEEN GATES........110 F
WIDTH OF LOCK.............22 F
DEPTH OF WATER OVER SILLS.......8 F
SINGLE LIFTS..........6FT. .TO. 11 F
NUMBER OF LOCKS................3

SECOND WELLAND CANAL
STARTED 1842 —— COMPLETED 1845

TYPICAL LOCK

TYPICAL VESSEL
LENGTH 140 FT. – CARGO CAPACITY 750 TONS

LENGTH BETWEEN GATES........150
WIDTH OF LOCK.............26 FT. 6
DEPTH OF WATER OVER SILLS.......9
SINGLE LIFTS.....9FT. 6IN. TO 14FT.
NUMBER OF LOCKS..............

THIRD WELLAND CANAL
STARTED 1875 —— COMPLETED 1887

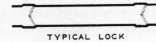

TYPICAL VESSEL
LENGTH 255 FT – CARGO CAPACITY 2700 TONS

TYPICAL LOCK

LENGTH BETWEEN GATES.......270
WIDTH OF LOCK.............45
DEPTH OF WATER OVER SILLS.....14
SINGLE LIFTS.......... 12FT. TO 16
NUMBER OF LOCKS..............

WELLAND SHIP CANAL
STARTED 1913 —— COMPLETED 1932-33

LENGTH BETWEEN INNER GATES___869 FT
WIDTH OF LOCK_____80 FT
DEPTH OF WATER OVER SILLS____30 FT. (REACHES 25 FT)

SINGLE LIFTS................46FT. 6
NUMBER OF LOCKS.. INCLUDING 3 TWIN____
TOTAL LOCKAGE.............325FT. 6

THE GUARD LOCK AT HUMBERSTONE IS 1380 FT. LONG BETWEEN INNER GATES

TYPICAL LOCK

TYPICAL VESSEL
MAXIMUM LENGTH 820 FT. & CARGO CAPACITY 25000 TONS AT 24 FT. DRAFT.

5.1   Comparison of lock sizes in 1932.

envision possibilities even beyond those realized on the Panama. In March 1911 George Graham, Minister of Railways and Canals, told the House of Commons about "something that may startle the ordinary individual" – an entirely new Welland Canal would be built with only two locks. Weller's idea was that the Ship Canal could have a mere two lifts, 800 feet (243.8 m) long by 80 feet (24.4 m) wide, each lifting ships 165 feet (50.3 m). The small number of locks would shorten the time each ship spent traversing the waterway. Moreover, Weller thought that the lower end or foot of each lock would be serviced by a gate of the "guillotine" type, with one huge gate being lifted and lowered out of the water on structures spanning the ends of each lock. (The upper gates would be of the double mitering kind.) This would be practicable, he thought, writing to Bowden in October 1910: "Such locks would, of course, be entirely beyond all precedent, but the more I study them the more inclined I am to believe that they would solve the problem in a most substantial, efficient and safe manner."[1]

The idea of vertical sliding "guillotine" gates lasted until at least 1912, when Weller was still pressing the notion on Bowden and was in correspondence with the Strauss Bascule Bridge Company of Chicago about such gates. The concept of a canal with only two such locks proved impractical, however, and Weller was soon planning for eight locks, three of which (those at the Escarpment) would be twinned. They would have *single-leaf* "rolling gates" – at least for the upper end of the locks. These gates would swing on a hinge at one side of the lock and rest in a recess cut into the lock wall; in other words, one single gate would span the whole width of the chamber. At the foot of each lock the gate would be 83 feet (25.3 m) high and 88 feet (26.8 m) long (fig. 5.2).

Weller believed that single-leaf gates were safer than the traditional *double* mitre gates when the lift of the lock was as high as he planned. Consulting engineer Alfred Noble reported in 1913 that, whereas he would personally adopt mitering (double) gates over single-leaf ones, "both forms are in successful use and either will give good service."[2]

And so, for at least seven years after construction began, the engineers assumed that, unlike the double-leaf lock gates of the first three canals, the locks of the Ship Canal would be single leaf. Weller's specifications for Section 1, dated 1 May 1913, described Lock 1 as having "two single leaf lock gates, one on the breast wall at the head of the lock and the other at the foot of the lock." The unwatering gates,

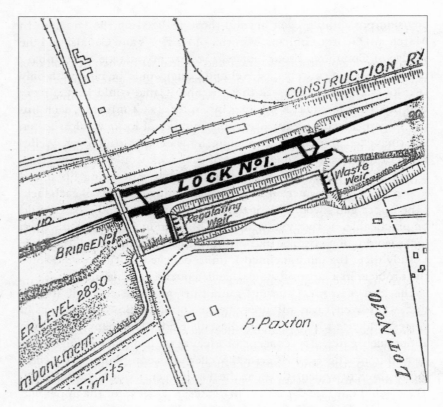

5.2 Port Weller. Original plan for Lock 1, showing single-leaf gates (the mitering symbol marks the unwatering gates).

however, would be mitered; i.e., double-leaf gates.[3] In April 1915 the concreting of Lock 1 began, with a recess on the east lower side for the withdrawal of a large single-leaf gate. So matters rested when construction was halted in 1917.

When building resumed after the First World War, Weller was replaced by Alex Grant and may well have been dismayed to see how his plans were subsequently altered. But changed "in mid-stream" they were, a surprising phenomenon given the expensive nature of this public works project but perhaps not so unusual, given the new waterway's great complexity and the insight and dynamism of the new engineer in charge.

CHANGING PLANS

One of the major problems Grant had to deal with when he took over the Ship Canal in 1919 was this question of the lock gates. He believed that the single leaves planned by Weller would be more unwieldy, would take up too much room in the lock chamber, and would take longer to open and close than mitre gates. In addition they would limit the length of each lock to 800 feet (243.8 m), whereas double-leaf mitering gates would allow for 20 more feet (6.1 m) of usable space in each lock. Mitering gates, moreover, would not be as heavy as single-leaf gates and would be therefore easier to position. As late as May 1919, a map of Twin Locks 6 showed the lower gates as single-leaf and the upper ones as double mitered gates.[4] In 1920 arguments against single-leaf gates were still circulating in the Department and no decision seems yet to have been taken.

Although documentation is lacking, Grant was probably the engineer who pushed for the abandonment of the single-leaf plan and for the use of the more traditional double mitering gates.[5] He was in correspondence with American engineers at Sault Ste Marie about single-leaf gates and visited that canal in late February 1920. In a letter of March 1920, the Ship Canal engineer F.C. Jewett, who was preparing a report for Grant on the state of Lock 1, referred to a phone call from Grant "affecting the type of gate to be used" on Lock 2.[6] In April 1920 Grant wrote to Bowden explaining his preference for double-leaf mitre gates: "they are more manageable in operation, easier and more quickly handled in case of accidents, and if equipped with [Gowan safety] horns their main disadvantage ... is to a large extent eliminated."[7] Finally, about the beginning of May 1920, Grant met in Ottawa with Bowden and with the St Lawrence canals engineer, D.W. McLachlan, and the three agreed to change the configuration of the ship canal's lock gates.[8]

At this time most of Lock 1's west wall and part of its east wall had already been built according to the single-leaf plan, which meant that, in 1922–23, gate recesses had to be cut out for the mitered gates while workers used explosives to take out a thousand cubic yards (764.6 m³) of finished concrete from the lock wall. The recess provided for the larger single-leaf gates then had to be reduced to suit the smaller size of the mitre gate leaves (figs 5.3 and 5.4).

5.3 Port Weller, 28 February 1923. Tearing out the recess in the west wall of Lock 1 after the plan to use single-leaf gates was abandoned in favour of mitre gates.

In opting for the traditional form of lock gates, Grant, Bowden, and their colleagues cannot be accused of conservatism because at the same time they were considering a daring and massive undertaking: the future twinning of all the locks on the new canal. Of course, from the start, the three lifts at the Escarpment had been planned as twin locks but in 1922 consideration was given to doubling all the locks on the new waterway. Bowden had visited the site in February of that year and had asked Grant if twinning were possible. In March Grant replied in a letter that the work was too advanced on Locks 1, 2, 3,

5.4   Port Weller, 1925. Interior of Lock 1, gates not yet hung, showing the mitre sill. The photographer, J.A. McDonald, has captured the intrinsic beauty of a structure never seen by any but engineers, contractors, and workmen. The simplicity of the massive lock walls, the perspective towards the far gates, and the precise symmetry of curves and angles of the mitre sill and dwarf walls (for guiding the cables of the gate-operating gear) appeal to our visual sense as they did to McDonald's.

and 7 for them to be twinned at the present time. At Port Colborne, however, little work had been done on Lock 8, so that it could be easily twinned. As for the other locks, "Future generations will have to solve the problem."[9] Nevertheless, a plan of Lock 7 shows the two alternatives (fig. 5.5).

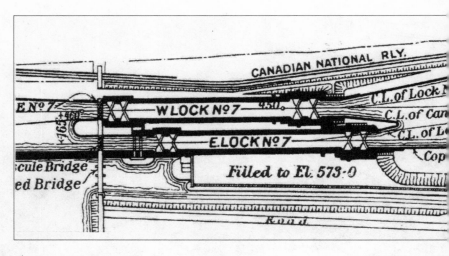

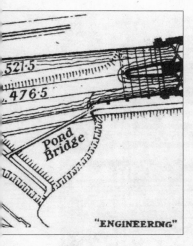

5.5 Thorold. Original plans for
Lock 7, showing the intended twinning.
Ultimately, only the three flight locks (4–6)
were twinned.

5.6 Thorold, ca. 1925. Twin Locks 4
under construction, showing the depth
of excavation, Blaw-Knox concreting
forms, and entrance to the conduits.
The technology of the 1920s permitted a
"head-on" attack on the Niagara Escarpment
as opposed to the lengthier oblique
approach taken by earlier canal builders.

5.7   Port Weller, 1927. A huge unfinished lock gate in place at Lock 1, dwarfing labourers.

According to a Departmental pamphlet of 1920,[10] the engineers also planned to remove the old stone locks from the first two canals at Port Colborne. As it turned out, however, "future generations" can still enjoy the sight of these two structures, for they were not demolished. Considerations of their historical value may have come into play for we know that Grant was interested in preserving certain older canal structures, but there is no documentary evidence as to who made the

5.8   Port Colborne, May 1928. Lock 8 almost completed, showing the twin set of gates, looking south from Bridge 19. The ladder must have been a challenge for some labourers.

decision not to remove them or when. The covered supply channel adjacent to the Second Canal guard lock was not removed possibly because it would still be of service. Conceivably, the walls of these two locks were deemed useful as piers for the approach spans to the two bridges crossing here at Port Colborne. Of course, experience with the removal of the Third Canal aqueduct and other earlier stone structures suggested that the process would have been time-consuming and expensive.

The average lift for the first seven locks would be an impressive 46.5 feet (14.2 m). Between Lake Ontario and the Escarpment the first three locks of the Ship Canal would gradually raise ships 140 feet (42 m) to the base of the cliff, where the three twin locks would carry vessels a further 140 feet (42.7 m). The locks' massive gates would be each 5 feet (1.5 m) thick; the lower gates, 82 feet (25 m) high, and upper gates, 35 feet (10.7 m) high (figs 5.1, 5.7, and 5.8).

Besides being much larger, the new locks differed from their predecessors in several other ways. For example, a horizontal passage or gallery, 6.5 feet high (1.98 m) and 3 feet wide (0.9 m), with connecting passages to the lock chamber, was built into both walls of each lock in order to moor boats when the water level was low. Spiral staircases connected these galleries with the surface.

THE AMAZING TWIN LOCKS

In June 1924, Herbert Hoover, himself an engineer and American Secretary of Commerce, and the US Waterways Commissioners visited the Ship Canal construction site, at which time a newspaper headline declared, "Deep Waterways Commission Amazed at Twin Locks" and "Visitors Marvel at Many Unique Features of Construction."[12] By the 1920s concrete was becoming more frequently used for large construction projects. Although in Ontario the Peterborough lift lock, erected in the new building material, had been completed in 1904, large concrete structures had not hitherto been seen much in Canada. Of course, Weller, Grant, and their colleagues knew that in England, the Manchester Ship Canal (begun 1882) had lock walls of concrete faced with brick and the Panama Canal's locks were of concrete.

These pioneering enterprises, however, were not always appreciated by the skilled working classes. The masses of concrete, which would replace stone as the basic building material in the Welland's locks, alarmed local stonemasons. Hearing of the choice of concrete for the new locks, the Bricklayers and Masons International Union No. 5 in London, Ontario, protested that stone was a better building material than concrete.[13] They feared that, not only would they be out of work if concrete was used, but also that they would themselves be reduced to toiling as unskilled labourers at lower pay and with lower social status. Moreover, the protesting stonemasons knew that this industrial-type labour deprived the worker of pride in his skills and left him remote from those who employed him "on the ground." The skills involved in putting down concrete were indeed different from those learned by stonemason apprentices. When concrete is about to be laid, for example, a "slump test" must be carried out to determine if the correct amount of water has been added to the mix. This cannot be done by a labourer on the construction site but must be carried out by men with an engineering education. On the Ship Canal, these technicians worked in the concrete testing laboratory, separated from the actual builders of the concrete locks. Engineers such as the Ship Canal's concrete inspector W.H. Waddell would probably have been familiar with the complex nine-hundred-page *Concrete Engineers Handbook*, by G.A Hool and N.C. Johnson, published in New York in 1918. Understanding this guide required a knowledge of scientific subjects such as chemistry.

On the other hand, the labourer on site required no special ability to understand the concrete with which he was building, whereas the stonemason, although without a university education, had learned through training and experience the physical qualities of certain types of stone and mortar. As the masons feared, the actual builders of the Welland Ship Canal's locks were much less skilled than those who built the locks of the Second and Third Canals. The former were well organized and vocal, but their protest proved futile.

The Department of Railways and Canals contracted with the Canada Cement Company in Port Colborne for the supply and delivery of 2,500,000 barrels of cement to be delivered as required until the canal was finished. The flight locks' walls would rise to a height of over 81 feet (24.7 m) with a maximum width of 46 feet (13.8 m). The flight locks' chambers were separated by 60-foot-thick (18.3 m) concrete walls, each about 3,340 feet (1 km) long. In these structures 1,170,000 cubic yards (894,529.2 m³) of concrete were used.[14] Taking into consideration the entrance walls of these locks, the concrete work of the flight locks would be about two miles (3.2 km) in length. The engineers accurately described these huge structures as "monoliths." Reinforcement of the concrete with steel was not usually practised in the lock walls, although it was employed around culverts, valve chambers, quoins, and sills; nor were the lock floors reinforced but instead were anchored to the limestone bedrock with bars because most of the lock walls were gravity structures founded on rock. In this way the engineers exploited the local geology. At the upper entrances of Locks 1 and 2, however, the entrances would rest on bearing piles.

The foundations of Locks 1, 2, and 3 would therefore be built extending down through clay to bedrock. In the case of the flight locks, however, the combination of clay and stone on the Escarpment had to be stabilized before construction began. On the other hand, the pit for Lock 7 was excavated entirely in rock. Although Niagara's subsoil rock was thus used effectively, its peculiarities also had to be considered. For one thing, it was not uniform in consistency. Building Twin Locks 4 at the Escarpment, Peter Lyall encountered shale, rock formed by the consolidation of clay; at Locks 5 and 6, he met beds of shale and sandstone; and at Lock 7 he found grey shale and limestone. Because shale or mudstone was often laminated or layered, any such rock which would support concrete structures could not be allowed to crack or disintegrate during construction. To preserve the rock face, when it had been cut to the configuration desired and all debris cleaned off, it was scoured with jets of water under seventy-five pounds (34 kg) of pressure and then scrubbed with brushes.

Work on the lock pits began very soon after the first contracts were awarded in 1913. At Lock 1 a temporary dam kept out lake water and excavation of the pit proceeded in 1914 (fig. 6.7). In that summer work at the site of Lock 2 began and the sites of Twin Locks 5 and 6 were stripped of the overlying earth and the Escarpment rock exposed (fig. 5.6). Excavation in the rock began in November with construction of Lock 6 beginning soon thereafter. Work on Locks 7 and 8 began after the war ended, but it was not until 1922 that pouring of concrete for the locks started again.

Although building the locks involved sophisticated engineering and complex equipment, sometimes the method used was simplicity itself. For example, at Twin Locks 4 during winter of 1925–26, the concrete floors were flooded to a depth of four feet (1.2192 m) to protect them from frost.

While concrete was now considered a more reliable building material than stone for structures as massive as the Ship Canal locks, it provided its own challenges. To meet them, a Cement Office and Testing Laboratory was opened in June 1921 near the construction railway track scales in Merritton (near the present site of the Seaway headquarters) with R.W. Downie as "Tester of Buildings Materials." Especially concerned about the effect that the ratio of water added to cement could have on the strength of the resulting concrete, Grant told Jewett in 1922 that if he discovered "collusion" between concrete inspectors and contractors' foremen to use "wet mixes when members of Engineering Staff are not around, they will be summarily dismissed by me."[15] Jewett was correspondingly alert to imperfection. In October 1924 he complained to his fellow engineer Cameron that crushed stone delivered to his sections was "the worst that I have ever seen." "The sample that I am forwarding was taken by a labourer who was blindfolded and turned around six times, told to dig fifty shovel fulls and throw them to one side and to put shovelfulls 51-2-3-4 and 55 in this bag."[16] Fortunately, most of the crushed stone used was in good condition.

In 1925 specifications for the lock gates were drawn up, which entailed much correspondence with suppliers and experts. The design work for the gates and their machinery was in the hands of Ship Canal engineer F.E. Sterns. In June 1926 the contract for the gate leaves was awarded to the Steel Gates Company Ltd of Montreal. The structural steelwork was sublet to Hamilton Bridge Works and the castings and forgings to Montreal Locomotive Works.

The gates had to be installed "in the dry," with cranes lifting them upright onto plinths in the lock walls. When completed, a leaf was jacked up, the plinths removed, and roller tracks substituted. The leaf was then jacked back to its quoin and lowered onto its pintle and anchored. This was painstaking, delicate work, as a gate could weigh as much as 500 tons (453.5 tonnes) (fig. 5.7). If machinery failed or mistakes were made in the process of installation, catastrophe could ensue. Installation began in March 1927 at Lock 1, followed by Locks 2, 3, 4, and 5. All the gates, including the spare leaves, were finished and/or installed by 1931 (figs 5.7 and 5.8).

THE CEMENT CRISIS

Construction of the locks faced several challenges, but perhaps the most irritating and unexpected was an unreliable source of that all-important building material – cement. When work resumed after the war, some cement which had been stored remained in fair condition, but other supplies which had absorbed moisture and solidified could not be used. But a worse situation awaited Grant and his engineers. Canada Cement, the Ship Canal's main supplier, could not provide the required amount of the product because they could not get enough coal as fuel for their own projects, either from Nova Scotia or from the United States. Their mills, such as the one in Port Colborne, were being shut down or working at reduced capacity. Grant therefore tried to limit the use of cement and to place his orders well ahead of time. Meanwhile, the Canadian National Railway authorities asked Grant if the Ship Canal project could spare any cement, while Grant, for his part, offered to buy cement from the Railway.

When not begging Canada Cement to increase deliveries, Grant told his sectional engineers how to ration out the available product to various parts of the site. For example, in August 1920 he instructed Jewett to close down concrete operations on the slope wall of the prism in his section, to reserve some cement for the construction of Bridge 5, and to lay off concrete gangs where necessary. Concern over the cement shortage was aggravated by the discovery that, at the Canada Cement mill in Port Colborne, vessels were being loaded with cement for shipment to the United States where a better price was offered. The story that Ship Canal contractors were working from hand to mouth for lack of cement reached the Toronto newspapers and caused a small uproar. T.C. Cain, a senior accountant with the Department of Railways and Canals who visited the Port Colborne plant, seems to have been able to put pressure on Canada Cement, which agreed to increase its output for delivery to the Ship Canal, including a daily delivery from its Montreal plant.[17]

Within two months, however, Canada Cement began to send too much to the Ship Canal contractors, one of whom begged Grant to tell the producers to stop sending two railway cars a day and limit themselves to only one car every second day. Given the contractor's limited storage capacity, the continuation of two cars a day, he said, "will overwhelm us."[18] All went well for several weeks until early November 1920, when Canada Cement started sending three cars of cement every day. This matter, too, had to be resolved by telegrams between St Catharines, Port Colborne, Montreal, and Ottawa.

In September 1922, however, sectional engineer F.S. Lazier reported to Grant that the contractor, the problem-plagued Peter Lyall, who by now required eight cars of cement a day for his section, was not receiving enough from Port Colborne. By this time, some contractors actually needed as many as twelve every day. And so Grant appealed to Bowden, who, in turn, pressured Canada Cement to maintain steady deliveries. But scarcely a month later the Port Colborne plant started to limit its shipments of cement to the entire project to only eight cars a day. Furious, Grant telegraphed to the Toronto headquarters of the company: "What is the meaning of this?"[19] Again, Canada Cement complied with Grant's requirements.

Grant also had difficulties with related equipment not being delivered on time. In October 1920 the concrete spouting plant, which had been ordered from Montreal, failed to arrive when needed. Grant's telegram to the manufacturer received a conciliatory but vague reply to which, already sorely tried by labour and concrete problems, the engineer in charge retorted: "Unless all the material ordered from you by Departmental Agents order number four hundred and twenty of twenty-third July is delivered here by the fifteenth instant, I will cancel the order and have the Department order the material elsewhere ... Do not wire or write excuses as they will not be considered."[20] Ten days later, after two months of being on the road, the equipment finally arrived.

Some of these problems might have been unavoidable even in the best of circumstances. Already in 1915 the problem of getting "first-class sand" for the concrete in the locks had emerged and was, said Weller, "an exceedingly difficult one to solve."[21] All of the sand from pits in the district was of an unreliable quality. Most sand came from St David's east of St Catharines but was unsatisfactory because clay or loam was mixed in with it. As well, iron oxide from Grimsby shale impregnated some of the sand, giving the resulting concrete of Lock 1 a pinkish colour. Luckily a large deposit of sand was discovered at the mouth of the Niagara River from which it was dredged and sent in scows to a large bin at Port Weller.

SOPHISTICATED MACHINERY AND EQUIPMENT

As with the excavation of the channel, the huge concrete monoliths of the lock walls were built with purpose-designed machinery. Concrete mixing plants were set up at each lock or at other placement locations, such as the dam between Locks 6 and 7. At every lock, Blaw-Knox "travelling forms" enabled concrete placement (figs 5.9 and 5.10) and were also used in the building of retaining walls on the canal's prism.[22] On the average, four days were required to fill such a form with concrete, after which two full days had to pass before the contractor was allowed to move it. Then another four days were needed to move the form to another spot. Moving such a contraption was a complex and dangerous matter, as the collapse of one of them in 1925 proved.

As well as the Blaw-Knox forms, steel concreting towers 150 feet (45.7 m) high, each weighing 300 tons (272 tonnes), operated on wheels running on tracks within each lock, moving at a speed of 30 feet (9.1 m) a minute. Especially useful on the flight locks, they were powered by steam engines, which also hoisted the materials (fig. 5.9).

5.9 Pouring the concrete, ca. 1929. A steel Blaw-Knox concreting tower, about 150 feet (45.7 m) high running on twelve wheels set on a ten-metre gauge track.

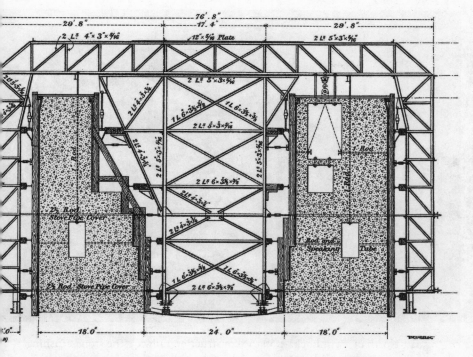

5.10 Another Blaw-Knox form. As in fig. 5.9, powered hoists carried wet concrete to the top of the structure from which gravity took it down through chutes to the selected site.

The contractors used inclined timber skidways covered with tallow to lower such towers from one lock to another, a process which could take up to four hours. These, too, could be unstable and could collapse in a high wind. In March 1923, for example, a gale blew down one of Lyall's concreting towers at the pit of Twin Locks 5, smashing it completely.

Among the suppliers of the equipment required to manufacture and operate the steel gates, Canadian firms predominated, although some were American subsidiaries. A few "giants" were awarded several contracts for both lock and bridge equipment but many local firms, which had acquired specialized experience in other fields, were involved. The Steel Gates Company of Montreal and the Herbert Morris Crane Hoist of Niagara Falls (Ontario) were two of these.

The machinery described above and the vigilant testing of the concrete paid off for the Welland's engineers. As the locks were going

5.11   North of Twin Locks 4 on the construction railway. The stone-crushing plant, a huge establishment, essential for the preparation of concrete.

up in 1924, a respected American civil engineer declared himself to be "particularly impressed with the good appearance of the concrete."[23] Repairs and maintenance have been necessary over the past eighty years but major failures of the lock walls have been few and far between.

Most of the cement came from the notorious Canada Cement Company in Port Colborne but the aggregate (hard material added to cement to make concrete) came from the rock-crushing plant (fig. 5.11). Here were produced 2,000 tons (1814 tonnes) each ten-hour day. The required sand came from dredging at the mouth of the Niagara River. In the summer of 1930, when it was no longer needed, the plant was entirely dismantled.

"QUEEREST CRAFT YET IN CANAL"

If a lock gate should be damaged or needed to be taken out for any purpose, a gate lifter was considered necessary. Such a crane mounted

5.12 The pontoon gate lifter (SLSMC). Alex Grant called it "the most dangerous machine that I ever had anything to do with."

on a barge used on the Third Canal was replaced in 1910 by a machine built by Matthew Beatty and Sons of Welland, but the mammoth size of the Ship Canal lock gates required a much more powerful lifter. Similar in principle to its predecessors, the Ship Canal's gate lifter was a self-contained unit, towed from place to place by tugs (figs 5.12 and

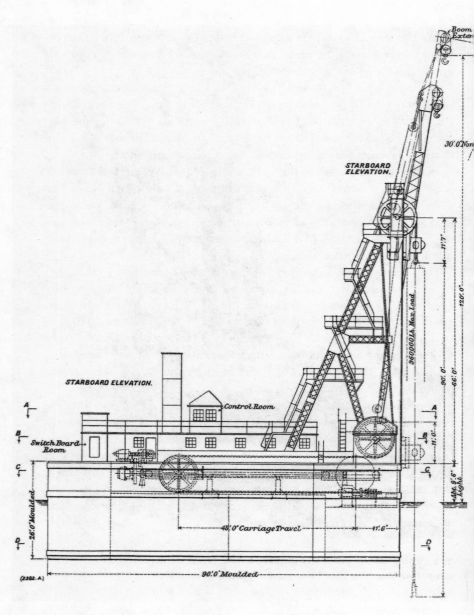

5.13 Diagram of the gate lifter, considered essential for lifting and placing the massive lock gates.

5.13). The simplicity of the machine belies the drama of its construction and delivery to the Ship Canal – a revealing example of the trials and tribulations of the waterway's engineers.

Planning for a "pontoon gate lifter" began in 1920, with engineers' plans accepted in 1927 and tenders called for in 1929. The contract for the hull was awarded to Collingwood Shipyards on Georgian Bay, that for the hoisting machinery to Canadian Allis-Chambers Co., and that for the electrical equipment to Canadian Westinghouse.

In fact, so complex was the basic contract that Collingwood let out a total of ten subcontracts. Included in this number were Drysdale Co. of Glasgow (the ballast and bilge pumps); William Beardmore & Co., also of Glasgow (the alloy steel forging); Emerson Walker of Gateshead-on-Tyne (the capstans). W.H. Allen Co., of Bedford, UK, provided the main engine and generating set.

The final cost was $1,500,000 – a large sum for the time ($21,134,831 in 2015 dollars). Its hoisting equipment was operated by electricity generated by a steam engine fuelled by oil. This machinery rested on a hull 90 feet (27 m) long by 66 feet (19.8 m) wide, weighing 1,226 tons (1111.9 tonnes). Capable of lifting the heaviest lock gate, its derrick rose 90 feet (27 m) above its deck. The *Welland-Port Colborne Tribune* described it as "the largest crane in the world, either stationary, moving or floating."[24]

Construction began in December 1929, with the contract calling for the finished vessel to be delivered to Port Weller by 15 August 1930. In April 1930 Collingwood reported that Allis-Chambers had made "very little progress" on the tower and hoisting machinery and informed Grant that "something drastic must be done to speed up this work, otherwise there be might be a great danger" of it not being finished on time.[25] Delays continued, with Grant urging Dubuc to take "immediate steps" to "compel the contractor to obtain better deliveries from their agents" so that operation could begin in the fall. By June, Collingwood thought that matters were "a great deal worse than we anticipated." Now, the shipyard blamed the Department, which, they maintained, had been "slow to check and return approved drawings."[26]

On 6 September, however, the lifter's main engine and generator, now installed, had a preliminary trial and Grant was told "everything ran very smoothly."[27] But still he worried, on 29 September urging the chief engineer to remind Collingwood that the lifter must arrive at Port Weller by 18 October at the latest. If not, the Escarpment locks of the operating canal would have to be kept open, which would delay completion of the new works on Section 3. Operating these locks for part of the next season would entail "considerable disadvantage and greater risk." He begged his Ottawa superior to "compel the contractors to bring the boat down to Port Weller this fall."[28]

Fortunately, the lifter sailed in October, with a crew of six. One tug, the JAMES WHALEN, would tow it, and another, the MUSCALLONGE, would travel along side, steering it. On 10 October Grant reported to Ottawa that the gate lifter was "floated" and was, he said, "being prepared for sea [*sic*]." After its uneventful journey, which Grant nervously followed by telegram and radio reports,[29] on 4 November the lifter "crawled into Port Colborne ... just before dusk," according to a local journalist, "looking like a battle ship stripped of its guns, swaying from side to side in the wake of the tugs."[30]

Although it traversed the canal and finally arrived at Port Weller without incident and was moored below Lock 1, nevertheless it was still incomplete and needed testing. For these reasons the completion date of the contract was repeatedly extended. Meanwhile, in December 1930 H.B. Smith, president of Collingwood Shipyard, protested: "There is a large sum of money due us under the contract, and we are suffering great hardship and heavy loss because of non-payment."[31]

Many more delays ensued until finally on 21 July 1931 the machine successfully lifted a 44-foot-high (13.4 m) gate leaf. Later, an 82-foot (24.6 m) gate was effectively raised. Even so, only in December 1931, corrections and adjustments having been satisfactory, did the Ship Canal formally take over the lifter. Finally in March 1935 the final payment was made to Collingwood. Alex Grant's mind could now rest, as the saga of the gate lifter – in his words, "the most dangerous machine that I ever had anything to do with" – was over.[32]

On the east side of the harbour at Port Weller below Lock 1, a small basin was built where the gate lifter would be drydocked for storage, painting, and repairs (fig. 4.2). Above the lock, a gate repair yard was built, starting in April 1928. Its concrete floor was lined with concrete pedestals upon which gate leaves could rest. In fact, a gate yard on this site was not part of any original concept because, at first, a marine railway was to be installed on the west side of the harbour as a way of moving gates into position at a gate yard. However, when studies showed that a railway would be expensive to construct and difficult to operate, the idea was abandoned in 1927. Instead, the aforementioned drydock was built. Here the lock gates would be floated by tug and lifted into position by the gate lifter, another example of the engineers' occasional change of plans. Port Weller Drydocks now occupies the site.

"CONSIDERABLE UNEASINESS"

Certain problems which the engineers faced during construction of the locks were unique to the Ship Canal's era and situation. For example, because of the halt to construction during the First World War, some concrete at Lock 1 had disintegrated and had to be removed before building could be resumed after 1919. On the other hand, Alfred Barrett and his fellow engineers in the 1820s would have understood and sympathized with the engineers' difficulties with Niagara's weather and climate. For example, in May 1919, the pit of Lock 1 had to be pumped out because it had been flooded to a depth of 15 feet (4.6 m). In February 1925 a freshet again filled the lock. At the other end of the construction site, Lock 8 was flooded by heavy rain in August 1928 and again in February 1929. The situation was exacerbated by underground springs seeping through the limestone bedrock into the lock excavation (fig. 6.14). On the latter occasion the installation of the lock gates was delayed because much of the contractor's equipment lay submerged on the lock floor.

Contractors frequently tried to carry on their work in the months of December through March but the Canadian winter had not changed since Barrett's time. At the site of Lock 7, for example, "extremely difficult weather conditions" caused by "the early freeze-up" in December 1929 retarded excavation.[33] Contractors, however, understood how to combat winter's bite with simple means. At Twin Locks 4, in the winter of 1925–26 the lock floors were covered with water to protect them from frost. On other occasions tarpaulins were employed during freezing weather to protect both the work and the labourers from frost and snow.

Using nature's own protective qualities, contractors also knew how to keep unstable rock from disintegrating. The foundations of Lock 1 lay directly on shale, which, when exposed, shrinks and disintegrates. But if kept continually damp it keeps its natural firmness. Because a secure bond between the lock's concrete floor and underlying stone was essential, the contractors tried not to expose the rock until just before the concrete was placed, leaving at least one foot (0.3 m) of stone unexcavated above that which would ultimately support the floor. When the concrete was ready to be placed, this remaining rock would be removed and the surface covered with concrete immediately. Thus subterfuge would foil Nature.

Elsewhere, the soft clay in the prism was a problem. In the summer of 1915, for example, the contractor at the site of Lock 3 had to abandon the clam shell shovel which had been equipped for the job and resort to hand labour to remove the clay. In 1920, however, hardpan was discovered at this site and piles had to be jackhammered into the earth to support the lock's concrete. Then in the spring of 1921 the stability of the bank behind the lock pit, part of which lay in the original bed of Ten Mile Creek, caused contractors and engineers "considerable uneasiness,"[34] necessitating remedial measures. Even late in the construction period, parts of the monoliths here were found to be moving due to the unstable ground beneath them. Elsewhere, in 1930, movement in the upper east and west entrance walls of Lock 1 was detected. The remedy was a solid slab of concrete laid down across the bottom of the upper entrance of the lock.

Even when concrete was poured and structures finished, cause for "uneasiness" remained. In September 1927, the upper west entrance wall of Lock 3 was gradually moving forward so that concrete struts would have to be installed in front of it (fig. 5.14). In 1931–32 the east abutment and pier of the approach to Lock 1's bridge also began to move, requiring further concrete buttressing. Landslides, the bane of contractors since 1828, still occurred, as at the site of Lock 2 in 1924, where a heavy concrete reinforcement had to be added.

At other sites, especially at the Escarpment where the Flight Locks were under construction, Niagara's rock had to be blasted. "Channeling machines" would drill blast holes into the rock at intervals, parallel to the canal's centre line and 20 to 40 feet (6.1 to 12.2 m) in depth. Heavily charged with dynamite, several would be fired at the same time, blowing up rock for steam shovels to remove. A smooth, vertical face would be left, against which the concrete walls of the locks could then be built. Such explosions were not welcomed by local residents.

As usual, not all the Department's problems in lock construction were meteorological or geological. The personalities and practices of contractors could be a problem. In 1921 Jewett had become impatient with the tactics of J.P. Porter on Sections 1 and 2. Little had changed by 1924, when Jewett found this contractor still working too slowly.

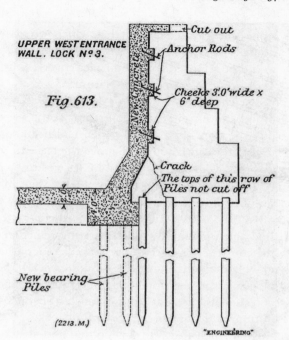

UPPER WEST ENTRANCE
WALL. LOCK N? 3.

Fig.613.

Cut out

Anchor Rods

Cheeks 3'.0'wide x
6" deep

Crack
The tops of this row of
Piles not cut off

New bearing
Piles

(2213.M.)

"ENGINEERING"

5.14 How to buttress
a cracked lock wall
with extra piles and
concrete.

Worse, Porter seemed to have a dangerous disregard "for drainage, for slopes, for anything that looks like holding up his latest set of ideas."[35] (Given the unstable ground on which Porter had to work, his caution was possibly justified. Jewett, for his part, was not known for patient forbearance.) Grant, too, could be brusque with contractors, as when in September 1927 he castigated Peter Lyall over aspects of the latter's work at the flight locks.[36]

Some of the lock builders' problems were quite beyond their control – in fact, out of the country itself. Harland Engineering Works of Alloa, Scotland, had contracted to supply motors for the lock gates and valves. As Grant wanted to open the canal in July 1930, it was vital that these be operative before that date. On 14 February 1929 Harland's agent in Montreal announced that there would be a delay in the arrival of this equipment in Canada. Unanticipated problems, including influenza, had occurred. "Surprised," Grant urged Harland's agent to expedite matters because delay was "cause for anxiety" and would "make things very bad for us here."[37] On 21 March two valve and gate motors were shipped from Scotland. More would have been

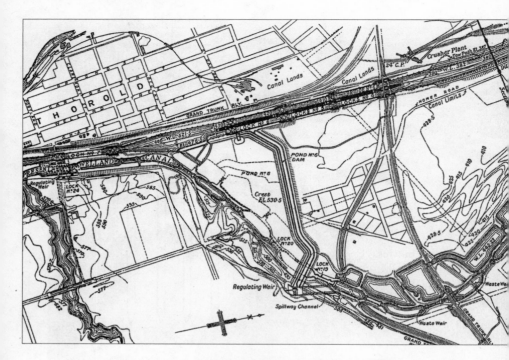

5.15   Thorold, ca. 1930: Lock 7 is at the left; the three double-flight locks near the centre with Lock 6's dam and pondage below. One lock of the Third Canal can be seen already submerged in the large pond. Other locks appear as the old canal winds away at bottom right. The gently curving bare patch at the top right of the map marks the route of the First and Second Canals.

sent but the sailing of the ship from Glasgow was advanced by one day, which gave Harland only six days' notice. Others would arrive on the next boat. Telegrams and letters flew between St Catharines and Montreal and presumably between Montreal and Glasgow or Alloa. Ultimately, the motors arrived in several shipments, some going via Saint John, New Brunswick, some via Montreal. Throughout April and May 1929 the machinery arrived piecemeal but, to Grant's relief, arrive it did.

Paucity of funding also retarded the excavation for the locks. Whereas most of the lock construction took place after the difficult days of postwar austerity, completion of the lock gate equipment was affected by the Great Depression, during which funding again became

5.16   Crossing of the Third and Fourth Canals. The new Lock 3 is in the foreground (site of the St Catharines Museum) with Bridge 5 and the Flight Locks in the distance. The present-day Welland Canals Parkway follows the line of the construction railway at the far right.

inadequate for the work planned. For example, installation of gate fender equipment had to be suspended at the end of December 1930 because money available from the 1930–31 construction appropriation had dried up. The work resumed at the start of the fiscal year 1931.

As with the excavation of the prism, operation of the Third Canal had to be considered during construction of the locks. The new water- way's Lock 7 was built very close to two locks of the Third Canal, ne- cessitating care lest the narrow barrier of earth between them should collapse (fig. 5.15). Moreover, the Ship Canal crossed its predecessor just south of the new Lock 3, at the old Lock 11, where the Third Canal began its slow climb, looping up the Escarpment (fig. 5.16). Here the operating channel would have to be blocked so that the Ship Canal could be cut through, a process which was postponed until the last stage of construction. To facilitate this procedure, the level of the reach south of Lock 3 was made identical to that of the Third Canal. During winters, moreover, work on the south entrance walls at Lock 3 was carried on as far as possible. In 1930 the banks of the older waterway were removed and a 14-foot (4.3 m) channel excavated, connecting Lock 11 with the new Lock 3. Through this passage, the Ship Canal from Port Weller to and including Lock 3 opened for navigation in April 1930. When navigation from Port Dalhousie ceased, ships used the new waterway up to this point and then turned into the older one to continue up the Escarpment. When the prism between Lock 3 and the flight locks was completed in 1931, the older canal was blocked.

At the same time, the lock construction process itself involved conflicts and delays. Concrete work at Lock 8 had to be curtailed in 1926–27 because of the need to get a temporary rail line over the lock site. At the flight locks in 1928–29, Lyall's delayed operations prevented much progress on the erection of the necessary control buildings. Except for two disasters at that site in the later 1920s (figs 9.1 and 9.2), however, accidents which delayed lock construction were rare.

Nonetheless, the huge concrete monoliths of the locks were built relatively quickly. Pouring of concrete at Locks 1 and 2 resumed in October 1922 and was finished by October 1924. Concreting at Lock 3 was carried on in 1924–26. Work at the flight locks and at Lock 7 began in October 1922 but was not completed until March 1930, very close to the projected opening date of July 1930. At Port Colborne, concreting on Lock 8 started in 1926 and was finished in 1929.

Of course, once the concrete was finished, installation of the gate operating machinery and the water-controlling valves was necessary. In the event, the full opening of the Ship Canal was postponed, as the waterway was put in operation in stages. In September 1929 Lock 8 was the first to be opened for navigation; then Locks 1, 2, and 3 were put in use after April 1930, when the GEORGIAN passed through up to the Third Canal junction, just south of Lock 3 (fig. 7.1). In November 1930 Lock 24 of the old canal at the Escarpment ceased operation and all ships of less than 18 feet (5.5 m) could use the full length of the Ship Canal. When the navigation season opened in 1931 ships 450 feet (137.2 m) long with a draught of 18 feet (5.5 m) were allowed into the new waterway. By the end of that year ships 650 feet long (198.1 m) and drawing 21 feet (6.4 m) were passing through the locks. Finally, by May 1932 vessels drawing up to 23.5 feet (7.2 m) of water and 700 feet (213.4 m) long were making the passage.

E.P. Murphy, engineer for Section 8 and perhaps a journalist *manqué*, gave a telling description of the formal opening of Lock 8 on 16 September 1929 (fig. 11.4). On "a typically bright clear Canadian Day," he wrote with pride,

> a large crowd of representative citizens of the Niagara Peninsula had gathered at the Lock to Witness the great event. Promptly at 2.40 P.M. Capt. John Manley, of the Boon Dredging and Construction Company ... pulled the operating lever, the gates swung open, and the steamer "Meaford" of the C.S L. [Canada Steamship Line] with all her bunting waving proudly in the gentle breeze, her siren sounding, and the band playing "O Canada" slowly steamed through the gates and the South end of the Fourth and greatest of the Welland canals was in commission: a grand tribute to Canadian brains and Industry.[38]

BUGS IN THE SYSTEM

While the completed locks were indeed impressive, at first their operation proved problematic. Even in the fall of 1929, during a trial run of Lock 1, air trapped in the culverts had caused geysers of water to erupt from the conduit wells, dislodging the gratings at the surface. As a solution, in January 1930 four air vents were chipped from the top of the main side-wall culverts to the face of the lock chamber walls. But in April 1930 the releasing of the trapped air through these vents caused turbulence in the water during filling of the lock. So a series of smaller holes were drilled throughout the length of each wall from the top of the tunnel to the face of the wall. Finished in March 1931, these had the desired effect.

The east lower gate of Lock 2 jammed on 12 September 1930, closing the canal temporarily. On 6 October, when a valve became stuck in the open position, Lock 3 was shut down for several hours, diverting traffic back to the Third Canal. Some complaints were heard about locks being filled too quickly, endangering ships.

Another problem was that motors operating the discharge valves caused such vibration that the upstream ends of the locks had to be reconstructed in 1932. In addition, the new gate leaves did not work well. When they were submerged during the filling of the locks in the spring of 1930, leakage into their air chambers was discovered, occasioning repairs to the bolts in the mitre ends of the leaves in the summer of that year. Deterioration of the original protective paint on the lock gates was noted and this, too, had to be remedied. Lock-masters required training in the efficient operation of the gates and valves, learning how, for example, to prevent ice from forming on the gratings over valve wells at Lock 8. Ships' crews also had to literally "learn the ropes." In September 1930 a rope fender was dropped by a passing ship into the cable pit at Lock 2, jamming its operation and causing a twenty-six-hour delay. These problems and other lesser ones were addressed in the early 1930s. Despite such snags, however, on the whole the new waterway worked remarkably well.

The plastic qualities of poured concrete were exploited by the designers of the Ship Canal to create lock-side structures that were pleasing to the eye. In her study of Americans' use of concrete as a building material in the 1920s, Amy Slaton finds an "absence of aesthetic intention"[39] in the resulting structures. The Welland's service buildings, however, were more than merely functional. Even structures which would not regularly be seen by the public, or even by many of the canal personnel, seem also to have been designed with a view to their aesthetic appearance. For example, of the weir at the large dam at Twin Locks 6, Cowan praised the "the symmetry of design which is so noticeable a feature of ... works on the canal."[40] These were the creations of the Department of Railways and Canals' own construction organization, which began work in 1927 (fig. 5.17). The powerhouse at Twin Locks 4, for example, the nearby buildings at ponds 6 and 7, and the machinery building at the west end of the safety weir, each in "streamlined" concrete with subtle decoration, were finished in 1931. On the other hand, new offices for the operating clerical staff were more domestic in design. The administration buildings at Port Weller and Port Colborne resemble suburban brick bungalows.

Electric power for the canal was supplied temporarily by the Hydro-Electric Power Commission of Ontario, but eventually the Ship Canal provided its own power from the penstock and turbines at the Escarpment locks (fig. 6.13). The locks and the reaches between them, 24 miles (38.6 km) in length, would be lit by electric lamps, in Cowan's unusually romantic words, "to at least the equivalent of full moon-

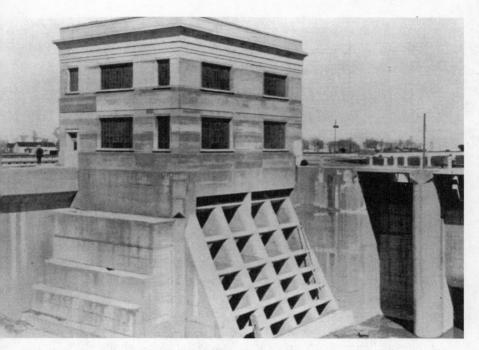

5.17 Port Weller. Water intake and valve house at Lock 1. These sleek reinforced-concrete structures were influenced by the contemporary "art moderne" fascination with geometric shapes and "streamlining," as in the decorative cornice.

light."[41] After February 1930 these lights were installed on the transmission line that ran along the west side of the canal. The new Welland would be a blazing swath of light across the Niagara Peninsula. But not before a bizarre discovery: when the crates for the power house's generators arrived in February 1932, they were found to be full of rats.

The gravitational weight of water, therefore, provided the power to illuminate the canal as well as to operate its locks and their associated machinery. This essential force, however, could prove dangerously intractable and required careful management.

CHAPTER SIX

Managing the Water

W hen we drive over the Ship Canal today on one of the many bridges, the waterway resembles a wide, placid river. If we look to the east of Locks 1, 2, and 3, however, we encounter torrents of white water pouring over the concrete weirs. Watching a lock empty, moreover, we can be stunned by the boiling turbulence of the water being released. The Ship Canal's builders had to find ways to control this natural, essential, but dangerous force (fig. 6.1).

Water management in William Hamilton Merritt's day could be complicated. The twentieth-century Welland Canal presented even more challenges involving water. As was the case with the Third Canal, the water used in the operation of the new locks had to be stored in ponds behind dams or weirs at which waste raceways would channel the surplus flow. Now, however, these would be much larger than any seen before on the Welland.

At the same time, unwanted water, such as that flowing in streams and rivers at right angles to the canal, had to be diverted under the waterway in culverts: another traditional solution to the problem but now requiring deeper and longer excavation or tunnelling. At either end of the canal, protective harbours had to be created or enlarged. Here, the Welland would be sheltered by breakwaters or piers from the turbulent waters of lakes Erie and Ontario. Such storms could damage these havens and, south of Thorold, raise the canal's water to dangerous levels. As well, the Welland's banks needed protection from the wash of the much larger vessels plying its reaches. More positively, at the Niagara Escarpment water was harnessed in a penstock and turbines to create electric power to move the lock machinery and bridges and to illuminate the waterway. Tonnes of potentially dangerous water had to be carefully "managed."

6.1 Thorold, ca. 1928. A view of Lock 7 under construction (looking south), showing the narrow – and dangerous – strip of land between it and the reach between Locks 24 and 25 of the operating (Third) Canal. (See also fig. 5.15.)

MAKING NEW LAKES

From the very first discussions of the Ship Canal's design, the engineers were aware that vastly greater amounts of water would be needed to feed the locks and to keep the channel operative. Of course, Lake Erie provided plenty of water, but how and where was it to be directed and stored? The southernmost part of the Third Canal was to be kept in operation to supply the new canal. Special attention would have to be given to the reach from Port Robinson north to Thorold, and particularly to those reaches on sloping terrain between the Escarpment and Lake Ontario, both to control the water flowing from Lake Erie and to store that water for use.

"Managing water" could become a very complicated matter. During construction itself, temporary dams were occasionally necessary, as at Lock 1, where an earthen wall was left between the works at the lock pit and the lake, so that the lock could be built "in the dry" (fig. 6.7). At the same time Dominion Dredging worried that Ten Mile Creek would be a problem, since initially it had been allowed to flow over the wall. The deeper the excavation went the more likely was a collapse of the earth barrier. Consequently, the contractor diverted the stream into a ditch which would turn it more directly into the harbour and thence to the lake.

The largest permanent dam on the Ship Canal was built at Twin Locks 6, where 84 acres (34 ha) of water would be stored to supply the flight locks. An earthen structure set on solid rock, it would be 3,300 feet (1005.8 m) long and 75 feet (22.9 m) high with a concrete core. The small lake which it created would follow generally the contours of Ten Mile Creek's upper valley, lying across the path of the Third Canal, submerging Thorold's cemetery and old Locks 20 to 22[1] (fig. 5.15). At the top of the Escarpment, old Lock 24 was replaced by a weir which would regulate the flow of water into the pond. When the water left the pond it would flow through Locks 16, 17, and 18 of the Third Canal, the gates of which were removed. The old locks themselves were supplied with new, small concrete weirs. At the new Lock 3, another large pond collected this water for use there. Little difficulty was encountered constructing this dam and the related pondage, although its completion was delayed by financial problems occasioned by the onset of the Great Depression. The problem of getting the canal over Chippawa Creek (which flows eastward into the Niagara River) again faced the engineers. Whereas an aqueduct had been constructed for the first three canals, a different solution was suggested for the Ship Canal. At first the idea was to build a dam across the creek at Port Robinson, to raise the level of the river by about 6 feet (1.8 m) to approximately that of Lake Erie. Because normal high water in the creek and normal low water in the lake were similar, the creek would be taken into the canal, supporting and controlling the water in the Deep Cut, the waterway's summit level. The dam would have a large overflow spillway and a regulating weir.

Such a plan had first emerged in 1828 when Merritt described how, "by throwing a dam over and construction of a lock in the Welland river [Chippawa Creek) below the entrance of the canal, and raising the locks two feet, water may be raised throughout the canal to a depth of ten feet."[2] Nothing came of this scheme because of the landslides on the Deep Cut in November 1828 and the resulting choice of the Grand River as water source. A similar dam across Chippawa Creek had been suggested in 1842 by Lieutenant-Colonel George Phillpotts (1790–ca. 1853), to raise the river to the Lake Erie level.[3]

This plan was revived by Weller in his initial suggestions for the Ship Canal. For $3.5 million, a dam at Port Robinson would be cheaper to build, he thought, than a new aqueduct at $4 million.[4] Acknowledging that the dam would flood about 1,600 acres (647.5 ha) of low-lying land, he noted that the river submerged the area every spring anyway and that the land was used only for pasturage.[5] He also claimed that many farmers in the area were using lands to which they held no deed and did not own.[6] On the other hand, Weller never seems to have fully grappled with another consequence of the dam: pollution of the domestic water supply of Merritton, Thorold, Welland, and St Catharines. A Departmental pamphlet of 1920 did recognize this problem and, as a solution, sketched a plan for a pipeline from Lake Erie to the town reservoirs.[7] This suggestion was motivated in part by the protests which erupted along the canal from municipal authorities.

For example, as soon as the plan became known, the city of Welland complained. In October 1913 the mayor and town clerk told the Department that local sewers would have to be rebuilt; two pumping stations would be destroyed; general flooding would be more likely. If a new aqueduct could not be built, they asked, would the Department pay for a new waterworks and sewage system? Such petitions continued well into the 1920s and the Niagara authorities were not alone. The Ontario Ministry of Highways was concerned about the flooding of the road which ran alongside the south bank of Chippawa Creek from Welland westward. Negotiations between the federal Department and with the Ontario Ministry of Highways continued with correspondence, estimates, telegrams, and meetings until at least October 1923. Private interests also made their voices heard. In 1923 a Toronto real estate developer abandoned plans to build a subdivision on land which would be flooded, claiming "great loss to us in principal, interest and taxes."[8]

Very early in his tenure as engineer in charge, Grant had doubts about the wisdom of this plan, writing to Bowden in March 1920 that if the dam were built, the "government would have to assume all liability

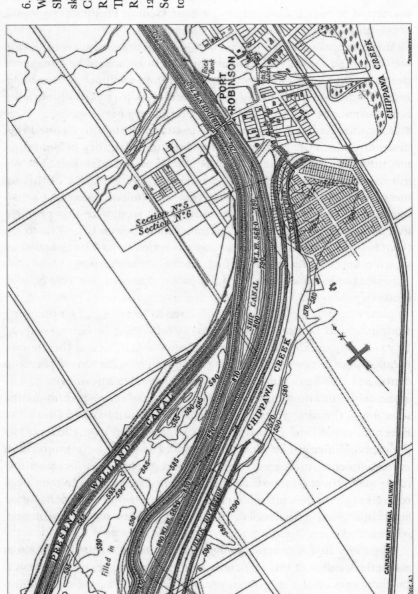

6.2 North of Welland, the new Ship Canal closely skirts Chippawa Creek (the Welland River), with the Third Canal, Port Robinson, Bridge 12, and the First and Second Canals' link to the Creek.

in connection with raising the roads ... and also innumerable unknown claims in respect to road ditches, culverts, and bridges ... put forward by the municipalities." Hesitation in Ottawa concerning the Port Robinson dam was first voiced in March 1920, when Bowden told W.A. McLean, deputy minister in the Ontario Ministry of Highways, that an "alternative plan which we have under consideration would not affect present elevations of the Welland River [Chippawa Creek]." Grant occasionally reiterated his doubts to Bowden until 1924. When the latter died in that year, his successor, A.E. Dubuc, was more receptive to Grant's views, agreeing to abandon the dam idea and to build instead a gigantic inverted syphon culvert to take the creek under the new waterway.[9]

So it was that, given the objections to the flooding, the potential of water pollution, and the threat of litigation, the idea of damming the creek was dropped. Not that the change of plan left the river untouched. Paralleling the new canal between Welland and Port Robinson, Chippawa Creek was realigned to straighten out two sharp bends in its course. The canal and the creek would continue to flow independently of each other but embankments would be placed on the east side of the new canal's channel, which would run parallel to the river on a higher level (fig. 6.2). At the site of the new culvert, the river was twisted onto a new bed in order to direct its flow through the culvert's tubes.

"DIFFICULT AND VERY DANGEROUS"

Alex Grant described the building of the syphon culvert on the Ship Canal as "a difficult undertaking and a very dangerous one."[10] This structure, which would carry Chippawa Creek under the Ship Canal (figs 6.3, 6.4, and 6.5), was a traditional solution to the "collision" of river and canal. The First Canal had been carried over the creek on a rickety wooden aqueduct; the Second and Third, on magnificent arched aqueducts. This latter crossing would have to be replaced because when the water level in Lake Erie was low, its draft was reduced to 12 feet (3.7 m), a depth which was already causing some of the larger ships now using the waterway to get jammed, causing delays in navigation. However, building a new, larger aqueduct in the traditional style was deemed impracticable because the new canal would be much deeper than the Third. A riverbed of greater depth would have to be excavated.

6.3   Welland, ca. 1930. The syphon culvert under construction (IV) with the aqueducts of the Second (II) and Third (III) Canals and the diversion of Chippawa Creek.

The syphon culvert, a remarkable structure, was planned to be built in the dry on the north side of the Third Canal aqueduct. Ultimately six large tubes, each 22 feet (6.7 m) long were laid down, parallel to each other, to carry the creek under the canal. These tubes, each of which was big enough to hold a railway locomotive, would connect on both sides of the canal with six vertical shafts, rising to the level of the creek bottom. A dramatic piece of engineering – using only the power of the natural syphon phenomenon.

In October 1925 contracts were awarded to Atlas Construction Co. for the building of the culvert itself and to E.O. Leahey and Co. for the excavation outside the culvert area, the latter work eventually sublet to Porter and Sons. Excavation of the intake channel to the west of the culvert site was carried on throughout 1926 until March 1927, when construction of the concrete tubes started.

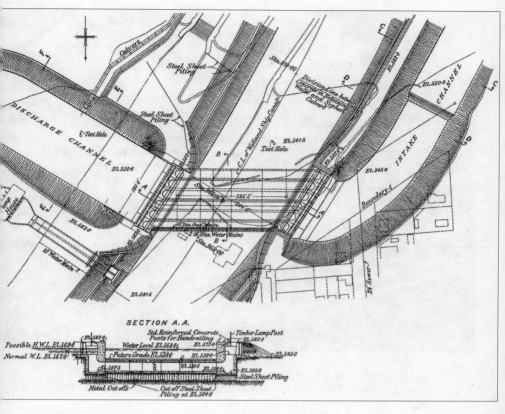

SECTION A.A.

6.4 Welland. The syphon culvert in a diagram which should be read upside down; i.e., north is at the bottom of the plan. Chippawa Creek is referred to as the "intake" and "discharge" channels. The aqueduct of the Second Canal is at the top, slightly to the left of centre. (The Third Canal aqueduct was demolished.) Compare fig. 6.3.

As Grant noted, building the syphon would prove to be the most challenging aspect of the new canal's construction. The contractors, supervised by E.P. Johnson, the sectional engineer, would have to excavate an open cut, which would be enclosed by a cofferdam extending around one end of the site and partly down two sides (fig. 6.3). This site, north of the older aqueducts, projected about 125 feet (38.1 m) into the route of the operating canal. In other words, the cofferdam had to be built about halfway across the navigation channel, the east

6.5   Welland, 1929. The syphon culvert, completed with ships already passing across it but with Chippawa Creek not yet directed through it. The entrance to the six concrete underground tubes is clearly visible.

bank of which was cut back to make space for shipping, but creating an awkward S-curve in the waterway which would prove hazardous to vessels. As for Chippawa Creek, the contractor diverted it 100 yards (90 m) to the north at its old junction with the canal, making it flow parallel to the canal and then turning it around to bring it to the syphon's intake. It would flow over the site of the lock, which had connected the Third Canal with the creek.

The local geology provided typical challenges. Before they found bedrock, the contractors met a shallow layer of sand and gravel, as well as a stratum of clay containing a few large stones. This clay was so unstable that if a 10-inch-wide (25.4 cm) tube was inserted, water rose quickly in that tube from 6 to 12 feet (1.8 to 3.7 m). At some test pits water flowed up at 70 gallons (265 litres) a minute.[11]

6.6   Port Robinson, 1927. Temporary lifting of the Canadian National
Railway bridge to allow E.O. Leahey's dredge STEWART to pass under it
en route to the worksite.

The large equipment, powerful but awkward, required to do the work
occasionally proved troublesome. Leahey, the contractor, brought in a
hydraulic dredge along the Niagara River and Chippawa Creek, but
at Port Robinson he found that a span of the CNR bridge there had to
be temporarily removed to allow the dredge to get through (fig. 6.6).
   As had happened with the locks, the original concept of the syphon
culvert was not implemented. The first plan had entailed building only
two tubes, 39 feet (11.9 m) in diameter, in rock beneath the canal. This
plan was abandoned because of the enormous quantities of excavation involved and the complex task of inserting the tubes through rock
with a concrete lining 158 feet (48.2 m) below the canal. This rock itself
was often soft shale, out of which, as noted above, water flowed from
underground springs under great pressure. Six tubes, founded on

piles established at a higher level than planned, were laid down in the open cut.

The contractors met with many crises during construction. As elsewhere, water itself was the greatest danger. On several occasions Lake Erie storms raised the levels in the operating canal, flooding the site. In addition, the cofferdam system proved unreliable. Piling began in February 1926 but in August the interlock between several piles failed, necessitating the driving of new piles. Then excavation of a test pit led to a tier of struts failing. Later, after some of the concrete monoliths had been poured, an expansion joint in one of them developed a crack, after which the great block of concrete, over 61 feet (18.6 m) wide and 30 feet (9.1 m) high, began to shift. Time-consuming repairs rectified the problem.

The S-curve in the operating waterway began to cause grief for ship captains and contractors both. In June 1926 the sectional engineer Johnson reported to Grant that he had seen some ships experiencing difficulty at the curve, yet he believed that most made the turn safely. Twenty-five ships had had trouble there in May and early June alone, but the list, he said, was "not as formidable as it looks" because traffic was very heavy at that time of year. No sooner had his report been filed than a ship hit the timber piles at the culvert site on 2 July and another struck them on 2 August. Soon afterward, a representative of the Dominion Marine Association wrote to the Department to say that the "situation is growing steadily worse."[12] To deal with the matter, a new row of piling was set up on the channel's east side, reducing the sharp angle of the older sheet piling. Nevertheless, in the spring of 1927 two more ships collided with the piling here. The Department agreed to pay for damages.

Other problems developed within the site itself. In August 1926, when the contractors began to pump water out of the excavated pit, now protected by steel sheet piling, some of the piles became unlocked and began to tilt inwards. The fault, said the contractors, was the soft ground, which tended to shift. They wanted to be reimbursed for the added expense entailed by the sliding earth. Johnson disputed this, and so the opinion of a New York City consulting engineer, Silas H. Woodard (1870–1961), was sought. Woodard affirmed the contractors' opinion that the substratum was unstable. In September 1926 the contractors' views seemed to be further validated when more of the sheet piling collapsed. Later in the month they experimented with a different kind of cofferdam, which ultimately held up well.

Problems continued. By the end of 1927, 41 per cent of the excavation was completed and 55 per cent of the concrete had been placed, but the elements continued to conspire against the contractors. In May 1928 fire destroyed one of the derricks working at the culvert site. Heavy rains in June caused a small slide, which weakened part of the piling and wiped out a dam between the creek and the excavation site. In January 1928 a southwest gale on Lake Erie raised the water level in the canal, sending torrents over the top of the culvert's cofferdam and shutting down operations.

Although the blasting of rock and the use of jackhammers at night expedited construction, this work provoked local protests. Welland residents were no doubt happy when, on 7 December 1928, ship traffic could be directed over the culvert and, on 6 September 1929, Chippawa Creek was diverted permanently through its new channel and sent underneath the canal. Now, however, the greater demand for water at the Ship Canal's summit level caused the current to flow very quickly through the Third Canal aqueduct, making it even more of a hazard to ships. In mid-1930 a channel had been provided for ships in the west half of the prism opposite the aqueduct, after which blasting of the old stone walls and arches began.

OTHER CULVERTS

The effect of building a canal across watercourses is the same as constructing a dam: the obstructed water will collect and flood possibly valuable land. Rivers and streams smaller than Chippawa Creek, such as Beaverdams or Ten Mile Creeks, had therefore to be directed under the Ship Canal through culverts. The apparently obvious solution of directing such streams into the canal itself was impractical because such inflowing water is uncontrollable and erratic and, on the downstream side of the canal, farms, industries, and communities which use that water would be deprived of an essential resource.

A reminder of the complexity of the system of natural watercourses and canals in the Niagara Peninsula, these culverts are underground and out of sight, and therefore are scarcely noticed by the public – unless they cause problems. Several streams had been sent under the first three canals in wooden or masonry culverts. With the building of the Ship Canal, the presence of two and sometimes three older artificial waterways with related culverts complicated matters considerably. For example, when the Third Canal between Allanburg and Thorold

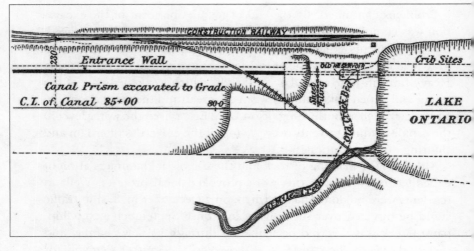

6.7   Port Weller harbour construction, showing the redirection of Ten Mile Creek and the temporary "plug" left in place to restrain the waters of Lake Ontario.

6.8 (*facing page*)   South of Thorold at the junction of the three canals with Shriner's and Beaverdams culverts, the safety weir and guard gates.

was closed, the low land between it and the Ship Canal would be used as a dumping ground for material excavated from Section 5. Not only would a new culvert under the Ship Canal be necessary but also an open ditch through this spoil-covered land. In this way Beaverdams Creek, which flowed into Lake Gibson (a hydroelectric storage pond atop the Escarpment southwest of Thorold) would continue to be channelled and controlled – or so the engineers hoped

Ten Mile Creek, which flowed north from the Escarpment near Thorold to Lake Ontario, presented a special problem. The new waterway would generally follow the valley of this stream but its route was crossed three times by the creek. This necessitated not only culverts but diversions of the creek's channel to protect the construction site, as at Lock 1 (fig. 6.7).

Three more of these water pipes under the new canal were important: for Shriner's, Beaverdams, and Davis creeks, which flowed eastward across the peninsula (fig. 6.8). The contractors would build a concrete culvert to take Davis Creek under both the Third and the

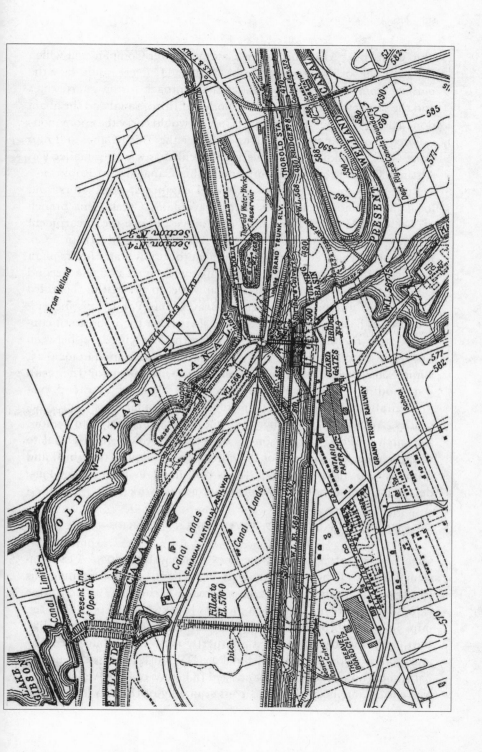

Ship Canal near Allanburg to the Cataract Power Company cut which fed Lake Gibson. South of Thorold, Shriner's Culvert would take the outflow from Marlatt's Pond under the approach to the guard gates and the safety weir and then under both the Third Canal and the abandoned Second Canal. Beaverdams Culvert would carry the eponymous watercourse under the new channel, under the Third Canal and into Lake Gibson. Adding to the plethora of culverts was the smaller Van Alstine's Culvert that passed under the Ship Canal at Port Robinson.

None of these watercourses provided engineers, contractors, and local people more headaches than Beaverdams Creek. This branch of Twelve Mile Creek flows from east to west above the Escarpment just south of Thorold. The Hamilton Power, Light and Traction Co. had dammed the creek at the Escarpment to supply water for its plant at Decew Falls around 1902. Between this cataract and the Second Canal, Lake Gibson was formed. Meanwhile, to the east of the Third Canal water gradually collected in Beaverdams Pond. Existing culverts could handle the overflow of freshets from the pond until construction of the Ship Canal began, when the low-lying land between the operating canal and the new canal was filled with spoil in 1923–24, wiping out Beaverdams Pond. Where was the water to go? The result was flooding on a scale never seen before in the neighbourhood. Not unnaturally, local residents blamed the Ship Canal construction activities. And so in November 1924 the contractor started to remove the earth covering the masonry culvert under the Second Canal to increase carrying capacity of the culvert system under the Third and Ship Canals. Although heavy floods continued, as in February 1925, delaying the enterprise, this remedy seemed to work.

DEFENDING AGAINST TWO GREAT LAKES

Great Lakes storms, such as the ones that regularly flooded the construction site at the syphon culvert in Welland and were dangerous to ships and mariners, could also damage harbours. The first three canals' engineers had provided piers or breakwaters at both lake termini in order to protect navigation, building sites, and human life. Port Colborne had functioned as a partly natural harbour since 1833 and would continue to do so. But Port Dalhousie, which also used a natural harbour, was to be abandoned in favour of Port Weller, which was entirely artificial. It would consist mainly of the two long break-

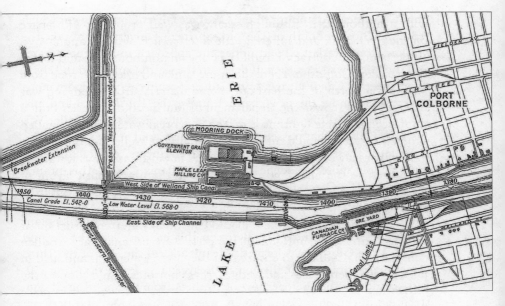

6.9   Port Colborne harbour, with the new breakwaters.

waters or piers that would stretch out a mile and a half (2.4 km) into
Lake Ontario. Converging slightly at the lake ends, these would be
1,200 feet (365.8 m) apart, while the new harbour itself would be 800
feet (243.8 m) wide.

The Department of Public Works began the Port Colborne harbour
improvements in 1900 (fig. 6.9). Weller was the first engineer in charge,
succeeded by Frank Lawlor (1901–03) and Alex Grant (1903–06). In
these years, the harbour was dredged to a depth of 22 feet (6.7 m). Two
breakwaters, one on each side of the harbour, had been completed by
1912, expanding on piers that had originally been built in 1833 and
constantly improved.

Powerful Lake Erie storms, however, could still damage any harbour
and wreck ships seeking its shelter. And so, across the southwest side
of the harbour, an extension to the breakwater was built 2,080 feet
(634 m) long, essentially an arm of the older barrier, on an approximately north-south axis, defending the new canal from the prevailing southwesterly gales. Its twenty-one reinforced concrete cribs were
built at Port Maitland, at first glance a relatively remote site but one
that was served by the Toronto, Hamilton and Buffalo Railway and

with a harbour that, although small, was well protected with space on the river bank and suffered little interference by navigation. A.W. Robertson, the contractor, built the cribs on pontoons here and towed them to Port Colborne. There they were sunk and filled with rock from excavation north of the harbour. Some material from dredging was brought in by scows. The Department of Marine and Fisheries built a reinforced concrete lighthouse on the new breakwater. This expanded protective system would differ from that at Port Weller not only in the generally east-west alignment of the piers but also insofar as it was not connected to the mainland, in contrast to the north-south layout of those at the northern harbour, where the piers would be built out from the shore.

The contractor used a new method in breakwater construction at Port Colborne. The bottoms of the cribs were of temporary wooden construction. Caulked to ensure that they were watertight and held in place by wooden braces and wedges, these bottoms would support the cribs when they were removed from the scows, and were left in place until the cribs were sunk, at which time they were released by means of ropes attached to the wedges. The wooden floors then floated to the surface and were used again. The contractor hoped that the rock fill in the crib would thus rest directly on the lake bottom and afford a more stable foundation for the cribs than if they had fixed bottoms.

By late 1924 the new Port Colborne harbour works for the Ship Canal were well advanced, but construction of the breakwater was attended by predictable difficulties. For example, Lake Erie storms in the winter of 1928–29 washed away part of the fill along the slope on the lake side of the breakwater. These gales could raise the water level at Port Colborne, flooding the site of the new canal and Lock 8, as happened on 1 April 1929.

Moreover, contractors faced the difficulty of improving the harbour while avoiding passing ships and allowing long-established businesses to continue some kind of operation. Canada Furnace Company and International Nickel Company of Canada, both on the east side of the harbour, had to make allowances for disrupted production and operation. New intake monoliths for their water supply had to be built. Canada Furnace's ore-unloading dock would also be reconstructed with cribs built at Port Maitland and floated to the site.

Although no such pre-established industries existed at the rural site of the Ship Canal's new northern terminus, Port Weller, building of

6.10 Installing stone and concrete protection on the Ship Canal banks, designed to prevent obstructive slides. As well, if a person slipped into the water, steps and ridges built into the concrete provided a foothold.

that harbour proved contentious nonetheless. Chief Engineer Bowden and John Weller, Engineer in Charge, did not see eye to eye on the matter of stone protection for the harbour[13] (fig. 6.10). In the spring of 1916 Weller wanted to proceed immediately with the placing of the stone but Bowden thought the matter should be considered further. In early May Weller began urging Bowden to proceed, and by 6 June he was warning Bowden against further delay in the work. In mid-June Weller went to Ottawa to speak to Bowden personally. Bowden showed him calculations of the expense involved hauling stone to the breakwaters. The mathematics had been done by E.B. Jost (b. 1879), then a young Departmental hydraulic engineer.[14] Weller, who thought that Jost was inexperienced, did not agree with his calculations. As he said later, they were "entirely erroneous and indicated a very great lack of knowledge," and warned Bowden not to accept them. His own judgment, he said, was "much better than any ordinary calculation." Back in St Catharines, he again protested Bowden's delay, describing the inadequacy of Jost's estimates and reporting that he had discussed the matter with contractors, who said that they couldn't do the work at the price quoted by Bowden. In the summer and fall, Jost, Bowden, and the Minister of Railways and Canals Frank Cochrane (1852–1919) each visited the Ship Canal site. These visits enraged Weller, who later wrote to Cochrane: "You took considerable pains to impress upon the Minister that both yourself and Mr. Jost knew so much more about Canal construction work than I did that my recommendation in the matter of placing this stone protection ... should not be considered and that I was very extravagant in my ideas of the cost of such work."[15] If Weller's description is accurate, his ire is understandable. Unfortunately, we do not have Bowden's view of the situation.

On 26 September Weller had already fired off a seven-page letter to Bowden accusing him of "interference" with his staff and of doing "great injury" to the work. In fact, said Weller, Bowden was "deliberately trying to jeopardize it."[16] On 14 October, Weller again begged Bowden for action on the embankments, and again on 7 November. Finally, Bowden announced that he would make his own arrangements with the contractors regarding the breakwaters and on 9 November, he arrived in St Catharines to do so.

After all this bickering, the stone protection work on the embankments at Port Weller harbour was closed down in March 1917 in the general stoppage of that spring. In April Weller fired his final volley,

6.11　Port Weller piers. A new northern harbour for the waterway, built with stone material excavated from the Niagara Escarpment.

6.12 Port Weller, 1914. The west pier under construction. Dredges, tugs, scows, and locomotives bring tonnes of earth and rock to fill concrete cribs sunk into Lake Ontario. Despite the structure's massiveness, much of it was smashed by a severe winter storm the next year.

writing a long letter (four and half pages, single spaced, typed, legal size paper) to Bowden in which he said, "I think it is well to herewith make a recital of the whole case and show in one document how your mismanagement of this piece of work has cost the Dept over $91,000,00 more than it would have been necessary to pay had my recommendation been adopted."[17] Altogether, over twenty-three letters and telegrams on this matter passed between St Catharines and Ottawa. Fortunately such disagreements were rare during the Ship Canal construction. It is impossible to know who was correct in this argument but the reasons for Weller's not being rehired in 1919 probably include this quarrel and his vigorous language.

By 1926 the breakwaters were largely finished and the quiet water between them could be used as a safe haven for vessels in stormy weather. Weller's considerable ego must have been salved when the Ship Canal's northern terminus was named after him. (No part of the waterway was named after Alex Grant, who served over fourteen years actively on the project, compared to Weller's mere five years.)

At Port Weller the two long piers, stretching out into Lake Ontario (figs 6.11 and 6.12), were under construction by 1914. Dredges would excavate the channel between them and into the harbour down to bedrock. Forty-three of the anticipated forty-six cribs were laid down by November 1923. Tromanhauser and Co., subcontractors for Dominion Dredging, built them at Port Dalhousie and, in the same pattern as at Ports Maitland and Colborne, they were towed along the lakeshore to their site. In 1920, all plant was moved to the west wall of the harbour at Port Weller. Temporary wooden trestles were built out in the lake on either side of the harbour from which hopper cars could start dumping spoil from the excavation of the flight locks, brought in by the construction railway. As the trestles were filled up, the dumping tracks were gradually moved sideways and the embankments widened. On the west pier, the Department of Marine and Fisheries erected a lighthouse with a foghorn.

The engineers were not blind to the dangers of unpredictable Lake Ontario. At Port Weller harbour, a heavy bank of earth was left to keep lake water out of the pit of the new Lock 1 (fig. 6.7). Even so, a pump had to be kept working intermittently to keep the lock pit dry. Nevertheless, Lake Ontario chewed away at the embankments being built at the new harbour. The winter of 1914–15 was especially difficult, as portions of the embryonic piers slid away, carrying portions of the trestle with them. Another storm that winter capsized the dredge DELVER while it was being towed to Port Dalhousie for shelter, rendering it out of commission for the rest of the season. Moreover, in that stormy winter, unusually low water in Lake Ontario inhibited the transport of cribs for the piers being built at Port Dalhousie, the harbour of which had to be dredged to allow them to be towed over to Port Weller. In the winter of 1924–25 lake storms and unusual ice conditions again retarded construction.

Sheer chance bedevilled the canal builders. For example, in 1916 one crib sank accidentally in the harbour and had to be refloated in 1919. In that year a ship collided with one of the piers in a fog, necessitating further repairs. Then in the spring of 1922 another crib sank while being placed and had to be retrieved. A trestle collapsed with loss of rolling stock in October 1923. Niagara's geology created problems here, too. On the outer slopes of the piers some of the fill material was sticky clay that was hard to dump efficiently so that the contractor resorted to using strong water jets to place it.

Unlike the difficulties with storms, nature was not to blame when ships' wash eroded the banks of the Welland. In the early twentieth century the larger boats, whose size had necessitated the rebuilding of the canal, also posed a danger to the security of its none-too-stable banks. Where the danger of erosion was greatest, therefore, the canal's banks were lined with a concrete wall a foot (30 cm) thick, extending from five feet below to five feet (1.5 m) above the water line. Elsewhere a layer of broken stone was put down on the banks (fig. 6.10). Some of this material arrived as gravel from the mouth of the Grand River, while parts of Lock 26 of the Third Canal and of a retaining wall of the old guard gate south of the new Bridge 12 were also used.

On the northern stretch of the canal, especially at Lock 2, the embankments themselves were often like dikes, supporting the prism above the surrounding land. Failure of these 30-foot-high (9.1 m) earthen walls could spell disaster for local farm- and homeowners, not to mention ships. Consequently those structures, as well as embankments at pondage areas, had to be made watertight. As had been done traditionally, horse- and mule-drawn wagons deposited layers of selected clays, during which work the animals' hooves compacted the freshly laid earth. As well, trees were planted so that their roots would stabilize the ground.

THE POWERHOUSE

The power of dammed-up water was essential to the operation of the Welland. The Ship Canal's designers also exploited its gravitational force to create electricity. All of the Ship Canal's power would be supplied from a building located just north of Twin Locks 4 on the canal's west side. Water would be drawn from above Lock 7 through an 8.5-foot (2.6 m) penstock that would run down the west side of the flight locks within the concrete of the lock structure. A surge tank 205 feet (62.5 m) high would stand at the concrete powerhouse (fig. 6.13). Built by Departmental labour, the latter structure was finished in June 1930 when the machinery was installed. The surge tank was completed several months later.

The powerhouse has stood for over eighty years and, now ivy-covered, looks very permanent. As with certain other features of the Ship Canal, however, in the 1920s its location was subject to debate. The plan, outlined by sectional engineer F.S. Lazier, in a memorandum of 1920, was to take water from the east end of Lock 7's pondage and direct it to the head of Lock 18 of the Third Canal. From here it would drop 100 feet (30.5 m) to a powerhouse planned for the top of

6.13   St Catharines. The powerhouse at the foot of Twin Locks 4. When built, it housed three 5,000-horsepower generators to provide electricity for the whole Ship Canal. Helping to control the flow of water to the powerhouse is a surge tower (a "differential surge tank") looming in the background.

the east end of the disused Grand Trunk Railway tunnel. "The masonry of this tunnel is in first class condition," said Lazier, and could bear the weight of a new concrete building above it. The turbines in that structure would discharge water into the tunnel from which it would flow into an existing channel to the pondage of old Lock 11.[18]

Taking water from above Lock 7 had advantages because more surplus water was available there than at Lock 6. Because most of such water came from Lake Erie, however, international political problems could develop. American opinion was already concerned that the new Welland might take too much water from the Great Lakes. "The United States engineers," wrote an Ontario Hydro official, "are ... carefully watching the power situation at the Welland Canal."[19] A

6.14 Thorold, April 1923. Water is a necessity for the operation of the canal but here it is leaking, partly frozen, into the pit of Lock 7. Elsewhere, too, it often caused difficulties by appearing at the wrong time and the wrong place.

controversy was already raging over Chicago's diversion of water from Lake Michigan and the Canadian and American governments were in negotiations over the efficient use of Lake Erie water. Ottawa had to reassure Washington that operation of the Ship Canal would not affect the water level of the Great Lakes. As for the Ship Canal engineers, they were encouraged to hold their cards close to their chests: "Avoid display of culvert plans," telegraphed Bowden to Grant in March 1923. (Grant had asked him if he should tell the CNR about the suggestion that a penstock be built into the walls of Locks 4, 5, and 6.) Grant

6.15 Excavating the channel, a Marion steam shovel owned by the Dominion Excavating Co. is mired in water and mud, ca. 1925.

was to assure those interested that the water drawn off was to be used only for Ship Canal purposes. Inquiries continued to be made about what Grant called "the controversial and international character" of the situation and he alerted Bowden to them. Both men made it publicly clear that Lake Erie, even at low water level, was not going to be threatened by any lowering of the summit level of the new waterway.[20]

While the Lock 7 plan would have been an ingenious example of recycling, it was never implemented. When the question of providing power for the lock gates and related structures became pressing in 1926, Dubuc asked Grant to look into the plan outlined by Lazier. Grant thought that at least until it was doubled, Lock 7 was the ideal site. In 1927 engineer Frank E. Sterns recommended a power plant at Twin Locks 4, an opinion supported by A.L. Mudge, senior electrical engineer, and A.T.C. McMaster, senior hydraulic power engineer. More support was obtained when, in July 1928, E.B. Jost (now an assistant engineer with the Department in Ottawa) encouraged Dubuc to develop hydro power at Twin Locks 4. These views seem to have swayed the chief engineer who, on 19 July, authorized the drawing up of specifications for the present powerhouse at the foot of the Escarpment.[21]

Water was a powerful natural force that the Welland's engineers and contractors exploited carefully and feared with good cause. But in constructing a major north-south waterway across the Niagara Peninsula, in an age of increasing highway and railway traffic, the problem of getting east-west communications across the canal proved an even greater challenge than in the past. Our next chapter describes how the builders confronted the issue of crossings – i.e., highway and railway bridges – never welcomed by canal builders and operators, but now more frequent and unavoidable than ever, as well as the myriad of under- and overground wires, cables, and pipes of telephone, telegraph, and water services.

CHAPTER SEVEN

Building Bridges

S till photographs cannot convey the dynamic nature of the Ship Canal construction site ca. 1925. Especially south of Thorold, where the Deep Cut was being dredged, tonnes of water flowed past cliffs of earth as high as 90 feet (27.4 m) that threatened to pitch into that water. Huge ships plied the existing canal in both directions, carefully avoiding collision with each other and with the dredges which eased their way into the channel with attendant tugs and scows awaiting their spoil. North of the Escarpment powerful steam loco- motives pulled long trains of boxcars and passenger cars across the widening prism, slowing down cautiously at the temporary wooden trestle bridges, while the construction railway rattled across its own temporary crossings. The noise of steam-powered shovels, draglines, and rock drills was punctuated by explosions designed to loosen rock. Perhaps only a sound motion picture could capture the vitality of the scene.[1] Over this changing land- and waterscape, designers, engineers, and contractors were required to construct permanent crossings.

The Welland Canal's builders had never been able to escape the problem of how to deal with east-west highways and, latterly, railways and their need to cross the waterway. Those men building the Welland Canal Company's channel in the 1820s had only a few such crossings to contend with but those building the Second and Third Canals faced an increasing challenge. By the twentieth century the problem was more acute than ever, as many more roads and railway tracks traversed the canal. Due to the emerging industrial economy and the increasing popularity of the automobile, land traffic on both rail and road cross- ings had increased tremendously, necessitating even more frequent bridges, a situation that would conflict with the burgeoning trade on the waterway itself. The main trans-peninsula highway, King's High- way 8, would cross the northern stretch of the new canal at Homer,

7.1   Port Weller, 21 April 1930. Looking north, Bridge 1 (a bascule) at the opening of Lock 1, with the GEORGIAN.

east of St Catharines, while, near Port Colborne, provision would have to be made for Highway 3. Less travelled roads included Lakeshore Road at the new Port Weller, the Thorold-Allanburg Road, and Highway 20 at Allanburg. Several major railway lines crossed the canal, while Sections 7 and 8, south of Port Robinson, saw a concentration of six road crossings and three railway bridges. Complicating matters was the fact that new internal combustion engines were heavier and faster than horses and buggies, and modern steam locomotives were lumbering leviathans, weighty and difficult to stop quickly. The new bridges would have to be durable, strong, and reliable structures – and much larger than in the past. Added to the problem was the growth of urban areas such as Welland on both sides of the waterway (fig. 10.6).

Providing bridges for railway lines had already challenged the Third Canal's builders. Faced with the growing size and weight of rolling stock by 1900, canal engineers already had to rebuild such crossings.

Moreover, Niagara's railways were now part of an international network that could not be disrupted without far-flung consequences. For example, the main line of the Grand Trunk Railway, by 1922 part of the Canadian National Railway, crossed the new channel at the foot of Twin Locks 4 to connect with New York State. Local railway lines were nearly as problematic. The electric Niagara, St Catharines and Toronto Railway, which connected Port Dalhousie with St Catharines, Thorold, and points south, crossed the Third Canal on a swing bridge just south of Thorold. This crossing would be the site of a new bridge but, until it could be constructed, a temporary structure had to be built. Such crossings had to be of the same strength and durability as permanent ones and entailed similar expense and care in construction.

Even by 1914 (the outbreak of the First World War), it was apparent that automobiles and trucks, themselves heavier than horses and buggies, would require highway crossings bigger and more complex than the older bridges. When an existing bridge was removed, a temporary crossing had to be constructed near the rail line or highway but not too close to hamper construction of the new bridge. In the fifty years since the Third Canal opened, the travelling population of Niagara had greatly increased. Industrialization had created a labour force that often needed to cross the waterway to get to work. In addition, the tourist traffic was growing, while the aforementioned automobile added to residents' mobility. However much people appreciated the importance of the Welland Canal to the local and national economy, they were impatient of delays occasioned by bridges being "up."

Driving along Highway 20 towards Allanburg and Lundy's Lane today, newcomers to Niagara may notice two towers looming in the distance.[2] These strange landmarks are the pylons of a vertical lift bridge, Number 11, which spans the Ship Canal. If the travellers drive south from here towards Port Colborne, they will find the otherwise flat landscape spiked with more of these towers marking the line of the canal. Given the many highways and railways that, already in the 1920s, crossed the Niagara Peninsula, these lift bridges and the less impressive bascule bridges, which also regularly span the waterway, were essential. To supervise their design and construction, the Department of Railways and Canals needed a new breed of experts: specialized bridge engineers. Possibly to their surprise, in the course of their daily work these engineers often found themselves involved in crises as much social or psychological as technological. As well, they discovered that twentieth-century Ontario required other forms of crossings such as telephone, telegraph, and hydroelectric cables of which the nineteenth-century canal builders had only an inkling. As did several other aspects of the Ship Canal, their original plans for highway and railway bridges changed and evolved from 1913 to 1930. Powerful railway companies and their demands and needs added to the canal engineers' challenges. Moreover, problems developed with the designers and contractors. Finally, as was also traditional, "the navigation" could not be interrupted during construction.

"THE CANAL WAS ON THE GROUND FIRST"

The Ship Canal's engineers naturally believed that the interests of shipping on the waterway took precedence over those of land transportation. They also maintained correctly that "the Canal was on the ground first," a point made by Grant in 1923.[3] However, reiterating the rights of ship captains over locomotives and automobiles did not preclude collisions of opinion. An incident in April 1931 at the newly completed Bridge 6 that took the Canadian National Railway over Twin Locks 4 is significant (fig. 7.2). When the bridge operators (railway company employees), working on instructions to direct all trains across the bridge at all times, held up the ERICSON for forty minutes, Grant telegraphed Dubuc for clarification on who had the right of way. The chief engineer, referring to the Canal Regulations and to federal legislation, replied in a telegram, "Navigation paramount to railway traffic."[4]

Nevertheless, another precedent was at work. The original Welland Canal Company Charter of 1824 had required the Welland's builders to construct bridges or lay down roads wherever major land arteries were disrupted. As late as 24 December 1925, this act of incorporation was cited by the *Welland Tribune and Telegraph* in an article which reported that the highway from Welland to Port Colborne was in a "dangerous condition" and that the government appeared reluctant to do anything about it. The writer noted that "in certain cases where the original road allowance was closed up there were no bridges built. The towpath was used and is in use today as a public highway to get from one bridge to another." The article continued, "There follows the indisputable fact that for nearly one hundred years the Government have maintained the former towpath from Welland South to Port Col-

7.2   Twin Locks 4, 1926. Bridge for the Canadian National Railway on its international line, an important thoroughfare that could not be obstructed.

borne as a public highway."[5] The government, therefore, should repair the highway. The town's case was a good one for, between April 1924 and December 1925, twenty-nine vehicles had accidentally left the road, two of which entered the canal.[6] "Make Somebody Do Something," cried a Welland newspaper editorial.[7] Eventually, the Ontario government repaired the highway.

THE BRIDGE BUILDERS

The statutory requirement to provide crossings for land traffic resulted in the fact that by 1931 twenty bridges had been built over the route of the Ship Canal. Eleven were vertical lift bridges, whose towers rose 165 feet (50.3 m) above water level (fig. 7.3). Bridges 8 and 15, at Thorold and Welland respectively, were swing bridges. The rest were double- or single-rolling lift, or bascule, structures. Five single-leaf bascule bridges were built, at Lock 1 at Lakeshore Road, Lock 2 at Carlton

7.3 Port Colborne, ca. 1930. Two typical lift bridges, one for Highway 3, one for the Canadian National Railway. At the lower right, locks of the Second and Third canals. The government grain elevator (1907) and that of Maple Leaf Mills (1908) are prominent in the background.

Street, Lock 7, the guard gate, and Lock 8 at Port Colborne. These sites reflect the fact that engineers preferred to install bascules where the canal was narrowest, as at locks. Double-leaf bascules were constructed at Bridge 4 (at Homer) and at Twin Locks 4. Fifteen of the twenty bridges were highway crossings, three of which also carried interurban railway lines: Lakeshore Road at Port Weller, Queenston Street near Homer, and Main Street in Welland, while five others took major railway lines over the waterway.[8] Two of the vertical lifts were built in the heart of Welland: Main Street (Bridge 13) and Lincoln Street (Bridge 14).

The designing firms were American. Bridge 6, a double-leaf bascule for the CNR at Twin Locks 4, was designed by the Scherzer Rolling

Lift Bridge Company of Chicago, which was granted the contract in May 1925. The other six rolling lift bridges and the eleven vertical lift bridges were planned by Harrington, Howard, and Ash of Kansas City, which received its contract in October 1925. However, the contractors who would actually build the structures were all Canadian: Hamilton Bridge Company of Hamilton, Ontario (for the seven rolling lift bridges), the Canadian Bridge Company of Walkerville, Ontario (for eight of the vertical lift bridges), and the Dominion Bridge Company of Lachine, Quebec, which was contracted for one vertical lift crossing, Welland's problematic Bridge 13.

Many of the companies that supplied equipment for the locks were also involved with bridge construction, particularly the steel and electrical firms. Canadian firms, including a number of local concerns, predominated. Along with names already mentioned were Cameron & Phin of Welland, Dominion Foundries & Steel (DOFASCO) of Hamilton, Sarnia Bridge, Hamilton Gear & Machine, and Frid Construction. Electrical equipment came from, among others, Ferranti Electric, Canadian Line Materials, Powerlite Devices, and Canadian Wire & Cable, all of Toronto; Canadian Ohio Brass of Niagara Falls, Ontario; Northern Electric of Ottawa; Packard Electric of St Catharines; Standard Underground Cable of Hamilton; Cutler Hammer of Milwaukee; and Eugene F. Phillips of Montreal.

This dry listing of names cannot convey the complexity of the bridge project, nor does it suggest the changes in plans that occurred between 1913 and 1930. Several men were mandated to confront such complexities. One of these was M. Brodie Atkinson (1879–1950), born in Quebec and educated at McGill. After much experience designing and inspecting bridges, he became engineer in charge of bridges on the Ship Canal in 1921. In this role he drew up the general specifications for the design and construction of all the crossings. He was a member of the Examining Board of Engineers that chose the types of bridges to be built, referred to consulting engineers, and supervised the contractors' construction. Also on the Board was Frank Sterns, who was appointed designing engineer, serving 1913–17 and after 1919.

Alex Grant and sectional engineers such as F.C. Jewett also had responsibilities with regard to bridge construction which involved dealing with contractors, labour, and communities, as well as those perennial elements of canal construction: water, rock, and earth.

AS THE BRIDGES WENT UP

Even before the steam shovels and mule teams began their work in 1913, it was apparent that construction of the Ship Canal would sever east-west road connections such as Thorold Stone Road to Beaverdams and Warner Road to St David's Road, both in Thorold. But would bridges be built for every severed highway? Grant was not always sensitive to the views of local citizens as, for example, when Port Colborne's mayor offered objections to plans for bridges in his community. "The public at large is paying for the cost of this structure and not the citizens of a small village," wrote Grant, "and therefore the interests of the public at large should be fully considered."[9]

In fairness to Grant, local residents could display contradictory or changing attitudes regarding the new canal's bridges. Whereas the Port Colborne mayor, the local MP, and businessmen petitioned for a highway bridge at Clarence Street, other residents wanted it at Fraser Street, a block farther north. Originally, certain Welland citizens were dismayed to think that their town might lose the Ship Canal to a route through Wainfleet to Jordan. Weller recalled the "very urgent opposition of Welland" to the possible loss of the canal. Speaking at a banquet in that city in December 1912, he said that "by the time the Welland ship canal was in operation, Wellanders might be very sorry that the Wainfleet course had not been followed. When the size of bridge necessary to span a three hundred foot water surface was considered, and the length of time that would be needed for swinging the bridge the people might find it somewhat inconvenient."[10]

When construction started on the route through downtown Welland, the city fathers expressed the hope that traffic across the canal at Main Street, the Alexandra Bridge, would not be blocked by construction. Moreover, they urged the building of two bridges in the heart of the city, at Main and at Lincoln Streets, the latter about eight blocks south of Main Street. From 1920 on, the mayor and the local MP badgered Ottawa for the quick execution of the bridge work, in particular the completion of the Lincoln Street crossing first. But work on the latter site (Bridge 14) was slower than expected and the locals protested. Therefore, in 1926 Canadian Dredging jacked up the Alexandra Bridge on piles, placed it on two scows, and floated it down the canal to serve as a temporary crossing at Bald and Division Streets (fig. 7.4). After Bridge 13 was completed in 1928, the provisional crossing

7.4   Welland, 1927. Moving the Alexandra Bridge (a swing structure) at Main Street in Welland to a temporary site until Bridge 13 was completed.

was taken down. Welland now had two downtown crossings without losing the Ship Canal itself.

As it turned out, Welland people eventually came to rue the day their parents campaigned for the Ship Canal to run through their city, with or without two spans, because, as the population and number of automobiles increased, the road bridges became an irritation. Traffic was frequently held up by the raising of the bridges, especially the one at Main Street, and complaints proliferated.

WHY VERTICAL LIFTS?

Had the engineers' original bridge plans been executed, Niagara's landscape would be different from its appearance today. There would be no vertical lift bridges because, initially, bascules and even the traditional swing crossings were favoured. Despite their disadvantages to shipping, John Weller envisaged the continued use of some of the Third Canal's swing bridges and expected most of the new structures to be bascules. In 1919 his replacement, Alex Grant, recommended a swing bridge for the Homer crossing and bascules elsewhere. In 1916 a Welland newspaper reported that the "highway bridge at Port Robinson ... will be of the bascule lift type, and work on the substructure is now in progress."[11] (It was built as a vertical lift.) In 1919–21 the Department carried out a study of bascule bridges in Chicago, Toronto, and Burlington Bay, and in May 1925 Grant, in a list of all planned bridge structures for Dubuc, did not mention vertical lift bridges at all but described the crossings as swings or bascules.[12] As late as August 1923, when Bowden asked the Scherzer Rolling Lift Bridge Company, the Strauss Bascule Bridge Company and Harrington, Howard and Ash to submit competitive designs for bridge superstructures, vertical lift bridges were still only one of three options and only one was actually planned.

The traditional swing bridges, which had been used to cross the previous canals, were out of favour with ship captains. For example, in February 1900 the Department received a petition from captains of vessels navigating the Third Canal setting forth the hazards to their ships created by the centre piers of such crossings. In that same month W.G. Thomson, Third Canal superintending engineer, urged demolition of the pivot piers and their replacement by steel bridges spanning the full width of the prism. As in the past, the increasing size – and now also the speed – of ships created the need for change. By 1914 many canal engineers believed that swing crossings were not the best type to adopt because, even if they pivoted on one bank and not in mid-channel, they took up too much space on lock walls and on the surrounding ground. If they pivoted in the middle of the prism, their guard piers or fenders could endanger ships. As it transpired, no such structures would be built, although two newer swing bridges constructed on the Third Canal would be retained.

Bridge 8 was one of these two Third Canal bridges incorporated into the new Ship Canal. Finished in 1915 for the interurban Niagara, St Catharines and Toronto Railway just south of Thorold, it had never been operated. The other example, which also turned on a pier in mid-channel, was south of Welland, where in 1910, having in mind the probably future enlargement of the Third Canal, the engineers built a new crossing for the Michigan Central Railroad. This span became

Bridge 15 of the Ship Canal but, although it had been built on a large scale, as traffic increased and ships grew larger, it in turn became a hazard. The problem was partly alleviated in 1929–30 by the dredging on both sides of the middle abutment or pivot pier to allow for navigation on two channels instead of the previous one.

Chief Engineer Dubuc seems to have been more interested in vertical lifts than was his predecessor and stimulated inquiries and research into their capabilities. In March 1925 Grant, on Dubuc's orders and accompanied by his brother, Gordon Grant, a CNR engineer, visited Chicago to inspect vertical lift bridges there. M. Brodie Atkinson, Frank Sterns, and H.B. Smart (also of the CNR) accompanied them. Atkinson seems to have been frequently in touch with engineers about vertical lifts elsewhere. For example, in 1928 a New York engineer wrote to him (presumably on his request) about the Köningshaven lift bridge in Rotterdam.

At all events, the choice of vertical lifts for eleven of the bridges was made only in late 1925. Each of these structures consisted of a central truss span that carried the road or railway, connected by a pulley system to huge counterweights located in towers set at either end of the bridge. These towers kept the span level as it was lifted. The concrete counterweights reinforced with steel balanced the span's load. Each was built in place, halfway up its tower, with a temporary flooring constructed for the purpose about sixty feet (18.3 m) from the top. Developed mainly in the United States, vertical lifts were widely used there. Among the reasons for their choice was the fact that they would give almost unlimited clearance for ships' masts. As the designers were drawing up plans for the vertical lift bridges in 1927, however, a rumour circulated that the new spans, even when lifted, would be too low and would endanger ships and impede shipping in general. Dubuc maintained that the 120-foot (36 m) clearance was sufficient, but American authorities protested.[13] Grant had already made inquiries of naval architects and shipbuilders on the height of masts on their ships and naval architects on the height required for wireless antennas. In the end the proposed height proved adequate.

The change of plan brought additional problems: those abutments already built to support a rolling lift bridge (as at Bridge 12 in Port Robinson) had to be modified to suit a vertical lift structure. Moreover, when a double-leaf bascule bridge was selected for Bridge 4 at Homer, examination of the concrete abutments built during the previous contract for this bridge revealed that the substructure was not strong enough to support the altered superstructure and that additional piles in the rear were needed as well as more concrete.

COMPLICATIONS DEVELOP

The work of studying the submissions of the American designers rested with the "Examining Board of Engineers" appointed in April 1924. This "Bridge Board" consisted of Sterns, Atkinson, and C.N. Montsarrat, an independent engineer from Montreal. Reporting to Dubuc, the Board travelled about, inspecting bridge designs, taking photographs, and preparing its conclusions. For example, in February 1924 they were in Cleveland studying the harbour bridges there.

Beginning in May 1924 the Board met nine times, usually in St Catharines. Typically, these engineers found that their work involved matters that did not seem technological or at all canal-related. Misinformation, communication breakdown, and rampant ego seemed to dog their work. When the Board failed to recommend Joseph B. Strauss's bascule design, Strauss (1870–1938), as president of the Bascule Bridge Company, kept the Board busy with his complaints about their competence and fairness. A representative of the Michigan Central Railroad had told the Board that "the Strauss Bridge makes a good structure if designed right, but there is too much material in the counterweight tower and it is ugly." (The Board had consulted other bridge experts as well before making their decision.) Undaunted, in September 1924 Strauss claimed that his submission for Bridge 4 at Homer was arbitrarily ruled out of competition because Board members were personal friends of some of his competitors. "Not one ... has ever designed a bascule bridge," he wrote to Dubuc. In high dudgeon the Board reacted vigorously, denying to Dubuc all of Strauss's allegations: "The entire letter is redolent with attacks upon the integrity, disinterestedness, and competence of the Board and of the Welland Ship Canal engineers, past and present, and violates the Code of Ethics of the Engineering Institute of Canada or any other recognized Engineering body."[14]

The Board maintained that Strauss knew that vertical lifts were to be considered as well as bascules and that he could have submitted plans for them. Although claiming to be offended and although he had submitted only bascule plans, Strauss announced that he would

7.5 Near St Catharines, the Homer twin bascule bridge (#4) has the counterweights placed under the span for aesthetic reasons – Highway 8 and later the Queen Elizabeth Way crossed the canal here. See also fig. 7.6.

soon submit plans for vertical lifts. In May 1925 he complained again to Dubuc about his not getting contracts for the Ship Canal bridges. Grant noted wryly that Strauss was "more of a lawyer than an engineer" and recommended to Dubuc that no reply be made beyond acknowledging receipt of his letters.[15]

In December 1924 the Board began to make recommendations to Ottawa for bridge types at various locations. At the Port Robinson crossing (Bridge 12), for example, they recommended a vertical lift, as designed by Harrington, Howard and Ash. For Bridge 4, at Homer, they wrote that a vertical lift, as suggested by the aforementioned firm, was "superior in certain engineering features to rolling lift [bascule]" but that "a rolling lift bridge ... would be preferrable at this site on account of its very pleasing appearance"[16] (figs 7.5 and 7.6). They probably considered the fact that this crossing would take the major peninsula highway linking the United States with Toronto and carrying many American tourists annually. The Bridge Board echoed a general

7.6   The Homer Bridge, ca. 1970, with leaves raised and the Garden
City Skyway, carrying the Queen Elizabeth Way (completed 1963) in
the background.

opinion that vertical lifts were ugly compared to the more graceful
arches or suspensions of traditional crossings. In 1919 Grant had already recommended a double-leaf bascule for this crossing rather than
a swing or vertical lift because it would be less expensive on the site
and was, he said, "pleasing to the eye."[17] Consequently the final design
for the Homer crossing installed the counterweights, normally placed
in such bridges above the roadway in a steel support, underneath the
level of the road on both sides of the canal, with the result that motor-
ists driving along Highway 8 often found that their automobiles were
half way over the canal before they realized it.

The Bridge Board's work was further complicated by the year-long
lobbying of W. Chase Thomson, a Montreal consulting engineer
(1866–1948?) to have them adopt his "Double Leaf Bob-Tail Swing
Bridge." In February 1924 Thomson wrote to the Minister of Railways

and Canals that the late W.A. Bowden had agreed that this type of bridge was suitable for the Ship Canal. Canadian engineers had designed it, he said, and "as you no doubt know, there has been considerable dissatisfaction expressed by members of the E.I.C. [Engineering Institute of Canada] that so much Canadian engineering work has recently been given to American designing firms." At the same time he wrote to Grant pressing for adoption of this type of bridge, noting that the cables on a vertical lift bridge were expensive to maintain and the bridge itself is "a most unsightly affair."[18] In March of 1925 Dubuc himself ordered the Board to consider not only vertical lifts but also Thomson's design.

In that same month Grant, Sterns and Atkinson reported to Dubuc. They found Thomson's suggestions "inadequate" due to errors in design. The vertical lift was better for railways because the land alongside was not encumbered when the span was open, as was the case with many swing bridges. The chief problem with Bob-Tail swing bridges, they said, was the need for protection from and for ships when they were open.[19]

Because vertical lift bridges were the first to be built in Canada, their design had an experimental aspect, which may account for some of the delays incurred in their construction. Surprisingly, moreover, the American designers committed errors in their submissions to the Department. Under pressure from Dubuc, who wanted to call for bridge tenders in April 1926, Grant castigated Harrington, Howard and Ash, noting that the Department was "very much disappointed in the time that you've taken ... You have caused us considerable annoyance and inconvenience."[20] Atkinson of the Bridge Board complained that, in the Board's work, "complications develop every day and have to be smoothed out ... Personally I will be very glad to get through with it."[21]

FURTHER HEADACHES FOR THE ENGINEERS

Although their abutments often were constructed as soon as the prism was completed, the superstructures of bridges were the last canal structures to be built. As was typical, once construction was under way Grant and his engineers encountered difficulties with contractors, who themselves faced special challenges. Where the new bridges were built across the operating canal channel, special situations developed

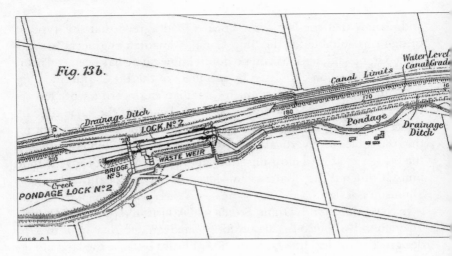

involving ship traffic and working in conjunction with deep water. Contractors much preferred to build "in the dry" but this was not always possible. Shortages of materials occasionally caused delays. Temporary bridges had to be built for railways and highways. Railway companies were annoyed when their schedules were disrupted by construction. "The navigation" could not be hindered and certain community amenities could not be undermined. Given these challenges, building the new, larger bridges proved as complex as building the giant locks.

As with the prism excavation and the locks, the actual construction of the bridges was carried out by private contractors rather than by Departmental forces, and hence was one step removed from Alex Grant's control – but not from his overall responsibility. The situation was even more complicated because the railway companies also weighed in with their needs and opinions on bridges. Problems over which Grant had no control were especially frustrating for this short-tempered and perfectionist engineer. For example, Bridge 1, a single-leaf bascule which would span the southern end of Lock 1 at Lakeshore Road, made slow progress through 1926–27 due to a shortage of steel, something about which neither Grant nor the contractor (Hamilton Bridge) could do much.

Especially Bridge 2, a vertical lift which would have taken Grantham Township's Church Road across the canal, taxed Grant's sense of fairness and diplomatic skill (fig. 7.7). The 1824 charter of the First

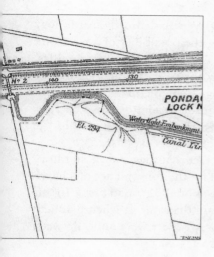

7.7 St Catharines. Bridge 2, in Section 1, intended to carry Linwell Road over the canal, was never built but appears to the right on this map in Cowan's *Welland Ship Canal*, 12, fig. 13b.

Canal compelled the canal builders always to construct bridges where roads were cut, and therefore on the new Ship Canal, between Port Weller and Lock 7 alone, there were to be five road bridges. The industrial communities of Merritton, St Catharines, and Thorold had grown up to the west of the new site, and the surveyed prism would also cut through thriving orchards and farmlands. Local east-west traffic of farmers, schoolchildren, businessmen, and tourists necessitated road bridges at Lakeshore Road (Lock 1), Linwell Road (Bridge 2), Carlton Street (Lock 2), what would later be Glendale Avenue (Bridge 5), and Peter Street (above Lock 7). Like the others, the Linwell Road crossing (Bridge 2) had been planned since 1913. Excavation and pile driving for its foundation were carried out in winter of 1914–15. Concreting of the west abutment was finished in 1915 and a temporary road diversion through the slope of the prism was constructed. The bridge, however, was never built.

What happened to this "bridge that never was"? The canal authorities had promised a bridge to local residents whose farms would be divided by the new waterway. When, in April 1923, residents detected hints that the bridge would not be completed, 105 of them petitioned the Minister of Railways and Canals to finish the crossing, which was, they said, "very much needed for the safety of the public traffic" – especially schoolchildren.[22] Nevertheless, by 1926 the canal engineers were having second thoughts and in 1928 Dubuc told Grant that Bridge 2 would not be built.

Concerned Grantham Township ratepayers had already met in 1927 and discussed the problem, considering the possibility of a road link on the east side instead of a bridge. The Read and Hack families, whose property was already divided by the new channel, vigorously petitioned the Department for the bridge's completion. In 1928, however, Dubuc decided not to build. Instead, Read Road (which runs between Lakeshore Road and Carlton Street on the east side of the canal) was laid out and paved in 1932 at Ottawa's expense.

The Bridge 2 controversy reveals the fact that, despite the statutory requirement, bridges would not be built for the convenience of a handful of local people. After all, "the canal was on the ground first." To this day, however, the bridge numbers remain the same as when planned. Twenty-one bridges were planned but only twenty were built. Between Bridge 1 and Bridge 3, there is no Bridge 2.

Nothing irritated Grant more than the inability of contractors to keep to agreed-upon schedules. Bridge 4 at Homer was finished in June 1928 but not before the contractors experienced difficulties with the terrain here. Typically, a nervous Grant harangued the Hamilton Bridge Company for their slowness in executing the contract. In January 1928 he complained about the company giving preference to other large contracts, such as the Royal York Hotel in Toronto, over the canal work, contracts which were "monopolizing your shops just now."[23]

To do him justice, Grant's bridge engineers were also disturbed by Hamilton Bridge's slowness. A good example is Bridge 6, actually two bridges, or a double-leaf bascule, crossing Twin Locks 4, to carry the Canadian National Railway over the double lock. Brodie Atkinson, Departmental bridge engineer and formerly a member of the Bridge Board, complained to the company about their inefficiency. In February 1929 he wrote to a colleague, W.W. Cushing at Hamilton Bridge, "strongly" recommending him to "put good draughtsmen on this work." Cushing replied: "Dear Mr. Atkinson: Re: Bridge #6 As Sir Thomas Mallory would say, – In sooth, Sir Brodie, your jest about putting good draughtsmen on this work liketh me not; for sooth, I put on this quest the best man with his hands as any that live, for wit ye well, I did it myself. Yours truly, Cush."[24] Fortunately, a sense of humour occasionally lightened the tensions of canal building for hard-pressed engineers, including those at Hamilton Bridge.[25] The bridges were finished in 1930.

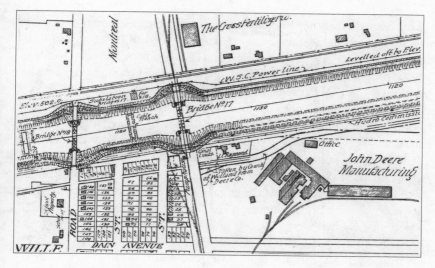

7.8   Dain City, south of Welland, sites of Bridges 17 and 18 with a cable trench and the Ship Canal power line.

7.9   South of Dain City, Bridge 18, "in action," allowing for the passage of a large laker, the TADOUSSAC.

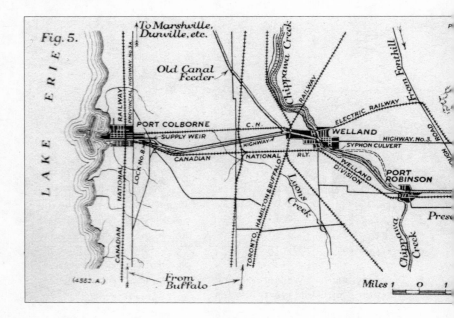

Fig. 5.

KEEPING THE TRAINS ON TIME

A special challenge for the contractors was the railway bridges, more problematic than highway crossings because of the tracks to be laid, the schedules that railways had to maintain, and the heaviness of the trains. In Ottawa Dubuc tried to appease the railway owners while reminding the contractors to keep delays to a minimum. In February 1927, for example, the chief engineer wired Grant: "Advise railways that Department will bear expenses due to interruption of contractors operations ... Also advise Hamilton Bridge that interruptions should be kept down to minimum possible and that expenses which appear to you unwarranted will be deducted from their estimates."[26]

A typical situation existed with the Wabash Division of the Canadian National Railway at the new Bridge 17 near Dainville (Dain City), which could not stop running because the larger canal was being built across its path (figs 7.8 and 7.9). Here the contractor developed a complex but successful way to keep the trains operating smoothly. In 1925 the old swing bridge with its railway tracks was floated off its setting onto barges and moved to a temporary site 159 feet (48.5 m) south of the original site.

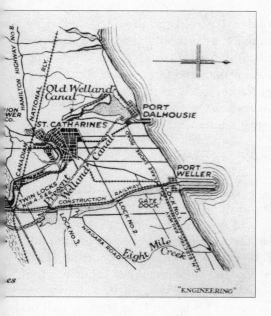

7.10   Route of the Ship Canal, ca. 1930, showing the complex network of railways and highways that needed to cross the waterway. For a more detailed view of one section of the route, see fig. 6.9.

THE TREACHEROUS CLAY (AGAIN)

As it had done often elsewhere and in the past, Niagara's geology undercut the bridge contractors' work. A good example is Bridge 4 at Homer, a double-leaf bascule that would carry Highway 8, later the Queen Elizabeth Way, and a branch of the Niagara, St Catharines and Toronto electric railway over the canal. The abutments were built before 1914 but, after work ceased during the war, a large landslide occurred in July 1917, pitching the east abutment about 10 feet (3 m) into the prism and throwing the piles on which it rested out of the vertical. After construction resumed in 1919, the prism's slope was flattened, the abutment dynamited, the rubble removed, and new excavation started on the troublesome soft clay. In 1920 the building of new piers started, only to be halted in 1926 when the structure on the west side shifted. Meanwhile, in 1922 clay on the nearby banks had partly buried a steam shovel while it was flattening the slopes. A dragline brought in to rescue the shovel also became stuck in a slide. The necessary flattening of the prism slopes here meant that the Homer bridge would have a long, clear span of 200 feet (61 m) and a total length of the bridge of 622 feet (189.6 m) (figs 7.5 and 7.6).

The notorious Deep Cut south of Thorold also provided challenges to the bridge builders. Its treacherous subsoil was a problem at the site of the new Bridge 12 at Port Robinson. During the building of the abutments here, quicksand was encountered three times. Sheet piling was installed to buttress the adjacent earth. Later, because of the unstable terrain, a heavy reinforcing concrete strut was installed in the prism between the piers to prevent movement in the substructure.

"NOT TO INTERRUPT THE NAVIGATION"

As in the past the engineers were concerned to keep the existing canal operating with minimal delays to shipping. Except for where the new channel cut between Locks 10 and 11 of the Third Canal, this requirement was not an issue north of the Escarpment, but south of Thorold, where the Ship Canal would be merely an enlargement of the Third Canal, the problem was often intense. For example, at Allanburg the existing swing bridge had become a hazard to navigation and was to be removed. The presence of the old bridge and the construction of the new meant that the channel was narrowed in two places and the increased velocity of the current in the canal began to prove dangerous to ships. Much of the work, therefore, was done in the closed season. In addition the banks here proved unstable, a cofferdam leaked and piles had to be redriven. Consequently, the structure was one of the last finished in 1930.

At the site of the new vertical lift in Crowland Township, south of Welland, the pre-existing span, Bridge 16 or the "Broadway Bridge," was a swing structure which pivoted on the west bank. In 1925 a channel for ships was dredged on the west side of the pivot pier so that the old east channel could be closed and the new east pier for the vertical lift could be built without interfering with shipping. This highway crossing was finished in 1928.

A DREADFUL AND DANGEROUS ROAD

Although the travelling public and business interests could be sure that when the new canal was completed it would be crossed by at least twenty bridges, the problem of getting highway traffic over the deepening, widening channel as it was being excavated marked the decade of the 1920s. In some cases a pre-existing bridge was moved to a new site to accommodate east-west traffic, as in Welland, but more often temporary structures, usually wooden trestles, were constructed. For example, from Lakeshore Road at Port Weller both road and electric railway traffic were diverted onto temporary wooden structures while the new bridge was installed at Lock 1. Nevertheless all traffic had to be halted for over a week in 1927. Bridge 3, at Lock 2 where Carlton Street crosses the waterway, was, like Bridge 1, completed without much ado in 1927, but a temporary trestle across the site was necessary to take the road across the deepening prism. At Queenston Street (Highway 8), traffic was directed onto an unfinished path through the prism, a situation which led a local motorist to complain about it being "a dreadful and dangerous road to travel over."[27] Even when a temporary bridge was installed here, "hummocks" were still to be endured until 1928, when the new bridge was ready for traffic. At Bridge 7, the Peter Street bascule over the southern end of Lock 7, a temporary crossing was constructed for the road traffic to use. In this case the wooden trestle dating from 1914 had to be entirely rebuilt in 1920, having decayed into a dangerous condition during the wartime stoppage of construction.

Some communities vigorously campaigned to keep cross-canal road connections open during the construction period. In 1924, for example, Humberstone Council petitioned Grant for a bridge to take Main Street across the new channel to connect the two halves of their community. They also asked for footpaths on the temporary bridges over both canals and, for the east side of the Ship Canal, they requested a road to connect with the provincial highway to the south.

Perhaps the most famous – or infamous – bridge on the Ship Canal was Bridge 13, which took Welland's Main Street across the channel. The municipal authorities had not wanted the new canal to bypass Welland, and so the city and its vicinity would have a plethora of bridges of which the vertical lift Bridge 13 was one of three largest on the canal, having a roadway 30 feet (9 m) wide. The most expensive of all the bridges to construct ($986,363.00 [13,592,298.92 in 2015 dollars]), it was unique on the waterway in that its towers were set at an angle to both the waterway and Main Street. Its construction also proved to be exceptional.

To minimize delays to road traffic, in March 1927, Canadian Dredging started to move the old Main Street swing crossing (the Alexandra Bridge) to the site at Division Street, where temporary substructures were prepared (fig. 7.4). At first the low water level in the canal hindered the move, but a week later it was successful and the moved crossing was soon in full operation on the temporary Division Street location. Construction of the new bridge was less smooth. In September 1927 the old substructures were removed and sites prepared for new east and west piers by dredging and driving foundation piles under water. The subcontractors, Maguire, Cameron, and Phin of Welland, floated the west pier crib into position and sank it without incident.[28] But the east pier crib, under construction, flooded prematurely and sank to the bottom. A timber cofferdam was built but, when it had been pumped out, it collapsed, killing three men.

This bridge, finished in 1930, became both a landmark in Welland and the bane of many residents' existence. Wellanders expected that the new span, more modern and more efficient than the old Alexandra Bridge, would cause fewer delays to street traffic. Unfortunately, a hint of what was to become chronic for the next four decades occurred when, just one day after the bridge opened, a major traffic jam developed on Main Street. Matters never improved. As the local population and land traffic rose, delays occasioned by the bridge being "up" became common. Much rejoicing prevailed when this stretch of the Ship Canal ceased to carry boats and the span was placed in a permanently "down" position in 1972.

PROBLEMS WITH CONTRACTORS

Grant hoped to open the Ship Canal in the spring of 1930 but was worried that the slowness of the Hamilton Bridge Company in constructing their crossings would make that deadline unattainable. As early as June 1927 he fussed that the contractor's "abnormal very slow progress" was "absolutely inexplicable to me" and probably revealed "want of interest" in their contracts. He told Hamilton that there was "no reason in the world why the ... four bridges cannot be completed by the 31st August next."[29]

The completion of Bridges 20 and 21 at Port Colborne was a particular headache for Grant. Although his worries over these crossings reflect his own high-strung sensibility, it is also true that by May 1928 Hamilton Bridge was one year behind their schedule. The company's representative explained that "it is very very difficult to obtain structural iron workers." In late January 1929 Grant told Dubuc that, of twenty-five men employed on Bridge 21, only six were ironworkers. In the same month the Department decided to extend the contract for

Bridge 21 until May of that year. Dubuc also visited Hamilton to investigate the delay and encourage speed. At the same time, when a Hamilton Bridge representative was in Ottawa, Dubuc threatened the company with denying them any further Departmental contracts and with a loss of their deposit and a 10 per cent retention. These threats seem to have had some effect because, by mid-February 1929, Grant noticed that Hamilton Bridge was employing "a better class of workman than they have had in the past." Still, it would be "impossible for the Bridge Company to adhere to the ... schedule," and, he added, "nothing that we can say to the officials of the Company has any effect on speeding up the work."[30]

Nevertheless, in March Grant noted that sixty men were working on Bridge 21 each day and that the company was again on schedule with that crossing. By April good progress was being made, for the west tower was fully assembled and riveted. Unfortunately, bad weather had delayed the placing of the concrete counterweight.[31]

In September 1927 Hamilton Bridge had also been granted the contract for building the superstructure of Bridge 20 for the Buffalo-Goderich division of the CNR at Port Colborne. A temporary supporting structure was in place by March 1928 and a start had been made on the span's steel work. Testing of the lift began at the end of April. But construction was slow and delayed other work on the canal. "Until this bridge is completed and railway traffic diverted thereto," Grant wrote, "the general contractor [Northern Construction] is delayed in the completion of his excavation and concrete work at the site of the existing diversion for the railway."[32] The Northern Construction Company had to wait until traffic was sent over Bridge 20 and a temporary bridge diversion removed. Rail traffic was moved from the detour to the new crossing at the end of August 1928. Finally, in September, the contractor could begin his rock excavation.

In 1930 a similar drama was enacted over Bridge 6, at Twin Locks 4 and at Bridge 9 at the guard gates. About the latter contract Atkinson, on behalf of Grant, harangued the contractor, writing that there should be "no excuse for not having this bridge completed in record time ... Allow no loose ends to accumulate,"[33] he ordered. The bridge was completed in 1930.

Dubuc, Grant, and Atkinson had their own responsibilities to fulfill and deadlines to meet but they may have overlooked some of the challenges faced by the bridge contractors. The railway companies in particular often proved difficult to work with. A disagreement between Hamilton Bridge Company and the Niagara, St Catharines and Toronto Railway over Bridge 1 at Port Weller brought work on the bridge to a standstill in February 1927. When Grant appealed to Dubuc to intervene the chief engineer replied in a telegram to Hamilton Bridge, insisting that interruption of railway traffic should be kept to a minimum and threatening that expenses from "unwarranted" stoppages would be deducted from their estimates.[34]

SLAPPING CABLES AND EXPLODING MUFFLERS

The engineers' and contractors' problems did not end when the new structures were completed and spanned the width of the channel. Months would pass before all the bridges worked smoothly. The railway companies, bridge operators, and local residents alike complained of problems with the operation of the new structures.

For the engineers, the most perplexing difficulty was that the counterweight cables on the lift bridges tended to slap together in the wind. Bridges 5, 10, 18, and 21 were afflicted with this "slapping ropes" problem, which was reported to Harrington, Howard and Ash in 1928. The designers set to work to remedy the situation, testing a rope clamp to separate the cables or spread them out. Installed in 1929, they seemed to solve the problem.

To alert land traffic to the impending closure of spans, Canadian Westinghouse supplied warning horns for the highway bridges. Unfortunately, these proved indistinguishable from the sounds of normal highway traffic. In 1930, moreover, the Thorold Fire Department was frequently confused by the siren-like horns on Bridges 9, 10, and 11, which, being similar to their own horns, would make them "run to the firehall for nothing."[35] Unwilling to change the sound of their sirens, the canal authorities volunteered to pay the town for new and different equipment. Similar alerts for informing the bridge operators as to when bridge leaves were in the nearly full or nearly closed position were so annoying to them that they refused to use them and turned them off.

On the lift spans the bridgemasters would work in the machinery cabin, located in the middle of the lift crossing. On Bridges 14 and 16 they were perplexed by faulty electrical equipment and complained of inadequate coal stoves in their cabins. On Bridge 17 the operator claimed that in January 1929 bottled water for storage batteries froze even though the containers were placed beside the stoves. On the other hand Atkinson found that on Bridge 7, on "a miserable cold day," he could not stand within two feet of the stove, so hot was it.[36] When rainwater endangered electrical equipment on Bridge 16, the bridgemaster reported a leaky roof. In 1930 the Board of Railway Commissioners claimed that the operator on Bridge 20 was unable to see approaching trains from his cabin. The sightlines, they said, were obscured by the cross members of the bridge. In the same year bridge gas engines were found to have exploding mufflers. All these issues had to be resolved before the new bridges became reliable and safe. In 1929 Homer residents complained of the noise made by the joint plates on deck of the new Bridge 4. "They certainly make some racket when east bound autos go over them," said Jewett.[37]

Other locals were more aggressive at the Homer crossing. In April 1930 Jewett noted the case of a "simpleton" who "edged his car beyond the wig-wag [warning signal]" and "considerably irritated" the bridgemaster.[37] Ship captains, locomotive engineers, bridge operators, and car drivers alike had to learn to co-exist with the new bridges.

WIRES, CABLES, AND PIPES

Other crossings of the waterway would become increasingly important to the engineers. As early as 1882 the Montreal Telephone Company had had to cross the Third Canal by submarine cables at four public roads. In 1899 the St Catharines Electric Light and Power Company, as well as Lincoln Paper, were allowed to lay pipes across the canal for fire protection purposes.

With the development of hydroelectricity at Niagara Falls, moreover, a number of power lines crossed the canal. At Killaly Street in Port Colborne, for example, the Hydro-Electric Power Commission's line crossed the waterway and a transformer station had been built near this site in 1912–13. The Ship Canal engineers decided to have the line cross the canal in a conduit under the channel. Elsewhere, such wires crossed between towers, carrying the cables high enough to avoid impeding ships' passage.[38] In addition, as use of telephones increased, their wires had to cross the canal, and here too underwater cables were more convenient and less subject to interference. Similarly, as municipal water systems expanded, pipes to carry water supply under the canal were approved.

The pace of technological development has increased, so that engineers have had to solve the problem of getting an ever-greater number of pipes, wires, and cables over or under the waterway. As early as 1936 at one single road/rail crossing of the canal, all of the following were in place: two storm sewers; one water main; two ducts for the Hydro-Electric Power Commission; one gas main; two cables for Bell Telephone; and one cable for CNR telegraphs. In addition the Department had on hand requests for a further four cables for hydro and four pipes for gas – all at one crossing. By 1956 cables for traffic lights had been added to the list.[39] And so it went.

Powerful personalities such as John Weller and Alex Grant, industrious engineers such as Jewett, and talented contractors such as the ill-fated Lyall have dominated our description of the Ship Canal's construction. Their expertise and dedication are undeniable, as are their inventiveness and persistence in the face of challenges both new and traditional. Yet on the gravelly slopes of the prism and in the deep and perilous lock pits, operating the hot, steam- and smoke-belching machinery was an army of labourers who took their orders from the aforementioned engineers and contractors. Many of them "soldiered on" for fifteen years on this technological battleground. None were decorated; some mutinied; many were injured; scores of them died violently. To their role we now turn.

CHAPTER EIGHT

"Facing their own kaisers at home"

When, as a twentieth-century "navvy," you reported for work with a Ship Canal contractor such as Lyall or Porter you might have found yourself with a group of strangers. Of course, depending on the season, you all dressed more or less alike – with soft caps, leather boots, and baggy trousers. On the other hand, many of your co-workers were from outside Niagara or indeed from outside Canada. You couldn't communicate with some of them for they did not speak your language. As for your boss, he spoke only English and had no patience with your non-comprehending comrades, but given the economic recession of the early years, the uncertainty of wartime, and the turbulence of the immediate postwar years, you were all glad to find any work (figs 8.1–8.7).

For such a common labourer or even a skilled tradesman in the lock pits or in the deepening prism, working on the Welland Ship Canal involved both traditional difficulties and some new experiences. Conditions of employment remained harsh, with outbreaks of disease and accidents common. Workers endured inadequate wages and long working hours, issues exacerbated by inflation and unemployment. The living conditions of single men were occasionally atrocious. Dependent on contractors or subcontractors for transportation, food, clothing, and accommodation, both married and single canal workers found their ability to obtain redress for grievances almost non-existent. Engineers and contractors, for their part, often seemed oblivious to the problems of day-to-day life and work "on the ground." Not surprisingly, therefore, strikes were common. On the other hand, the Ship Canal's Medical Service was a successful official effort to alleviate some of the labourers' plight. Still, canal labourers building the new waterway often found their lives complicated and challenging.

WORKING ON THE WELLAND

As had been the case on past canal construction in Niagara, thousands of men worked building the Welland Ship Canal. A precise total may never be calculated but we do know that in July 1919 the entire work-force, including the engineering staff, numbered 2,786, and in August 1924 over three thousand individuals were employed.[1] Most were hired by the various contractors on the site but "Departmental forces" were used on some projects, such as making the wooden unwatering gates, 1925–27. The Department of Railways and Canals also required white-collar workers such as draftsmen, designers, and architects, including the sectional engineers who worked in the Welland's headquarters in St Catharines or at sites along the canal, as well as numerous cler-ical and secretarial personnel (fig. 9.6). By the 1920s this force had also grown in number, had to be fairly reimbursed, and, because they were usually from outside Niagara, had to be housed in decent accommodation.[2]

Due to demobilization and the conversion from wartime to peace-time production, the years 1919–20 saw much working-class unemploy-ment throughout Canada. Given the hard times of this immediate postwar era, the federal government was under pressure to provide work for as many men as possible. In Niagara, 1919 was a difficult year for local industries and in the spring of 1920 local businessmen predicted that conditions would be worse in the coming winter. Con-struction of the Ship Canal, therefore, was resumed partly as a relief scheme to provide employment, especially for war veterans. At least five hundred of these "returned men" worked on the Ship Canal in late 1919.[3] In mid-December 1920 the federal government authorized the extension of contracts with Dominion Dredging, Baldry, Yerburgh & Hutchinson, Canadian Dredging, and Doheny, Quinlan & Robertson, stating that "the work on the Ship Canal should ... be kept going in order to give employment to as many men as possible."[4] This involved winter work as far as conditions would permit.

The unemployment problem continued in 1921. On the operating canal, the overseer at Dunnville wrote to his superior in March that he "never saw so many men looking for work."[5] The Department of Labour now discouraged Sunday work, but significant was Lazier's memorandum to Grant in July 1921, in which he noted that, although he did not himself approve of Sabbath labour, many workers were

8.1 Near what would become Port Weller, 1911. Surveyors working out the route of the new Ship Canal. A broad-brimmed hat kept you cool in the humid Niagara summer and a horse was still the best transportation over uneven farmland. These "white-collar" workers were essential to the completion of the Ship Canal, but the actual construction was done by armies of skilled and unskilled labourers (note the necktie).

"perfectly willing" to do overtime or even straight time on Sundays.[6] Contractors, too, were under pressure to provide work, as explained by A.M. German of Canadian Dredging in September 1921. The situation in Welland was "extremely bad," he said, citing requests for more jobs in the coming winter from the local government, from the Great War Veterans' Association, and from unemployed men themselves. Canadian Dredging, however, had no further work to offer.[7]

By 1922 the Queenston Hydro project was nearing completion, a situation which proved beneficial to the Ship Canal employers because they no longer had to compete with the Ontario government's higher wage scales, but now more Niagara men were out of work. In January 1922, faced with the swelling of its welfare rolls, St Catharines asked

8.2   Ship Canal labourers with their mules, the hooves of which were less likely to become stuck in Niagara's clinging mud than the wheels of motorized equipment such as trucks, whose extrication cost time and money.

the Department to find a way to provide more work on the Ship Canal. In fact, into at least 1925, Grant and the contractors continued to feel pressure to provide employment. Late in that year Thorold's mayor wrote to the minister describing how many men laid off in the fall were now applying to the town for relief. He cited fifty "urgent" cases of married unemployed. It was, he said, a "considerable hardship on our town to take care of these men."[8]

WAGES AND HOURS

For those who could find work on the Ship Canal, the issue of adequate pay and suitable hours was of paramount concern. By December 1918, the cost of maintaining a family and a home in Canada had increased by 46 per cent over the 1916 level.[9] Especially in 1919, inflation sky-rocketed but wages were not increasing, so that the real income of many Canadians had declined. To help remedy the situation, the federal government periodically announced "Fair Wage Schedules," based on local conditions in industry and business for the guidance of employers.

The situation in Niagara was complicated by the presence of the Hydro-Electric Development at Queenston. Here, not far from the Welland, another canal was being built, which involved similarly skilled builders and labourers. Already in 1920, the Ship Canal engineers were critical of the Hydro Commission, which, lamented Grant, "yielded to the importunities of its employees and granted increases of wages."[10] Naturally, workers compared wages and hours, and found that Hydro men were paid more for less work. Consequently, until at least 1922 the Hydro Canal situation tended to regulate the treatment of labour on the Ship Canal. Under provincial government pressure to build their canal quickly, the Hydro engineers entered an agreement in early 1919 with the Niagara District Trades and Labour Federation which established an eight-hour day and forty-four-hour week with higher pay for overtime. Many Ship Canal workers naturally expected and demanded the same pay for similar work. In August 1919 the Welland's authorities agreed to labourers' requests but the result of shorter working hours was loss of output for contractors and loss of income for certain workers, some of whom became dissatisfied. Discipline declined and men resigned. Some even asked to have the ten-hour day again.

Lampard of the construction railway and sectional engineers Lazier and Johnson reported inadequate labour supply throughout 1920, a problem partly due to the tendency of Niagara municipalities to embark on construction programs in the summer months and to offer relatively high wages to men working on those projects. As Jewett put it, "the Welland Ship Canal forms a favorite recruiting ground for employers of summer labour."[11] In the later 1920s, the International Nickel Company, Canada Cement, and Canada Furnace, all at Port Colborne, attracted iron workers and mechanics away from the Ship Canal operations. Comparison of hours and wages, moreover, made for a continually unhappy workforce. The Winnipeg General Strike had already fuelled the Canadian labour movement. Perhaps inevitably, therefore, a general strike erupted in September 1919.

Ironically, due to inflation and to union activity, by 1921 all classes of labour had actually enjoyed an increase in earnings – at least on

8.3   Dain City, ca. 1928. Workers – possibly members of the Mohawk First Nation – at a lift bridge, probably 17.

paper – usually doubling those of 1913. A few workers, such as carpenters and qualified locomotive engineers, were earning more in real income in 1929 than in 1921. Nevertheless, by 1929 the average wage had declined by about twenty cents an hour. Moreover, in 1925 the federal government's Fair Wage Schedule had actually involved a general reduction of rates. Perhaps the most telling example of the fluctuating nature of remuneration is that of waterboys, who earned fifteen cents an hour in 1913, twenty in 1920, twenty-five in 1922, and fifteen again in 1927. Since most trades on the canal were now set at nine hours a day, many men were working fewer hours but for less pay. By the end of the '20s, however, the steam had gone out of the labour movement, trade union membership had declined, and the new schedule was accepted by Ship Canal workers because of the abundance of labour available.

Regardless of any Fair Wage Schedule announced by Ottawa, contractors on the Welland usually sought to pay less than the government recommended. For example, in 1922 the Minister of Labour,

James Murdock (1871–1949), reprimanded J.P. Porter because his wages did not meet the standard of the current schedule. Murdock also received complaints in that year concerning Peter Lyall, who had allegedly been ignoring the government's suggested rates. In practice, however, most contractors managed to pay labourers the rate prevailing in the district, even if this was below the level suggested in the Fair Wage Schedule.

The question of wages was inextricably tied to working hours, which, in most labourers' demands, loomed larger than rates of pay. Throughout the construction period the ten-hour day tended to prevail. Exceptions, however, were many, both over time and from site to site. In 1913 most labourers worked ten hours but certain others, such as steam shovel firemen, worked twelve hours. Men could be expected to work night shifts in the summertime. Ten hours was still the norm in 1921, with the exception of, for example, dragline operators, who worked eleven hours, and locomotive firemen, who worked twelve. In some cases a twelve-hour night shift prevailed, coupled with a similar day shift, the only breaks being for meals at noon and midnight.[12]

The year 1919, when construction resumed, saw many variations in the length of the working day. On Section 1 the men worked an eight-hour day but on Section 2 half the men were working ten hours. On Section 4, 81 per cent worked a ten-hour day, and on Section 5 all worked ten.[13] Despite the agitation of labour leaders for a standard eight-hour day, many workers preferred to work ten because of the greater income they received. In May 1923, for example, fifty-eight labourers sent a petition to J.P. Porter requesting the ten-hour day. Labour activists suggested that the men were coerced but, given the cost of living and the low wages, many labourers may have credibly sought the longer hours.

At all events, by 1925 the ten-hour day was generally established. In that year, however, the Minister of Labour imposed a nine-hour day with time-and-a-half for overtime at the prevailing rate of wages for all classes of labour, except carpenters, who would have eight-hour days. Meanwhile, on the Ship Canal contractors cut wages to correspond to those paid in the Niagara District. Typically, the unskilled workers suffered the most severe cuts. By this time a defeatist attitude tended to prevail on the canal site and few protests occurred.

After the stock market crash of October 1929, the Great Depression had less effect on the Ship Canal's construction than might originally have been expected. Most of the waterway's vital features were almost finished. Grant discovered, however, that funding began to be constricted; hence certain aspects of the project were cut back temporarily or otherwise delayed until Ottawa found the money to continue. Still, Grant was encouraged to try to find as much employment for those out of work as possible. From the viewpoint of the labourers on the ground, the canal again became a make-work project, much as it had been in 1919–20.

To cope with the growing unemployment crisis, the federal government in March 1930 permitted the eight-hour day with "half holiday" on Saturdays but banned overtime except in emergencies. By April of 1930, however, construction railway labourers were still working a ten-hour day. Appropriations under the Act for the Relief of Unemployment in September 1930[14] made more work possible and assisted in the final completion of the canal. The powerhouse at Twin Locks 4 could be finished as could the laying of water-tight material on the dam at Twin Locks 6, as well as certain trimming and sodding. The contractors still at work agreed in principle, trying to give as much employment as possible and to use local men only.[15] Various expedients were tried, such as using two half-day shifts, offering work on alternate days, or using manual labour instead of more sophisticated machine-trained men.

The navvies were not the only men affected by the new stringency. From March 1932 no raises in salary were to be allowed to canal office workers in the foreseeable future. Then, as the Ship Canal neared completion, a reduction in the number of all kinds of employees became necessary, which added to the unemployment problem as Niagara became part of the larger national crisis.

"IN WATER UP TO THEIR WAISTS"

By 1919 various legislative measures had improved the quotidian experience of canal labourers as Ottawa gradually assumed more responsibility for the more vulnerable members of Canadian society.[16] Despite such benevolent intervention, however, working on the Welland's construction still required grit. Although twentieth-century contractors and engineers understood more about hygiene and the origins of disease than had their forebears, the working environment was not appreciably better than it had been one hundred or even fifty years

8.4 At the Lock 7 site in 1926, without protective headgear, construction workers toil at a cold, damp, and dangerous rock excavation.

earlier. Not only was the labour dirty and dangerous but, in the early twentieth century, it demanded nerves of steel. The work site was filled with the pounding of steam-powered hammers, the clatter of riveting machines, and the rumbling and screeching of heavy machinery of all kinds, not to mention the acrid odours of various construction materials – and the pleasures of deep, clinging mud (fig. 8.4).

Of course, some improvement in working conditions on great public works had occurred since the building of the Third Canal in the 1880s. In 1899 the federal government had passed an Act for the Preservation of Health on Public Works and in 1913 established the Ship Canal Medical Service. As well, in September 1924 the Department of Railways and Canals formed a Health Board to supervise the medical, sanitary, and first aid services on the Ship Canal site and to enforce the Public Works Health Act there. The members were federal Department of Health inspector Dr J.J. Heagerty, engineer E.G. Cameron, and Dr John McCombe, head of the Canal's Medical Service.

Even before the exigencies of the Depression made hand labour a useful make-work strategy, however, some of the excavation was still done manually, not much differently from the work on the First Canal and in highly uncomfortable circumstances. For example, in 1914 Baldry, Yerburgh & Hutchinson had men digging the pit of Lock 2 with picks and shovels. With the fine ethnic distinction typical of contemporary opinion, a Toronto journalist wrote: "A good many of the men who braced Flanders' and Belgium's hardships in mud and wind and rain, are doing the same thing on the ... [Ship Canal construction site]. Men must work in water up to their waists, and Canadians and Britishers are doing things that the Italian navvy passed up with disdain."[17]

An added challenge was Niagara's climate. In September 1920, for example, Lazier reported that on Section 4 the prevailing hot weather had "caused heat prostrations among the workmen."[18] There were other unexpected discomforts. In July 1923, for example, men building Shriner's Culvert south of Lock 7 were temporarily blinded by fumes of hydrogen sulphide gas. Operations were stopped until a blower pipe was installed.

As had their nineteenth-century predecessors, Ship Canal workers frequently succumbed to disease. In July 1921 and August 1924 typhoid fever struck, especially at Port Colborne. Smallpox broke out at the syphon culvert site in 1927–28. Both Ship Canal and local political authorities were reluctant to accept any responsibility for such outbreaks. To John W.S. McCullough, chief officer for the Ontario Board of Health, Grant asserted that "the Canal works are in no way responsible for the outbreak of the [typhoid] epidemic" of 1924. McCullough told Grant, however, that the dredges of the C.S. Boone Co. at Port Colborne were discharging fresh sewage near the intake of the town's water supply and "very likely contribute to the trouble." The matter reached Ottawa when W.M. German, MP for Welland, wrote to Dr Heagerty to assure him that C.S. Boone was not responsible for the typhoid outbreak. Nevertheless, Boone was told to stop the practice[19] and some sort of clean-up seems to have been undertaken, because typhoid did not recur. Compulsory inoculations and isolation of patients also helped.

RESISTING THE KAISERS

If, for the majority of labourers on the Ship Canal site, the basic day-to-day issues had not changed since the Third Canal was under construction, what had developed was their literacy and self-confidence. Beginning in the 1880s, the Canadian union movement had grown and by 1900 membership had developed accordingly. During the First World War, the federal government prohibited strikes and lockouts for the duration but, partly because of this policy, labour union membership in Canada doubled and, given the shortage of labour, an employees' market prevailed and wages were temporarily high. Influenced by the British labour movement and the 1917 Russian Revolutions and less hamstrung by the fear of poverty and unemployment, workers became more militant and some, more radical. Already in 1916 Canadian workers began to be skeptical about the purposes and operation of the Great War, which seemed to be carried on for the benefit of profiteers and politicians. In 1916 a strike wave swept the country.

In September and October 1918 Ottawa tried to ban radical organizations and to forbid strikes. The intensely conservative Arthur Meighen, prime minister in 1920–21, seems to have been shocked at the newly militant labour movement. Fearing Bolshevism, he strengthened the Dominion Police and the Royal North-West Mounted Police. More constructively, he appointed a Royal Commission on Industrial Unrest in 1919, which recommended the eight-hour day, unemployment and accident insurance, and legal collective bargaining. But the commission's report was too little and too late because the former measures only increased the workers' sense that "Prussianism" was not limited to Berlin.

After the war, moreover, a glut of labour meant hard times for many proletarian families, as unemployment was high. Most "navvies" remained unorganized. Sectional engineers and contractors on the Ship

8.5   Future site of Twin Locks 4, 1914. Italian labourers laying track for the construction railway. Such immigrants usually worked diligently but occasionally only partially understood the contractors' orders.

Canal were less than sympathetic to workers' interests. Some war veterans, who had thought they were fighting for democracy in Europe, discovered, in the words of the historian James Naylor, that "they were facing their own kaisers at home."[20]

Often, the canal workers were ready to meet the challenges. In July 1923, when Ship Canal carpenters believed that contractors were not observing the recommended wage schedule, they sent a telegram directly to the Minister of Labour in Ottawa. Also typical of the new workers' confidence was a letter written in 1922 by Charles E. Young of Port Robinson to W.H. Sullivan, principal assistant engineer, in St Catharines:

Dear Sir. I am writing to you on behalf of the ["some" inserted] men on section 5 of the Welland Ship Canal to find out if there is a government wage scale for this year out as the Canadian Dredging Co. has put out a schedule from a 10 to 15 cent cut per hour from last year. I would like to know if the government is going to set a scale of wages from the first of May for this year will you kindly let us know? and oblige yours, etc.[21]

Although we cannot be sure that Young was himself a labourer, the "pro-active" tone of the letter reflected a newly alert and knowledgeable working class that would not passively accept perceived injustices.

"THE UNPLEASANTNESS OF 1919"[22]

These words of engineer Jewett were an understatement because in that year the Ship Canal was wracked with labour unrest which, although not attended by as much violence, was of a sort unseen since the 1840s. In fact the entire Niagara district was affected by national and international labour troubles, as was the country as a whole. The Winnipeg General Strike of 1919 had lasted six weeks, ended with two violent deaths, and terrified the Canadian establishment. The Niagara District Trades and Labour Federation (NDTLF) vigorously tried to represent workers with the strike as their favoured instrument. Meanwhile, unskilled workers resented the preferential treatment apparently given to skilled ones. Immigrant workers were suspicious of the native-born labourers, the contractors, the engineers, and the government. Few if any workers trusted the contractors, who, like the sectional engineers, were hostile to signs of working-class independence. With typical sarcasm, in June 1919 Jewett wrote that, on Section 2, "a very large percentage of both mechanics and labourers ... [are] possessed with the idea that they are working too hard and not getting enough for it."[23] In Niagara these issues were exacerbated by the Hydro-Electric Power Commission's policy of offering shorter working hours to its labourers. When, in April 1919, Grant met with the commission's superintending engineer, H.G. Acres, with a view to having the HEPC extend its working hours, he received no support. On 25 July 1919 a meeting of government officials and contractors' and labour representatives was held at St Catharines. The eight-hour day and forty-four-hour week, including time-and-a-half for overtime work, were ratified by both the Department and the contractors. The leaders of the NDTLF approved. But among the labourers, misunderstanding, rumour, and internecine squabbles prevailed. Many workers believed that the new system would take effect almost immediately on 1 August or might be retroactive to 1 May, which was not the case.

Some canal labourers, however, were dissatisfied with the eight-hour days. Immigrants were especially committed to making as much money as possible and did not resent longer hours if a higher income was involved. According to one estimate, 78 per cent of the Canadian Dredging's "foreign" labourers requested a ten-hour day.[24] By early August 1919, however, "the delay by our Department in taking this matter up in an expeditious manner," wrote Lazier, had "caused a lot of unnecessary excitement among all classes of labor." Such "excitement" had already arisen in that month of 1919, when wildcat strikes broke out. Some of Section 3's immigrant labourers stopped work and roamed the site urging the rest of the men to quit. At Lock 7, Lazier reported: "On Saturday morning 2nd inst. [August], there were no foreign laborers at work, but about eight o'clock a large number of them appeared at the upper entrance of Lock No. 7 where carpenters were at work and threatened to drive them off the job. At this time a few pieces of coal, stones and sticks were thrown by the crowd at one of our locomotives going to South end of the Section."[25] Reflecting the hysteria which consumed much of Canada following the outbreak of the Winnipeg General Strike, the canal authorities expected the worst and called in armed constables, thus exacerbating an already tense situation.

Was the description of these men as "foreigners" correct? Of the approximately 2,230 men on Sections 1, 2, 3, and 5 in August 1919, only about 703 (or less than one-third) were immigrants.[26] On the other hand it seems reasonable that workers recently arrived from Eastern or Southern Europe, embittered by conditions in their homelands, inspired by the revolutionary events in Russia and Germany in 1917–19, and encouraged by the Winnipeg General Strike, were more likely to be leaders in these strikes. "Immigrant workers," notes Donald Avery, "demonstrated a capacity for effective collective action and a willingness to defy both the power of management and the state."[27] Events in Niagara seem to support this generalization.

On Section 3, Lazier had about seventy special constables recruited from co-operative labourers, contractors, and members of the engineering staff. They were sworn in by the Thorold Police Magistrate and armed. A machine gun was obtained from the St Catharines armour-

8.6 Workers at the dredge FUNDY in 1930, with a nine-ton rock. The relationship of the boulder to the workers suggests the often perilous nature of Ship Canal construction. In this case, drowning was a possibility.

ies, guards were posted, and "No Trespassing" signs were erected. Faced with this show of force, by 4 August 1919 most of the labourers returned to work on Section 3.

However, on Section 2 that day, pitmen and labourers working around the steam shovel refused to continue. Next day, led by immigrants, they assembled at Carlton Street, near Lock 2. Their attempt to enter the lock pit was resisted by foremen and skilled labourers. Jewett, like Lazier, had sixty special constables sworn in and supplied with a machine gun and rifles. Also on 4 August disturbances broke out on Section 1, to which strikers from Section 2 paraded, calling on the men to stop work. Sectional engineer Johnson, too, resorted to constabulary aid and by 14 August most of the labourers were working again.

Aware of the divisions among the labourers and knowing that most of the men wanted to continue working, the NDTLF did not condone these walkouts and on 3 August the union leaders advised the strikers to return to work until the Department had pronounced on the wage question. At a 5 August 1919 meeting in Ottawa between Minister of Railways and Canals J.D. Reid, Minister of Labour G.D. Robertson, Grant, and contractors' representatives, Reid finally publicly authorized the HEPC pay rates for Ship Canal workers. The new rates would be retroactive only to 1 July 1919, not 1 May, as the union believed Reid had promised.

The confused situation was aggravated when the guards were armed. Some men claimed that shots were fired at or over the heads of strikers and considered this a deliberate provocation. At a St Catharines meeting of 8 August, the union leaders denounced what they believed to be the "brutal and uncalled for display of militant force."[28] A day later they sent a telegram of protest to the deputy minister.

The use of military force to suppress a stike by canallers was not unusual in North America, as witnessed by the crushing of a violent protest by workers on the Beauharnois Canal in June 1843. The arming of the guards in this 1919 case, however, seems to have been much exaggerated and no shots ever seem to have been fired near labourers. In fact on Section 1 arms were never distributed. However, on Section 2, as a test, two rounds were fired into a ditch and another into the canal bank below Lock 2, volleys which, overheard, may have frightened nearby workers. On Section 3 half the rifles were never loaded and, while the machine gun was fired at the machine shop, it was merely to test that it was in working order. The guns were returned to the armouries by 11 August, on which day employees of Baldry, Yerburgh & Hutchinson, contractors for Section 2, issued a declaration to the effect that the NDTLF's statement about the use of a machine gun was "absolutely false."[29]

The cessation of the wildcat strikes did not betoken contentment. At that 8 August meeting of their members in St Catharines, the NDTLF denounced the schedule of wages and hours announced by the Department. They maintained that this schedule broke a promise made to union leaders by Minister Reid that the canal rates of pay and hours, the same as those on the Hydro project, would be retroactive to 1 May 1919.

The engineers may be forgiven for feeling perplexed when, on 21 August, petitions began circulating on the work site, which the workers were urged to sign, requesting a return to the ten-hour day. The source of these petitions remains questionable, for it was alleged that the contractors themselves prepared several of them. Some workers voluntarily put their names to it, "but many others were forced to sign it to keep their jobs" and union men felt that the contractors were "taking an unfair advantage."[30] Peter Lyall in particular was accused of making his employees sign under duress. Both Reid and Bowden were aware that some degree of coercion from contractors might have existed and told Grant to remind them that the men must be totally free to choose. No coercion was used, said Grant on 4 September, writing to Reid, adding that the contractors simply needed reliable information.[31]

When the ten-hour day was reintroduced as an option, the workers were divided among themselves. The situation was even more complicated by the fact that some workers believed that, if they worked for ten hours, the extra two hours beyond the eight would be considered overtime and that they would be paid time-and-a-half. Others accepted the ten hours as entirely straight time.

Annoyed by this perceived coercion of labourers, the lack of clarity about the eight-hour day, and the aforementioned sense of government's betrayal, on 11 September 1919 the NDTLF announced a general strike all along the Ship Canal construction site. Grant was probably correct when he noted that "from the half-hearted manner many of the men stopped work ... the case appeared to be a family fight between the men and their leaders as to the number of hours per day that should constitute a day's work."[32] In the hope that a sufficient number of men would return to justify continuing the work, he encouraged the contractors on Sections 2 and 3 to continue operating for a few days. When few labourers reported for work, he closed down Section 3 on 13 September and Section 2 on 19 September. All the plant on these sections was laid up and small tools and unused material were put back in storage. As the strike continued, Sections 1 and 5 were closed down early in November, due as much to exhaustion of the parliamentary appropriation as to strike activity.

Meanwhile, for the sake of the local economy and employment, both municipal governments and union leaders wanted to see the strike end and to have construction continue throughout the winter. Several meetings were held in the early fall of 1919 in an attempt to restart the work. Representatives of trades, veterans, St Catharines City Council, and the local Board of Trade met on 2 October. A telegram was sent to Ottawa urging the government to give a fair hearing to the workers' grievances. Grant was invited by the Great War Veterans' Association to another meeting at St Catharines on 5 October. The result of this gathering was the dispatch of a deputation to Ottawa to inquire into the possibility of getting construction going again. The problem of funding arose because Parliament would have to vote a new appropriation for the work. Meanwhile, many of the contractors' foremen had found work elsewhere and would have to be replaced.

Although some men did return to work and the project limped along on a limited scale through late fall and early winter, the strike did not formally end until 8 February 1920 when the NDTLF announced its conclusion. Labour unrest continued, however, when in late May 1920 workers on the construction railway's sand bin refused to work on Sundays except for double time. By July, however, full-scale construction could begin again and Grant rejoiced: "We are beginning to make a small start here once more and when once under way I hope we will have peace and quietness throughout 1920, as I never again wish to experience the labour troubles that we had here last year."[33]

Labour disputes did indeed subside during the remaining time the Ship Canal was under construction. But economic conditions were bad during the winter of 1920–21 when businesses closed or cut back production drastically, throwing men out of work. On the canal site rumblings of discontent were heard in August 1922 when the steam shovel crews on Section 4 struck, demanding higher wages and better pay for overtime than Peter Lyall was prepared to offer. Again, Grant was alarmed by the level of threatened violence.

Problems continued in 1923, and the issues were the same as in the past, although the threat of violence diminished. The steam shovel men on Sections 1, 2, and 3 and the construction railway labourers at Port Weller struck. Typically, carpenters complained that contractors were not observing Ottawa's Fair Wage Schedule. Porter sent Grant a petition which he claimed was from workers who wanted the ten-hour day instead of eight. Meanwhile, with the declining influence of the

8.7 Port Weller, ca. 1928. Like miners underground, these workers are building a conduit (for admitting and releasing water) in the wall of Lock 1.

NDTLF, working conditions did not improve and in 1930 they became appreciably worse.

The justice of either side's cause is not the point here. Given social and economic conditions in their homelands, however, some of the immigrant workers were accustomed to taking extreme measures. In addition the Canadian authorities were inclined to balk at giving in to any kind of intimidation, however mild. Individual personality also played a role. When annoyed, Grant was not inclined to a moderate response, as his language during the 1919 crisis revealed.[34] Later, in 1921, he dismissed union spokesmen as "parties styling themselves representatives of the workmen here employed."[35] Such complaints about labourers were based in part on the views of Lazier, sectional engineer on Section 3, who throughout 1921 criticized canal workers as being lazy and foremen as "not having yet adjusted themselves to a condition unknown for several years and some of them lacking the ambition to do so."[36]

The engineers' and contractors' attitudes to their workers had much in common with contemporary Canadian views about labour organizations and about immigrants. Such opinions could influence safety regulations – or the lack of them – on the Ship Canal site as well as the living conditions of the workers, the subject of our next chapter.

CHAPTER NINE

Ameliorating Disaster and Squalor

Clearly, working conditions on the construction sites of the Welland Ship Canal were difficult. When they tried to organize and to improve their lot, twentieth-century navvies faced suspicion and hostility from their employers. Their situation was often complicated by the fact that many of them were immigrants, some of them were illiterate in any language, and their Niagara neighbours were prejudiced against most "foreigners." Moreover, when they returned daily from the work site, they faced living conditions that were substandard (fig. 9.5). The calamities that occasionally befell them in the canal prism or the lock chambers were probably due in part to their lack of English-language skills and in part to the indifference of most engineers and contractors to the working conditions of any workers, including "aliens." On the other hand, the labourers' lives were ameliorated by the authorities' Medical Service.

THE ALIEN FOREIGNERS

In June 1919 the *Toronto Star Weekly* reported that, at the end of the east pier at Port Weller, "workmen speaking many languages collected loose stones and piled them into ... [a] circular mound as a monument" – a "tower of Babel."[1] With hundreds of immigrants seeking and finding work in its deepening prism and developing lock pits, the Welland was characterized by a cacophony of accents and languages. For example, a list of appointments to the construction railway in the summer of 1922 shows that of the seventeen names, three are Anglo-Celtic, while the rest are Ukrainian or Polish.[2] By 1928 the workforce was even more ethnically mixed. A landslide in Thorold in that year killed Joseph Dumoulin and Mike Kozar and injured five others of various backgrounds.[3] Similarly, a newspaper account of the lock gate collapse of the same year is telling: "Women, whose husbands or sons were employed near the location of the accident, hastened to the scene ... Many of the women were of foreign extraction, their highly colored dress lending the only touch of color to the tragic scene."[4]

As had been the case during the Third Canal's construction, one of the largest groups of immigrant labour came from Italy (fig. 8.5). At least eighteen Italians were killed during construction, a number equalled only by native-born Ontarians. (Of the European immigrants, the next largest number of accident victims were Hungarian.) In places such as Sicily the soil had been ruined and landlords oppressed their tenants. After 1900 this "southern question" drove more and more Italians to emigrate and, after 1913, in which year 27,704 Italians arrived in Canada, their presence predominated on the Ship Canal construction sites.[5] That number waned during the war as many returned home to defend Italy but rose again in the 1920s. Most of the Italians made Toronto their port of entry and base camp. Willing to accept hard labour and temporary seasonal employment, they would travel from Toronto's "Little Italy" to Niagara every summer. Some, however, settled permanently in the area. For example, Benedetto Collini came to Canada in 1912. His wife followed in 1921 and they established a farm at Port Weller. Among their nine children was fourteen-year-old Antonio, who worked as a water boy on the Ship Canal and was killed falling from a concrete wall in 1927. Like so many immigrant labourers, the Collinis spoke little English and were illiterate even in Italian.[6] Another Italian fatality was Frank Berardi, killed in 1930 on Section 3. Berardi had left a wife and three children in Mangone (Cosenza), Italy.[7] The diversity of backgrounds caused problems, especially of communication, and could lead to accidents, sometimes deadly.

At every level of Niagara – and Canadian – society at this time, prejudice against immigrants was common. From the earliest days of Ship Canal construction some engineers expressed revulsion at employing non-British workers. Weller was horrified at the prospect of being "reduced to using Italians" during the crisis of 1917. Just as in the 1840s, local people were alarmed at the arrival in the neighbourhood of workers speaking with strange accents or not speaking English at all. In January 1914 certain farmers of Grantham Township, in which the canal's northern stretch was being built, asked for police protection from "the depradations of the foreign element" who were allegedly cutting wire fences to get to and from work. Local residents feared "wholesale thievery" from their fruit farms in the coming summer.[8] Xenophobia peaked during the First World War when fears of sabotage led to questions being repeatedly raised in the House of Commons concerning workers on the operating canal who were of German origin. In the postwar period locals expressed annoyance when immigrants seemed to be given canal jobs over native-born Canadians. Accusing "foreigners" of making and selling bootleg whiskey, a Thorold resident wrote to Robert Borden in 1921, asking, "Is it fair when our Canadian boys fought and gave their heart's blood to be turned down now and the foreigner given the work on Section 3 of the New Canal under construction?"[9]

The engineers and contractors had some sympathy with such attitudes, resenting what they regarded as interference by men who were seen to be citizens of a foreign country. Moreover, because they believed immigrants were infected with political radicalism, they often exhibited hostility to efforts of any labourers to improve their wages, working hours, or working conditions. The engineers, in particular, had a great fear of the labour movement, believing it to be "revolutionary" and they had a profound suspicion of "foreigners." They used this term to describe labourers from Europe whether or not they were landed immigrants or had become Canadian citizens but also to indicate undesirable connections with the United States. In that regard, the Industrial Workers of the World (IWW), which was American-based, was often considered by engineers on the Ship Canal and elsewhere to be the most potent threat to stability on the work site, although the movement seems to have had little impact in Niagara.

The engineers' dislike of "foreigners" was reflected in their desire to employ native-born Canadians, especially veterans, over immigrants. "Let go the majority of the foreign labour gangs on Section 4," wrote Grant to Lazier in May 1922, "and replace them with the best returned men in the labour gangs of Section 3."[10] Lazier complied, dismissing immigrants in preference to Canadian, British, or married men. When the Great Depression struck, non-British or foreign-born labourers were again the first to be let go, a policy which was followed on public works elsewhere in Ontario at the time.

The federal government encouraged the hiring of veterans in preference to other applicants for any vacant position so that in 1919 most of the engineering staff, for example, consisted of "returned men." For its part, the Great War Veterans' Association (GWVA) was vigilant in defending the right of "returned men" to have jobs over immigrants, even if the latter were naturalized Canadians. In January 1921 the association notified J.D. Chaplin, MP for Lincoln (in Niagara), of its recent resolution that foreign-born workers, of whom there were too many employed on the Ship Canal, should be fired and replaced by British-born workers. One engineer did not share in the general anglophone xenophobia. Irritated by the Veterans' Association campaign, Jewett found it "little short of disgraceful that naturalized citizens are constantly being discriminated against by resolution manufacturers." In June 1921, when the GWVA again protested the hiring of "foreigners," which to them included Québécois workers, Jewett protested, finding such a view of French Canadians "contemptible."[11]

"Foreigners" who worked on the Ship Canal's construction, however, were not always immigrants willing to work there: some were interned "enemy aliens." When labour shortages arose during the First World War, many of these prisoners of war were shipped from internment camps to industrial centres or construction sites throughout Canada, wherever workers were needed. In 1916 Weller and his engineers faced a disturbing decline in available labour, since many men had resigned to join the armed forces and some Italian labourers had returned to Europe. In June of that year, therefore, the authorities announced that interned "enemy aliens" would be assigned to labour on the canal. Two hundred and twenty-one Austrians and Bulgarians were brought in from a camp at Kapuskasing in northern Ontario. Put to work at carpentry, concreting, and digging, they proved to be "excellent workmen," said a local journalist. They were distributed among several contracting firms and housed in the contractors' barracks.[12] The "Austrians" were actually immigrants to Canada, usually Ukrainian-speaking people from Galicia or Bukovina in the eastern part of the Austro-Hungarian Empire – ironically, with little sympathy for the Habsburg government, one of Canada's enemies.[13] Although they laboured under armed guard, they were paid at the same rate as regular workers. In April 1916 many of the Bulgarians working on the piers at Port Weller struck for more pay. In a panic the authorities called in the militia, about fifty of whom showed up with fixed bayonets. The strikers surrendered and the men were lined up and searched, as were the boarding houses. In August of that year a similar problem developed with "Austrians" working on Section 3, sixty-five of whom refused to work any longer, fearing that their home government would cut off allowances to their families. They were returned to Kapuskasing.

On the other hand, unlike in earlier times, intra-ethnic disputes were relatively rare on the Ship Canal construction sites. An important exception was a riot at Port Weller in 1916 between Russian and Austrian labourers, in which "blood and booze flew like water." The *St Catharines Standard* found the incident made good copy: "One man was seriously injured and two others cut about the head and chest in a general fracas among the foreigners on No. 1 section of the canal yesterday, following a riotous celebration of the Russian Christmas Day. A number of Austrians, from the east bank of the canal, inflamed by racial hatred, crossed over and tried to break up the celebrations of the Russians ... Both parties, it seemed, were also 'inflamed' by alcohol."[14]

ACCIDENTS

The Ship Canal's Medical Service submitted Annual Reports to Ottawa concerning accidents and deaths on the work site. According to these records, 118 men died violently during construction of the new waterway (figs 9.1 and 9.2). In recent years, however, research by local Niagara historians suggests that the total number of deaths on the job was possibly as high as 137[15] (see Appendix III).

Minor injuries and cases of illness were treated either at first aid stations on the construction sites, in the main hospital at Homer, in the field hospitals, or in the workers' homes.[16] Because of the greater size of structures and of machinery, accidents were often more devastating than in the past. For the victims who survived, newer legislation such as Workmen's Compensation was welcome and accidents were better recorded. The sectional engineers were required to fill out forms to document whenever an accident occurred. Data filed in this way included personal statistics, ethnic background, and how the person was injured or died. Local journalists, too, were more assiduous in reporting accidents. The Medical Service also kept records, so that we know that in the year 1924–25, for example, accidents on the site increased, with 109 men being treated at the Service's hospital at Homer and thirty-one at Humberstone. As the pace and extent of construction mounted, the numbers continued to rise. In 1925–26 115 men were treated at the Homer hospital, and twenty-four at Humberstone; and

9.1   Twin Locks 4, 12 August 1925. Collapse of a Blaw-Knox concreting form, which killed eight men. The accident happened while the form was being moved from the site of Twin Locks 4 to that of Twin Locks 5.

in 1926–27 a total of 171 men were treated at both hospitals. "Strangely enough," wrote Dr John McCombe (1873–1945) of the canal Medical Service in April 1930, despite the decrease in the amount of construction in the year 1929–30, the number of accidents did not decrease proportionately. The figures were actually somewhat higher than in the previous year.[17]

In 1927–28 McCombe reported that the majority of fatalities that year (fifteen in all) were due to workers tumbling from walls of completed structures in the northern end of the site or into the deep excavation on Section 6 or to drowning.[18] In 1929–30 Grant noted that at this stage of construction, the men were "required to work in unusually hazardous locations such as on lock gate and bridge construction and equipment installation at the lock structures."[19]

Several other factors contributed to the high number of injuries and deaths. A contemporary journalist opined that the many fatalities notable already in 1924 were due to the large number of workers involved

9.2 Twin Locks 6, 1 August 1928. Collapse of a lock gate. A crane carrying an end post for the 500-ton steel gate crumpled, killing ten men and injuring twenty others.

in the project and to the prevalence of "very unskilled labour."[20] To a degree, this is true but a twenty-first-century labourer would deplore the fact that steel-toed boots and safety helmets were still unknown in the 1920s. Machinery was larger and more complex than fifty years before so that blows from heavy objects such as the booms of cranes, falling timbers, or collapsing concreting forms, could easily kill their victims. Descriptions of accidents are a chronicle of fractured skulls, pelvises, and spines, occasioned by heavy blows or falls from a great height. The lock walls, under construction or when completed, were very high, 35 to 45 feet (10.7 to 13.7 m), so that falls from them to the concrete floor below were usually fatal. For example, James McCoy of Beamsville died of a fractured skull when he fell down a valve pit at Twin Locks 4 in 1928. A similar accident two weeks earlier left a more fortunate George Innis of Beamsville with only internal injuries. The use of dynamite charges, much more powerful than in the past, was exceptionally hazardous. At Allanburg in February 1928, for example, one and one-half tons of explosive used to shatter rock detonated prematurely. "The explosion came with dramatic suddenness," wrote a local journalist. "There was no warning. A loud report, as from a mighty cannon, and the ground on which the men were standing broke up like matchwood and huge boulders went flying skyward. In fifteen seconds it was all over. What was once a flat surface on the earth is now a pile of boulders and stone, piled fifteen feet high in some places." Two men were killed in the explosion and several injured, "hurled beneath huge piles of the shattered rock."[21]

Workers were often labouring on or over water, with the result that a misstep could end in drowning. For example, in 1926–27 four out of eleven fatalities occurred when men fell off boats or scows.[22] In May 1929 a Canadian Dredging scow at Port Colborne overturned, drowning William Stanbury. The 1927 collapse of a timber cofferdam at Bridge 13 in Welland threw men into the water, drowning Robert Lethbridge, Henry Nealis, and Achille Bisson. Especially after 1928, when water was let into parts of the new prism, drownings often occurred.

The banks of the prism were much higher than in the past and, if they collapsed, could crush labourers. Moreover, huge pieces of clay could have the consistency of rock. The 1928 landslide that killed two workers included "tons of heavy blue clay ... [which] plunged from a point near the top of the 90-foot canal bank" down onto ten men laying a track for a tramway on the channel's floor. A journalist reported that the scene was "one of almost unbelievable mud ... having the appearance of an immense quagmire, due to the heavy rains of late."[23]

Because hydroelectricity was now widely used in construction equipment and would be used to power the lock gate machinery, electrocutions became more common. In June 1930, for example, three men were killed at Thorold near Bridge 9 as they were putting up a wire-braced extension ladder at the guard gate substation; the wind wrenched the ladder out of their control and up against a high-tension wire. In other cases, luckier men escaped with mere burns.

Linguistic barriers hindered communication about safety matters. Because they could neither read written instructions nor comprehend directions spoken in English, some labourers found themselves in life-threatening situations. A February 1928 explosion on Section 3 near Thorold killed two workers, including Carlo Blanco. Among the injured were other Italians, Patsy Boniferro and Joe Attobello. Labourers who spoke only Italian may have misunderstood English instructions because, at the coroner's inquest, testimony was given by Attabello, who had to act as translator for his co-workers. Occasionally the engineers acknowledged the existence of non-English-speaking workers as when, during a 1922 strike on Section 4, Lazier put up posters in Italian banning labourers from the site.

Two accidents deserve to be recounted in some detail because they show the danger and complexity of the Ship Canal as a workplace (figs 9.1 and 9.2). On 1 August 1925 Lyall was moving a Blaw-Knox steel concreting form from the centre wall of Twin Locks 5 to Twin Locks 4. A cable broke so that the whole form skidded down sideways off the runway, collapsing in a mass of steel, planks, and timber. Twenty men were buried in the falling materials and three were killed. Worse occurred on 1 August 1928 during the installation of gates at Twin Locks 6. Men were working at riveting and bolting in the unfinished gates when a crane supporting one of the gate leaves fell into the lock pit, tearing out the scaffolding on which the men were working and sending the gate leaf itself crashing down on other labourers. Twenty-three men were injured and ten men died, "crushed in most cases beyond recognition."[24] Working on bolts inside the gate, William Walters, who suffered only a gashed forehead, recalled: "The crane at the top leaned over and then crashed onto the gate. As the gate fell the first thought that flashed through my head was to jump to the cement 30 feet below. Then I thought better and stayed where I was. It was fortunate that I

9.3   St Catharines. A tombstone in Victoria Lawn Cemetery commemorating "two sunny Jims" killed in a Ship Canal construction accident.

did, if I had jumped I would most certainly have been crushed. As it was I rode in the gate and practically escaped."[25]

In January 1933 Grant sent to Dubuc a list of fatalities entitled "IN MEMORIAM," with a view to having it included in Cowan's forthcoming collection of his articles for the journal *Engineering*. Dubuc replied:

> I do not think it desirable to include in the reprint the names of those who were killed during the construction of the Welland Ship Canal and whose names were listed on the sheet headed "IN MEMORIAM" enclosed with your letter of January 17th. This feature has no particular relation to the purposes of a Reprint Volume, and in any event the Department has under consideration the erection on the Ship Canal of a suitable Tablet commemorating those who were killed during Construction.[26]

Possibly Dubuc believed that it would be politically unwise to publish such a list in Cowan's collection. At all events the book contains only

THIS HAVEN
WAS CREATED TO
COMMEMORATE
ALL THE PEOPLE
WHO LOST THEIR
LIVES WHILE
BUILDING OR
OPERATING OUR
WELLAND CANALS

9.4   St Catharines. Headquarters of the St Lawrence Seaway Management
Corporation (Western Region). Hidden in a small grove of trees, to date
this plaque is the only public memorial to men killed building the Welland
Ship Canal.

cursory mention of accidents involving injury or death to workers. The
tablet he mentions was never erected (but see figs 9.3 and 9.4).

THE WORKERS' CAMPS

Although many of the labourers were itinerant or from outside Niagara, the Department took no responsibility for the housing of most of
them. Because they were usually the employees of the contractors, not

9.5 A labourers' "camp." Temporary housing provided by the Department of Railways and Canals or by the sectional contractors. The quality of this accommodation varied widely.

of Ottawa, the federal position was understandable. Offers from several would-be operators of boarding houses are in the Departmental files but the authorities seem to have ignored them. "Camps," consisting of boarding houses or "barracks," were operated by the contractors, who often adapted existing structures (fig. 9.5). For example, at Port Robinson in 1919 the contractor rented an older house and hired a cook to prepare meals. At Thorold in the same year, two frame buildings were built on Wellington Street, with dining rooms and lavatories to accommodate about eighty men, "one being for native and one for foreign labour."[27] In this case the men ran the commissaries themselves. The segregation of immigrant labourers was repeated at a camp for "foreign" workers that opened in 1920 on Section 3 in Thorold. In the same year another camp opened east of Lock 3, where men were working on the watertight embankments at the lock's pondage. At Allanburg an old store was rented as a boarding house. Other camps were located on Carlton Street and on Lakeshore Road near St Catharines.

On one occasion, a concerned engineer urged contractors to improve accommodations. For example, in 1920 Jewett, in charge of Section 2, encouraged the contractors Baldry, Yerburgh & Hutchinson to build an addition to the Carlton Street "bunkhouses" to house a library and reading room, which seems to have occurred.

And so, occasionally, the canal labourers' living conditions, although intolerable by twenty-first-century standards, were better than on earlier canal construction sites. In 1920 a journalist reported that "in the canal boarding houses, the very best of food is supplied. 'The meals we get would cost about two dollars a throw in a city restaurant' declared a husky dredge man working at Port Weller."[28]

Conditions could vary dramatically along the site, however, and some of the barracks proved to be distinctly substandard accommodation. In September 1924 Dr Heagerty, chief inspector for the Department of Health and co-founder of the Ship Canal Health Board, ordered J.P. Porter to clean up his Port Weller camp by, among other things, chlorinating the water supply and installing screens on all windows and doors on the kitchen and dining room. The inspector made several trips over the work during 1925–26 and was satisfied on the whole with general conditions, "but was not enthusiastic over the Sanitary arrangements of several of the contractors." Heagerty reported the matter of "Porter's houses" to Ottawa:

At Lock No. 3 ... there are two old farm houses which are occupied by about forty men ... and which should be immediately condemned as they are totally unfit for human habitation. Both houses are in a complete state of disrepair. The roofs are leaking, plaster down in rooms, walls broken and devoid of plaster and paper, window panes broken and missing, windows boarded up, floors filthy, dining-room and kitchen combined ... and all over there is a bad odour. The rooms occupied as bedrooms are filthy and most uninviting; broken plaster, broken panes and boarded up windows, unmade beds, filthy floors, meet the gaze in every room. In one of these houses there is over a foot of water in the cellar and the moisture is constantly absorbed by the walls. There is an odour of mildew and decay in all of the rooms. Both houses are overrun with rats.[29]

Porter, however, did not comply and so, the following month, the Board established a permanent sanitary squad of men from the construction railway staff to supervise execution of its instructions. Their duties went beyond inspection and enforcement because Cameron, the

Health Board engineer, told the railway's supervisor to "select ... two intelligent men who are reasonably handy with hammer and saw, but at the same time are not above using a pick and shovel."[30]

Unfortunately, Heagerty and his squad were hamstrung by inadequate legislation. When he described to Cameron the unhealthy conditions prevailing in Porter's camp, he complained that the Public Works Health Act did not give him the power to close Porter's "houses." He had asked the Ontario health authorities to act and was awaiting new legislation.

"A GREAT DEAL OF ILLEGAL SALE OF LIQUOR"

During the First World War federal and provincial legislation was introduced prohibiting the sale of alcoholic beverages. Typically, these laws only drove the buying and selling of liquor on or near the canal construction site underground. The problem was one that previous canal builders would have recognized. So too would they have known the futility of corrective measures.

After violent disturbances in January 1916 the *St Catharines Standard* reported that "there is said to be a great deal of illegal sale of liquor [on the new canal], and the foreigners are openly laughing at the attempts of the government to control the situation."[31] Jewett reported to Grant in November 1920 that "the Ontario Temperance Act is being violated with increasing frequency in and about the camps on this section [2] and to the serious detriment of the work." He advised, moreover, that the whole canal site from Port Weller to Thorold be "cleaned up," because the problem of "blind-pigging" (the illegal sale of alcoholic beverages) was widespread. Nothing seems to have been done, for in August 1923 Porter wrote to Grant describing two houses and a barn situated between the construction railway and the canal which were a "nuisance through the fact that the occupants of same are using them as the headquarters of a boot-legging establishment."[32] Nevertheless, the problem of alcohol abuse was less intense than it was a century previously.

"THE HERO ON A PEACE BASIS"

Whereas thousands of "blue-collar" and "common" labourers built the Welland Ship Canal, its construction also required the hiring of

9.6 Thorold (?). Ship Canal sectional office workers. The number "272" suggests an expropriated domestic property.

a small army of "white-collar" workers: designing, mechanical, electrical, and hydraulic engineers, not to mention the sectional engineers. The latter were flanked by assistant engineers (junior and senior), auditors, secretaries, clerks, and four photographers. Drawing up the plans and specifications were draughtsmen, rodmen, and assorted clerks. Some of these men were local residents, while others came from outside Niagara (fig. 9.6).

Although their lives were by no means as rigorous as those of the labourers, the living and working conditions of the canal's office workers provoked the *Toronto Globe* to lament the problems faced by "the hero on a peace basis."[33] Single employees were accommodated in canal-side structures such as the building which is now the Lock Seven Inn on Chapel Street in Thorold or what became the handsome Welland Club in that city. Still, Grant and the Department had to deal with issues that many an engineer would have thought were beyond his sphere. In the early 1920s, as construction was recommencing after the strike of 1919, the accommodation of these men proved difficult. In March 1920 Lazier described to Grant the problems of married men on his staff, such as C.W. West, who could not find apartments or houses in or near Thorold. Vacancies were rare and rents were high. "It is certainly not fair," he said, "that our Staff ... should be required to pay the exhorbitant rentals demanded by the profiteering landlords of this town."[34] The situation was complicated by the fact that some houses expropriated by the Department and suitable for engineers' or draughtsmen's families were still occupied by permanent residents not yet evicted. Grant set about discovering the names of the tenants in such government-owned houses and, because the records contain no more complaints, we assume that Lazier's men and their wives and children found suitable homes. When Section 8 was opening up in 1924, however, a similar problem occurred. Sectional engineer George Kydd reported to Grant that the superintendent of the Northern Construction Company was, "like many others, unable to get a house for himself in Port Colborne."[35] In this case, however, probably because the contractor was perceived to have more resources than a draughtsman, no action seems to have been taken by the canal authorities.

Alex Grant ran a tight ship and was not sympathetic to office workers who had to dwell at a distance from their workplaces. In 1921 he sensed a problem on Section 6 in Welland, where some of E.P. Johnson's staff were living out of town, in St Catharines and Thorold, a situation which he would not tolerate. Such employees, he said, must live in Welland, Allanburg, or Port Robinson. Similarly, those working on Sections 6 and 7 must also live in Welland. Later that year, little seemed to have changed for Grant told Johnson that he wanted such men to live "within a very reasonable distance of their work." Employees who lived far away arrived at work late and left early: "Their minds are on the clock and not on their work."[36] Anyone in Johnson's office who lived in Thorold, for example, must move to Welland.

Grant was not totally insensitive to his employees' difficulties, for at least two examples of his fair-mindedness exist. When in 1920 a draughtsman started work two days after a deadline for a pay raise for men in his classification, Grant suggested to the Departmental comptroller "that the regulation pertaining to annual increases might be elastic enough to permit of his increase becoming effective October 1 instead of January 1."[37] On another occasion, in August 1921 he petitioned the deputy minister for overtime pay for his office staff. Because the plans for re-letting Section 3 were being drawn up, his men had to return to work "after supper" from 8 until 11 p.m. He pointed out that since February they had been working from 8:30 a.m. to 6 p.m. every day including Saturday. The overtime rate was approved.[38]

Not that the Department paid such men well. While undoubtedly better remunerated than most manual labourers, canal office employees received salaries which were notoriously lower than those paid in the private sector. Consequently, the Civil Service Commission, responsible for hiring the Ship Canal's engineering staff, experienced difficulties finding properly qualified people. In fact, said Lazier, many "laborers and trades workers of this vicinity ... [are] in receipt of higher remuneration than the scale paid our staff."[39] Added to Grant's problems in the year of the general strike, 1919–20, was the behaviour of many office staff who, believing that the Ship Canal would never be finished, sought better pay elsewhere and gave notice.

The working environment of these men was not princely. In most cases the sectional offices were converted houses. At Allanburg, for example, "the stone house" was repaired and renovated in 1919 as the engineers' office and single staff accommodation for Section 5. It burned in December, destroying the personal effects of the men who lived there, although all the records were saved as well as some furniture.

THE MEDICAL SERVICE

By the time the first steam shovel hoisted a load of Niagara's clay in 1913, legislation was offering more work-site security to Canadian workers. The federal Public Health Act already required the provision of medical and services on public works sites, such as the Ship Canal. Such legislation continued to be enacted in the early years of construction. In Ontario, for example, an act of 1914 established compensation for injuries sustained by workers. Federal employees were covered by similar legislation in 1918[40] and a federal Department of Health was established in 1919.

The canal Medical Service had been set up in 1913, directed by Dr John McCombe (1875–1945), who had been the National Transcontinental Railway's doctor for ten years. As chief medical officer he operated the service on Sections 1, 2, and 3 until 1917 when the war closed down operations. Re-established in 1919 to include the whole site, the service was funded by monthly deductions of $1.00 from each employee's paycheque to cover all medical needs except those covered by the Workmen's Compensation Act. The fees of workers directly employed by the Department were paid by the government.

By 1914 McCombe supervised the construction of hospital buildings on the north side of Queenston Street, between St Catharines and Homer, close to Victoria Lawn Cemetery. Here his staff consisted of a medical superintendent, two other doctors, a matron, a nurse, a cook, and an orderly. The "Homer hospital" was extensive, including the institution itself, the doctor's residence, a chicken house, ice house, store shed, and barn, all situated on twenty-two acres with cherry, apple, and mixed orchards, a "grapery," and a meadow.[41] Field hospitals were built at Thorold, Welland, and Humberstone. In the latter town a lot on Ramey Avenue near the north end of Lock 8 was expropriated in February 1924 for a hospital with ten beds and a resident doctor with nursing staff. In 1927 a frame cottage in Welland was expropriated and moved to Aqueduct Street near the syphon culvert. First aid stations were set up in contractors' offices and, at the height of its work, the Service had the use of three automobiles, one motor ambulance, and a "speeder" (a track maintenance car, which could be used in medical emergencies).

On the 1919 resumption of work on the Ship Canal and McCombe's return from overseas service, Bowden offered him his former position as chief medical officer and the use of the hospital and farm together with equipment at the nominal rental of $1.00 per year. McCombe would receive the deductions from all employees and endeavour to carry on the service on these receipts. When the doctor found that it was impossible to make this income cover the expenditures, Bowden arranged that the Department should carry the Service and allow him a salary equal to his former army pay. However, after 1922 McCombe took over the Service on his own account, forgoing all salary and leasing the land on which the hospitals stood. He retained profit from receipts after having paid the expenses of the Service. By 1926 McCombe was operating the service independently of the Department of Railways and Canals.

A review of McCombe's problems takes us to the heart of the construction site and to the core of problems endured by some of the labourers, contractors, engineers, and auxiliary staff on the Ship Canal project. In the mud, dust, and noise of the lock pits, less educated or immigrant labourers, for example, were not at first enthusiastic about McCombe's service. When an outbreak of typhoid fever occurred on Section 8 in 1924, McCombe provided inoculations for the workers in that area. About 60 per cent of them, however, were (in Grant's words) "more-or-less antagonistic to the idea of being inoculated."[42]

Some had no idea of what to do in an emergency. To partially remedy this situation a "first aid detachment" was appointed by the engineer of each section, consisting of workers (probably veterans) with first aid training. A prize of $25.00 would be awarded each month for the most satisfactory first aid detachment. In August 1919 the inaugural prize went to the machine shop workers on Section 3. This admirable system was in danger of foundering because some men in charge of the first aid boxes proved to be incompetent. In 1923 the Ontario Workmen's Compensation Board urged Grant to train workers in their use and McCombe agreed to offer courses.

The doctor also encountered resistance from contractors, who "grumbled a little at being obliged to carry out the orders" of the Canal Health Board or the federal Department of Health.[43] In some cases they did not comply with sanitary regulations. One of McCombe's first endeavours was to install "fly-proof latrines" along the site but the Department of Health had to order the C.S. Boone Company to install a "sewage disposal receptacle" on each of their Port Colborne dredges in 1924. On another occasion in that year, the Canal Board of Health reprimanded Porter for his lack of compliance with their instructions and notified him that they had established a "permanent sanitary squad" to carry out all their instructions. Cost of any necessary work would be charged to the contractors concerned, who must allow the squad reasonable access to all parts of the work.

From at least 1928 only about one in five of the contractors turned over the monthly deductions from their workers' paycheques to the Medical Service. For example, Canadian Dredging and subcontractors Broderick Brothers, Hill and Sibbald, and Ontario Construction did not do so. When explicitly asked to remit the funds, the contractors demurred. The problem continued into 1933, and the records do not suggest whether or not all eventually paid up.

In fact McCombe encountered resistance at every level. Refusing to accept responsibility for the health of construction workers or for unsanitary or dangerous conditions on the work site was not limited to contractors. Even Grant was reluctant to acknowledge any responsibility for Ship Canal construction in the outbreak of typhoid fever in Port Colborne in 1924, when fresh sewage discharged from dredges working directly over the town's water intake was found to be the cause.

The construction site was inevitably a complex and an occasionally disorganized place. In the case of accidents, it could prove impossible to deliver first aid quickly to injured men. For example, in June 1919 Benjamin Price fell into a lock pit. Possibly because of the long delay in getting aid to him – the ambulance which came to the scene was horse-drawn – he died. Grant therefore recommended and Bowden accepted the use of a car powered by gasoline on the construction railway to serve Sections 1 to 4. By July 1919 this "speeder" was in regular use. The sectional engineers would provide for its storage.

The problems of the Medical Service were not entirely medical. Occasionally they reflect the feisty personalities of the men in charge of construction. In 1922 a row erupted between the Service's matron, Miss M.O. Boulter, and the probably exhausted engineer Jewett over the aforementioned "speeder." In September 1922 when McCombe was away, Boulter wrote to Jewett concerning complaints she had received about the slow service of the ambulance. Jewett, who was responsible for housing and maintaining the "speeder," wrote back: "I have kept your speeder in operation – serving your department and my own and without expense to you. If you think it has been altogether a pleasure I wish to assure you to the contrary." He told Boulter that he relinquished all responsibility for it and that she could house the speeder in a shed at the headquarters of the sectional contractor, Porter. This brusque reply drove Boulter to write to Grant, asking if he could "help me over an unpleasant stile." She noted that workers on Sections 1 and 2 were becoming "obstreperous" when the speeder, based in Section 3, was not arriving quickly enough during emergencies. Grant assured her that Jewett would continue to operate the speeder until McCombe returned, at which time the doctor could house the ambulance with Lampard, head of the construction railway.[44]

As construction neared completion, the Medical Service was gradually scaled down. The Humberstone hospital was closed in December 1927 and in 1930 McCombe began to reduce the number of employees in the service. The wards in the Homer hospital were gradually closed partly because the few patients there complained of loneliness.[45] By June 1932 the Homer hospital had fully closed, although the Medical Service continued on a much-reduced scale. The first aid station at

Thorold was maintained until the end of October 1932, when all aspects of the Medical Service were terminated. Companies still with contracts to fulfill made arrangements with local doctors.

A BALANCE SHEET?

The officially recorded human cost between 1913 and 1932 – at least 118 deaths – did not go unnoticed in the Niagara area. On the occasion of the ceremonial opening in 1932, they were commemorated by an elegiac poem in the *St Catharines Standard* (Appendix VI). As we write this, however, no public memorial to those killed in the Ship Canal's construction exists, save for a small plaque obscurely located at the Seaway headquarters in St Catharines (fig. 9.4). Richard White describes the workers on the Grand Coulee Dam Project on the Columbia River, 1933–1942, as "oddly depersonalized in even sympathetic accounts."[46] Perhaps inevitably, most of the Ship Canal "navvies" remain impersonal statistics.

Our readers might therefore believe that the building of the Welland Ship Canal brought much more human misery than contentment and prosperity to Niagara. Such a view would be unwarranted, not only because most major public works result in human injuries and temporary community dislocations, but also because the Ship Canal project, like its predecessors, was a stimulus to employment, industry, and community development in the area. Moreover, descendants of some of the construction labourers often look back with pride on their great-grandparents' contribution to the Welland Ship Canal.

The on-site difficulties we have chronicled, however, were echoed in the tension that often arose between the waterway builders and residents and businesses of the adjacent communities. Although the engineers were sometimes reluctant to listen to complaints from neighbouring towns, some them worked to overcome the tension between canal construction and the local community's needs. In fact, they strove to make the canal precinct a landscape of which Niagara citizens could enjoy and take pride in. Such are the topics of our next chapter.

CHAPTER TEN

"A settled and established community"

Addressing a Welland audience in 1912, Weller claimed that building the Ship Canal would present more challenges than did the construction of the Panama. The latter waterway "was built in the wilderness," he said, "whereas the Welland ship canal will have to adapt itself in many instances to the present physical and commercial conditions of a thickly-settled and long established community."[1]

Weller was correct. As in the past, the canal builders would have to consider several problems that their project would inflict upon the local population. Now, however, the scale of disruption would be much greater. Niagara residents would endure the flooding of farmland and suburbs, the noise of construction, and the possible pollution of domestic water supplies. Local governments now had to face the prospect of rebuilding water purification plants and moving reservoirs. Industries, too, complained of disturbances to their water sources and to the basic operation of their enterprises. In addition, agricultural land was damaged, while homes and businesses were expropriated or demolished (figs 10.1, 10.2, and 10.3). One whole cemetery had to be moved. In chapter 7, we saw how families in Grantham Township suffered the loss of the projected but never built Bridge 2.

Yet the general public was fascinated by the canal-building project and flocked both from within Niagara and from abroad to inspect or tour the site. In fact, written inquiries came to the St Catharines office from around the world. Meanwhile, the canal engineers made an effort to beautify the finished waterway as a linear park while also trying to preserve some of the earlier Welland Canal sites as historic monuments. And so, despite being profoundly disruptive to the lives of Niagara people, the engineers tried to have the canal adjust itself to local interests.

10.1   McCalla's Park, ca. 1910. A pleasant recreational area lost when this section of Ten Mile Creek (at what is now Port Weller) was devoured for construction of Lock 1 of the Ship Canal.

One of the new, but simpler, issues confronting the engineers was adapting the canal to local electrical communication systems. Cables and pipes for gas and water services as well as telegraph and telephone connections had to be installed in conduits or armoured submarine cables under the canal or over the waterway on towers. Communities had to endure temporary changes in service as when, for example, at Port Colborne the overhead hydroelectric wires crossing Killaly Street

10.2   An endangered barn on the edge of the Ship Canal prism. In other places, farms were divided by the new canal route.

were found to be too low to permit the passage of the contractor's large Bucyrus shovel. A temporary diversion was made farther south until the shovel had worked past the original crossing. The Bell Telephone trunk lines on the east side of the Third Canal along Fraser Street in the same community had also to be temporarily diverted to an elevated crossing – all of which was disruptive, as Weller said, to a settled and established community.

"WATER SEEPING ..."

The immense size of the project and the greater volumes of water released or blocked made flooding a constant concern. Not since the building of the First Canal was "drowning" of adjacent land, homes,

10.3 Port Colborne, ca. 1910. These government buildings and business premises were demolished when Ship Canal construction swallowed up East Street. On the other hand, the older locks have survived to the present day.

and farms such a problem. The plan to deliberately inundate areas around Welland aroused community resistance. But flooding could also be accidental, if no less disturbing to Niagara residents. Some people felt deeply aggrieved at what they believed was the ruin of their fortunes by the Welland Ship Canal. For example, Mr and Mrs Grundy of Humberstone wrote to Grant in 1927:

> You perhaps think you did not do much damage and it dont *matter* much. Well there was our *Vegetables, Flowers, Rotting Fruit* trees *rotting* at the roots; besides the *soil* being impoverished, the *fence* Posts rotting and falling over – the water seeping in *cellar* – water seeping in *wells* our *drinking* water spoiled. Our son had diphtheria last winter ... I think we are letting you off *easy* with *200* dollars but we need it *now* not when we are *dead*. Please let

10.4 Thorold, 1916. Flood at Allanburg Stone Road, caused by blockage of the Beaverdams Culvert. The result of such disasters was claims for property damage not always honoured by the Department of Railways and Canals.

us know if you can settle with us before Christmas and oblige. [Emphasis in the original.][2]

In this case, the Haun Drain north of Ramey's Bend was declared to be the cause of the problem but the Department of Railways and Canals refused to accept any responsibility.

The most severe flooding occurred in the Beaverdams area, south of Thorold (fig. 10.4). The first instance was in the late winter of 1915–16. The cause of the problem was the blockage of the culvert carrying Beaverdams Creek under the Third Canal. Basements were flooded and the Beaver Wood Fibre Company suffered serious water damage to its plant. Certain farmers and the builders Battle and Martin added their voices to those affected. John Weller was reluctant to identify either the operating canal or the Ship Canal construction as responsible for the floods. In a letter to Battle and Martin, he referred to the "alleged flooding" at Beaverdams and pointed out that abnormally heavy rains had caused floods "all over the country." He did state, however, that the old culvert would be repaired in the coming summer.[3] Claims against the Department for damages caused by flooding and further incidents at this site continued until the late 1920s.

Alex Grant had some personal experience of canal-related flooding. On one occasion, when he was driving from Welland to Port Colborne with several canal engineers, "we got marooned in our car ... due to high water in the canal. We were in a bad plight for nearly two hours before being rescued by a car and truck from Humberstone. S.W. gale with snow – Cold."[4] However, in 1927 Grant, like Weller before him, evasively referred to the "alleged flooding of lands along Beaverdams Creek by reason of the Welland Ship Canal works."[5]

Despite the engineers' reluctance to accept responsibility for the flooding problem, certain practices by contractors may have in fact helped to cause it. For example, at the site of the Thorold Reservoir in 1922, a crane and shovel dumped spoil into Marlatt's Pond, raising the water level. As a partial corrective, Grant had his engineering staff patrol the culvert system during flood periods. By 1930 he had also come around to suggesting that the Department pay all damages to local residents.

"DISAGREEABLE AND NERVE-WRACKING"

Although the canal construction provided jobs and a degree of prosperity for local towns, it could also disturb residents' sleep. In May 1924 the town clerk of Thorold asked Grant to ban Lyall's use of pile drivers at night. Similarly, Welland's Board of Health complained to Grant in 1927 about a jackhammer working all night at the syphon culvert site. The noise was "very disagreeable and nerve-wracking," said the Board, and a "real menace to health in this community."[6]

The explosive sounds of blasting were also hard on the ears of local residents and – worse – presented the chance of real danger to life and property (fig. 10.5). After drilling holes in rock near Thorold in 1915, contractors inserted dynamite in them and, because as many as fifty-seven holes could be fired at one time, detonated thirteen tons of explosive. These heavy blasts "caused considerable complaint," wrote Weller, noting that he ordered the contractors to reduce the charges.[7] In June 1930 blasting on the west abutment of the old Alexandra

10.5   Ramey's Bend (north of Port Colborne), 24 March 1928. Underwater blasting of rock, a noise nuisance and occasionally a threat to businesses and persons.

Bridge caused damage in Welland when earth and rocks flew up into the air and one man was slightly injured.[8]

North of Port Colborne, Humberstone had similar problems. Blasting operations disturbed the recuperation of patients in the field hospital there in 1924 and caused local damage in September 1925. The village's solicitors accused the Northern Construction Company, who denied any responsibility. The company employed an official to deal with all damage claims but, as the Humberstone lawyers said, "This is all right as far as it goes, but the property owners of the Village ... much prefer not having their property damaged at all."[9]

In neighbouring Port Colborne, a firm building the new post office in 1926 feared that blasting by Northern Construction would cause slow-setting mortar in the brickwork to shift. Elsewhere in the town, plaster in homes was damaged. A local resident had been warned of planned blasting and so stayed away from her apartment on the day when a rock the size of a volley ball crashed into her unit. Also in 1926 the Highland Scotch Distillers claimed that their roof was destroyed by the contractor's blasting and that therefore they could not install machinery or open for business until repairs were made. For their part, the contractors pointed out that because the new distillery's owners were aware of the risk involved in building their enterprise close to the canal construction site, they refused to pay for damages. The Department promised to fund the repairs.. We have seen how the Pilkington Glass Factory south of Thorold was damaged in 1924.

On at least one occasion, the blasting of one contractor disrupted the work of another. In 1928 Canadian Dredging fired a large blast at Ramey's Bend, north of Humberstone, which resulted in a surge of water wiping out part of the Northern Construction Company's trestle to the south, damaging their trackage and powerlines, and blocking the channel as well. In 1926 the Dominion Marine Association believed that the sound of blasting at Ramey's Bend prevented ship captains from hearing each other's signals and asked for placement of a semaphore at each end of the curve and at the Humberstone bridge. Dubuc maintained that the blasts were very short and refused to consider semaphores.

A whole catalogue could be compiled of small nuisances to canal-side communities consisting of mishaps involving equipment. In the summer of 1930, grass fires caused by sparks from construction railway locomotives were "burning up the whole country," said Alex Grant, exaggerating.[10] Fortunately such blazes were soon contained and extinguished. In 1923 one of Porter's cranes being moved on the construction railway broke a trolley wire of the Niagara, St Catharines and Toronto Railway at Lock 1, delaying traffic on this commuter line. In 1926 a pipe of Port Colborne's waterworks that crossed the canal's prism was broken by the contractor's dragline. This sort of disruption to municipal water supplies was probably the most irritating of all.

MUDDY AND DANGEROUS WATER

In several communities, problems with domestic and industrial water supplies were contentious issues, causing considerable inconvenience, to say nothing of a possible threat to public health. Welland faced a particular dilemma (fig. 10.6). Potential conflict existed between the city fathers' desire to have the new canal run through their community,

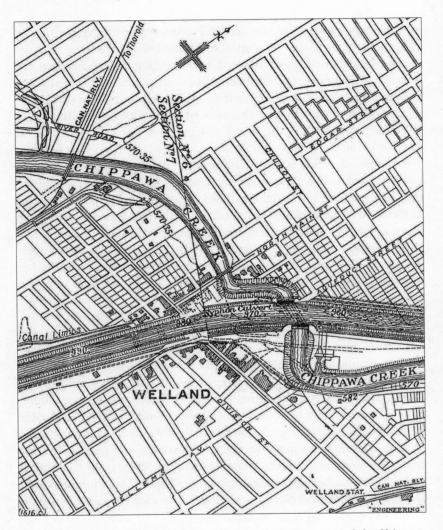

10.6   Welland. The syphon culvert area. The city fathers wanted the Ship Canal to follow the route of the Third Canal, directly through the heart of the city but came to regret its divisive results.

with the perceived economic advantages, and the disruption which construction and operation of the new waterway would entail. It did not help that John Weller was not above tweaking the local authorities' self-interest. In late 1913 when Welland's mayor wrote to him expressing the town's fears, he replied:

I have yours of the 3rd inst., in reference to the Width of the proposed Ship Canal through the town of Welland, and in reply would say that the new canal will undoubtedly require a great deal more room than the present one, as I pointed out on several occasions to the people of Welland when they were so anxious to have the canal go through the town instead of to the west of it, as I once proposed.[11]

Of particular concern was the domestic water supply. Canal-side towns feared that the new waterway, while being built and when in operation, would pollute their domestic water, which came from the channel. In 1912 Weller suggested to Bowden that a pipeline from Lake Erie should be built to overcome the problem. Connected to this issue was the proposed Port Robinson dam on Chippawa Creek, which could pollute the water supplies of Thorold, Merritton, and St Catharines as well.

Already in 1919 canal towns were experiencing water pollution. In May Thorold and Merritton complained that the contractors' method of spoil disposal in the Beaverdams area was fouling their water supply and asked Bowden for an early start on that pipeline from Lake Erie. But Grant told Bowden that the turbid water coming out of taps was caused by spring rain and increased canal traffic and not by overflow from the disposal area. In June 1920 complaints recurred as residents again found their water dirty. A Thorold resident could not see the bottom of his bathtub when he filled it with water.[12] Grant again attributed the muddy water to rainfall and not to dredging. On the other hand, in 1926 E.G. Cameron noted that the contractors' hydraulic dredges could stir up "a considerable quantity of very fine silt" which could be put in suspension in the canal's water and carried northward to be taken into municipal waterworks.[13]

Dirty tap water in homes was not the only problem. Many in Port Colborne feared that C.S. Boone's dredging had caused the typhoid outbreak there in 1924. Controversy over this matter led to the creation of the Welland Ship Canal Health Board, while the Department of Health ordered the contractor to install a sewage disposal unit on each dredge. Railways and Canals also co-operated with local authorities. In 1926, when the water supply for the east side of Port Colborne was disrupted again by construction, the Department laid down a temporary main around the new east harbour wall.

Another crisis erupted in Welland in December 1925 when residents were warned to boil all water for drinking and domestic purposes until further notice. The canal engineers had inserted a provision in the contract for Section 7 that allowed the City of Welland a period of a year in which to provide a proper filtration plant before dredging operations would begin. Welland began to take the necessary steps to remedy the situation by planning a new plant near its existing pumping station. In late 1925 dredging was postponed until the spring of 1926 to allow the municipality time to finish its construction. Completed and put into service in July 1926, the plant proved successful in supplying safe water to the city. In May 1929 placing of concrete started in the permanent intake to a new pumping station, which was completed in September of that year, taking water from the Ship Canal.

The plan to dam Chippawa Creek at Port Robinson would have raised its water level by more than 6 feet (1.8 m). In 1913 Welland's mayor told the Minister of Railways and Canals that if the creek were dammed, the town's water would be contaminated. Correspondence between the Welland authorities, the Ontario Board of Health, and the Department of Railways and Canals continued throughout the early twenties. On-site reports were drawn up and in 1924 Welland's mayor conferred with Bowden in Ottawa on the matter. By early 1924 Grant, beginning to doubt the wisdom of damming the river, drew up a report in July of that year in which he suggested an inverted syphon culvert to take the river under the canal, a solution which assuaged local fears.

Other communities where the domestic water supply was affected by construction had to move or build new reservoirs. For example, Thorold began its new one in October 1921, west of the safety weir and guard gates, completing it one year later. Many individuals, however, still received their home water supply from wells, which now seemed to run dry more frequently or were poisoned with undesirable chemicals. For example, in Humberstone in 1924 water that flowed out of seams of rock and flooded the canal prism and lock pits was not filling up local wells as it normally did. At least ten wells in the area ran dry that year while in others the normally pure water had become sulphurous. Local residents held the blasting of the rock cut on Section 8 responsible. The Provincial Board of Health urged the local government to build a permanent waterworks, which Humberstone did by January 1926, with Departmental assistance.

The canal contractors' use of dynamite was also said to be respon-sible for unsettling wells in Allanburg in 1931, a problem which pre-vailed until at least 1933. The water at a local school's well was said to be unfit even for cattle.[14] As twenty-first-century Canadians have discovered, however, the source of water pollution is often difficult to pinpoint. Although some canal engineers acknowledged the pos-sibility of the Ship Canal's role, most were determined to protect the Department from litigation. Only rarely did Ottawa make restitution.

PROBLEMS FOR INDUSTRIES

The turbidity of water taken out of the Second Canal was also a prob-lem for manufacturers, who used the Welland's water for washing and other procedures. The paper mills of Thorold, Merritton, and St Catharines were especially affected. Although in May of 1919 Grant had denied any connection between construction practices and water pollution, by December of that year he conceded that the dredge PRIMROSE was responsible for muddying industrial water. With no improvement in the situation by 1926, Interlake Tissue, Provincial Paper, and Lincoln Pulp and Paper took out an injunction against Canadian Dredging, Atlas Construction, and E.O. Leahey to restrain them from emptying muddy or polluted water into the Ship Canal, from whence it could flow into their water source, the Second Canal. The contractors' lawyers responded by suggesting that the govern-ment should terminate the mills' leases. Otherwise, because it was im-possible for the contractors not to stir up the water, if the injunctions were granted, work on the Ship Canal would have to stop. The prob-lem seems never to have been fully resolved as complaints were made as late as November 1930.

If dirty water was a problem for these mills in 1919, four years later, in 1923, they faced the prospect of no water at all. In that year, when the Ship Canal engineers considered totally dewatering the Second Canal, a concerted protest arose. The matter was serious because a number of mills, notably the aforementioned paper-producing fa-cilities, used the canal's water in their processes. The St Catharines Chamber of Commerce discussed the matter and drew in J.D. Chap-lin, the local MP, to support their cause. A reprieve was granted but, by mid-century, changing technologies and the closing of some of these concerns reduced the use of the Second Canal. By the 1970s the old waterway was nothing more than a sewer for industrial waste.

Other industries in canal-side communities were also adversely affected by construction. To allow the excavation of the prism south from Fraser Street in Port Colborne in 1925, the Canadian National Railways had to abandon its station, water tank, and other buildings, and build a new station and freight shed with sidings west of the Third Canal. Excavation for the new east harbour wall at Port Colborne intercepted the International Nickel Company's water intake. In 1925 INCO therefore laid a pipeline from the intake of the nearby Canada Furnace Company to a junction with the original intake pipe on Erie Street. As for the latter enterprise, also located on the east side of the harbour, it had to close down in June 1926 for the construction of new dock facilities. To the north, in 1930 the Electro-Metallurgical Company's dock in Welland South found its operations disrupted for the building of a new dock, as did the Ontario Paper Company near Thorold in 1929. Ultimately, these industries benefited from the Ship Canal but their managers had to guide their enterprises through a difficult transition.

During the construction period, shipping on the Third Canal faced new, if temporary, obstacles. Dredging operations required more attentive piloting of vessels. The most difficult stretch of the canal was at Welland near the syphon culvert construction site where the operating channel was twisted into an S-curve, causing ships to collide with the piling. In April 1928 the Dominion Marine Association complained to L.D. Hara, superintending engineer of the Third Canal, about the "confusion of noise and many whistles at Welland" and asked for the installation of a semaphore there. Grant told Hara that he had visited the site frequently and found no need for a semaphore at the syphon culvert site. Ships could see each other's approach clearly enough. For his part, the only whistle he heard was the twelve noon one.[15]

LOSSES AND DAMAGE

Construction of the Ship Canal dramatically changed the landscape in Niagara and considerably altered the built environment. Businesses, farms, and homes had to be dismantled and moved. Those that remained were occasionally damaged from blasting operations. Recreational sites were obliterated (fig. 10.1). Expropriation of land could mean that residents were deprived of long-held property, a traumatic event even when compensation was offered. Sometimes local people

10.7   Future site of Twin Locks 4, 1926. Temporary bridge for the Canadian National Railway on its international line, an important thoroughfare that could not be obstructed.

refused to abandon completely their homes when their land was expropriated. For example, in 1912 Richard Emmett's house, which stood on the line of the Ship Canal just east of Merritton, was placed on rollers and wooden rails and moved from what would become the east to the west bank of the Ship Canal, near Bridge 5 at Glendale Avenue. Emmett's farm, however, remained divided.

In 1919 the Town of Thorold took legal action concerning the destruction of a sewer and waterpipes, impaired electric lighting service, damaged concrete and plank walks, two demolished Ten Mile Creek bridges, and severed roads and highways. Much of Wellington Street, for example, had been obliterated as the CNR right of way had to be expanded to the west of the Ship Canal, depriving several homes of their front access to the street. Other houses here and on nearby Chapel Street were demolished or relocated.

Such disruption of community life occurred everywhere along the line of construction as the working lives of local people and the services on which they depended were affected. When, in Port Colborne in 1925, the Canadian National Railway station was demolished, so too was the post office and custom house with its fine woodwork and mansard roof (fig. 10.3). Railway schedules were potentially inconvenienced, but in several instances temporary crossings were built for the lines (fig. 10.7). In Welland the J.H. Crow Building, on the north side of West Main street, was torn down to make way for the retaining wall and abutments of Bridge 13.

Sometimes the consequences of canal building were less obvious but more long-lasting. Throughout Welland, retaining walls on both sides of the prism were built to prevent the community from literally slipping into the channel. St Andrew's Presbyterian Church, built in 1889, stands on the west side of the canal, very close to the bank of the wider new channel. Despite the installation of a strong retaining wall, the building has experienced ongoing problems with the stability of its foundations.

On other occasions, the inconvenience to local residents was only a nuisance but, especially if repeated, could become a profound irritation and considerable expense. In 1915, for example, construction workers removed fences from farmland with the result that horses and cattle strayed onto railway tracks and were killed. Weller had the fences replaced at no cost to the owners but the problem persisted and in 1919 three cows were killed by a locomotive near Lock 3 because of fences removed by contractors' men. In 1925 a farmer in Crowland Township could not harvest his hay because of the stakes which Ship Canal surveyors left behind and which, obscured by the tall grass, had twice broken his reaper. Grant agreed to investigate.

The government was not totally deaf to local authorities when they asked for special consideration. Upon requests from residents, the Department built a loading dock north of Lock 3 to serve St Catharines and improved roads in the Thorold area. On the request of the City of Welland, the Department filled in the abandoned bed of Chippawa Creek east of the Second Canal aqueduct to prevent it from collecting stagnant water. When Port Colborne complained about the traffic problems created at the north end of busy West Street by the existence of the forebay of the old supply weir, the Department partially filled it with rock and covered over the rest of the channel.

Canal building in Niagara inconvenienced the dead as well as the living. The Third Canal's construction had already been disruptive to a cemetery in Thorold (see *This Great National Object*, chapter 8). When Ship Canal construction in the Thorold area began, the town's major graveyard at St Peter's Church, which lay on the site of the future pondage for Twin Locks 6, was doomed. The cemetery contained between nine hundred and one thousand graves. Therefore, in 1923 the contractor Peter Lyall acquired new coffins for the removal of the bodies, some of them United Empire Loyalists who had helped to found Thorold, and their associated tombstones to Lakeview Cemetery atop the Escarpment. In 1926 the graveyard's former site was flooded. In 2009, however, when the pondage was drained, human remains were unearthed, suggesting that not all coffins had been removed.

Despite the disturbing implications of this scene, Lyall's efforts imply a certain respect for communities disrupted or damaged by the Welland's construction. Even more illustrative of some canal engineers' sensitivity to the damaging effects of their work was the effort to surround the new canal with a park.

CHAPTER ELEVEN

Parks and Publicity

Construction of the Ship Canal did not occur in a geographical vacuum. Indeed, some Niagara residents may have rued the day John Weller began to supervise the first excavations. Some of the engineers, including Alex Grant, however, were concerned to build more than a functional, efficient ditch for large vessels. They were also alert to the value of "good p.r." about their canal. They agreed with a Canadian observer of the work that the beautification of the great ditch would be "a work of national importance."[1]

THE CANAL BEAUTIFUL?

Criticizing the work on the First Canal in 1828, the engineer John MacTaggart had recommended that "trees ... should be planted thickly along the banks of the Deep Cut, to support the rim."[2] In fact the banks of both the First and Second Canals were sodded, while for the Third Canal the area near the locks from Port Dalhousie to Lock 25 was planted with trees and the sides of the prism were faced with stone or were planted with grass and wild clover. So, too, the banks of the Ship Canal were planted with trees and covered with sods. As in the past the tree plantings were designed to prevent erosion of the banks and to protect ships from the prevailing wind. The Ship Canal, however, was also the site of a far-reaching and, unfortunately, abortive project of "reforestation" that, surpassing this limited definition, would have created a magnificent linear park from Port Weller to Port Colborne. The work of the "Forestry and Maintenance Branch" reflected the zeitgeist and offers some insight into both the minds of the engineers who built the canal and the attitudes of contemporaries.

The creation of public parks and the beautification of the grounds of government buildings and other public installations had been under way in Europe and North America since at least 1893, when the "City Beautiful" movement was inspired by the World's Columbian Exposition in Chicago. The Canadian Pacific Railway maintained a "Forestry" department, supporting greenhouses and nurseries for the purpose of embellishing the grounds of its stations. The Grand Trunk and the later Canadian National Railways also had such gardens. At the turn of the century parks and boulevards were being established in several Canadian cities. For example, in Ottawa the Rideau Canal Driveway was being developed. In and around Niagara, after a century and a half of logging, forest removal, and canal building, the development of public gardens was becoming popular. Frederick Olmsted (1822–1903), the prolific landscape architect, had designed public parks in St Catharines and Buffalo. The Niagara Parks Commission was in the process of creating a parkway along the Niagara River between the lakes. Considering the growing tourist trade, prominent Niagara people were encouraging improvement of all the canal precincts with gardens.[3] An awareness of the growing public interest in the new canal may have inspired Alex Grant when he championed the work of the "Forestry Branch" on the Ship Canal.

"WHEN MEN MAKE A CANAL THEY MAKE A DESERT"

So wrote a Toronto journalist in June 1929, going on to describe the effects of Ship Canal construction:

> It is a massacre of many miles of smiling meadows, a hideous disembowelling of towns as well as of country. For the last sixteen years a great army of human moles and earthworms have been running through the Niagara peninsula, the garden of Ontario, if not of Canada, an especially huge furrow and burrow. It is one of the world's marvels of engineering, but it is also one of the world's greatest landscape lesions ... an ugly incision in beautiful vineland and peachland.[4]

Such purple prose was not far off the mark. According to contemporary reports, the contractors left debris, ruined derricks, and wrecked steam shovels, rotting cement bags, rusted and twisted rails, crumbling workers' barracks, and great mounds of useless clay strewn

11.1   At Port Weller, a Forestry Project nursery, part of the plan to create a park along the banks of the Ship Canal.

about. Especially north of Thorold, meadows, orchards, and wood-lots had been disfigured by large spoil dumps and former wetlands had been filled in with excavated material. The Escarpment waterfall of Ten Mile Creek, a popular "beauty spot," had been destroyed, as was the stream's entire valley.[5] "The job had been going on for fifteen years," said sectional engineer Jewett, "and it looked like the dickens."[6]

The idea of creating parkland along the Ship Canal was supported by both Grant and Jewett. Of course, these engineers were not blind to the non-technological advantages of a canal beautification scheme. They knew that an attractive waterway was a good advertisement for their skills and accomplishments. And so Jewett named W.H. Waddell to be in charge of the new Forestry and Maintenance Branch, a fitting appointment because, as concrete inspector, Waddell was familiar with the making and placing of concrete, one of the messiest processes in the canal's construction and a practice which had played a major role in the uglification of canal-side lands.

The canal parkway concept, therefore, was an outgrowth of the effort to clean up the waterway's precinct. In 1927 the Forestry and

11.2 Port Weller, ca. 1930. A Forestry Project greenhouse and garden. All that remains of the project today are the rows of trees planted along the channel banks to act as windbreaks and to secure the dike-like banks of the waterway.

Maintenance Branch was created, although with no official authority for the name (figs 11.1 and 11.2).[7] Waddell had one assistant and a time-keeper and reported to Jewett, who seems to have instigated both the cleaning up and the planting of trees. It was Jewett who drew up a memorandum in 1927 on the need to protect boats from the wind and the banks from wave action and natural erosion. Creating small forests along the canal would suppress the growth of weeds and have potential commercial value as timberlands. As well, he noted that "public sentiment" now expected that large-scale works such as canals should not be left looking like a "battle zone." Without using the term, Jewett believed that the beautification of the Ship Canal was a public relations endeavour. Creating parks along the two older waterways as well as the new Ship Canal would "reflect favourably on the Dominion, on the Province, and the District," he wrote. "After all, the public sees the watchcase rather than the 'works.'" Moreover, "a well cared for property is more easily maintained, as the pride of the employees is stimulated and with it their efficiency." A year later, Jewett described another benefit of the newly launched Forestry Project: "in various ways better relations have been established with adjacent property owners; which cannot but result in less trespass and irritation in the future."[8] An element of pedagogy was involved, too. In 1928 Waddell reported to Grant that "lead labels have been made, and stamped with the common and botanical names of all trees found growing along the canal right-of-way, and will be attached to said trees. This idea will prove instructive and universally interesting to the general public."[9]

A LINEAR PARK

The canal-side tree and sodding program surpassed anything attempted in the past on the Welland, and soon evolved into a massive scheme to plant not only groves of trees but also shrubs and flower-beds along the waterway. The adjacent pondage would become lakes with wetlands, sown with wild rice, creating bird sanctuaries. The work began in the spring of 1927 and the first item on the agenda was to improve the appearance of the "battle zone." Cleanup and maintenance from Port Weller to the Canadian National tracks in Section 3 were undertaken, as well as draining, road building, fencing, salvage work, and brush clearing. Waddell started some landscape gardening and transplant areas. He saw to the planting of several thousand large trees, 8 to 10 feet (2.4 to 3 m) high on Sections 1, 2, and 3, and the reforesting of certain areas with thousands of hard- and softwood trees. Six nurseries, one seedbed, and an arboretum for rare trees were established in the northern half of the canal. In 1928 five more nurseries were opened.

In early spring 1928 orders were placed for further equipment and seedlings, and planting continued. Waddell reported regularly to Grant, usually through Jewett. In the fall of 1928, in the name of the Forestry Branch, he submitted entries in the St Catharines Horticultural Society's annual exhibition and won several prizes, including one for cut flowers. A complex "Development Plan for Reforesting and Beautifying the Welland Canal Zone" was drawn up, dated 12 June 1928, which proposed that the trees planted should be mostly native trees of Ontario, including walnut trees and rarer species native to the southern part of Ontario. Fifteen species of hardwoods and eight of coniferous trees were listed.

In the fall of 1928 Waddell went further, envisaging a "Lake to Lake National Boulevard Canal Park" with not only botanical gardens and arboretums but also bird sanctuaries and a "fish-stocked blue-waterway from Lake Erie to Lake Ontario." He outlined his plan in a confidential letter to E.G. Cameron, principal assistant engineer. "In Canada," he wrote, "the Welland Ship Canal will be Canada's national park and show place."[10] To this end, in 1929 a large greenhouse was built on Lakeshore Road near Lock 1, with departmental labourers constructing the concrete foundation and the works building, and the local firm of Lord and Burnham erecting the glass superstructure (fig. 11.2).

By 1930 over 321,000 trees of various kinds had been planted. In that year alone 150,000 bedding plants and annuals were set out along the canal.[11] The aforementioned Departmental nurseries supplied the plants but some shrubs came from a nursery in nearby Fonthill. The Ontario Forestry Branch, which had already undertaken an important province-wide reforestation project, supplied free of charge over 24,000 hardwood transplants and seedlings including elm, ash, and maple, and frequently gave advice and inspection, also gratis. Canal staff visited the Ontario Forestry station at St Williams, Ontario, which provided seedlings and cuttings again free of charge. On occasion, however, material was imported, as when Chinese elm seedlings were ordered from a nursery in Denver, Colorado.

Some of these trees, such as Carolina poplars and weeping willows, were chosen because they were rapid-growing and well suited to their role as windbreaks and anchors for the banks against slides and erosion, such as on the Port Weller piers. On the northern section of the waterway stretches of the canal would be supported by dikes, as near Carlton Street in St Catharines where ships ride high, vulnerable to the prevailing wind. Tree plantings in such areas were considered a necessary safety measure.

Between the stands of trees were beds of flowers (perennials, annuals, and bedding plants) which would soften the harsh look of concrete monoliths. The sodded areas would be punctuated with blossoming shrubs which would provide seeds and berries for birds. The locks, bridges, and harbours as well would be embellished with such gardens.[12]

The project drew widespread interest and support. The superintendent of Niagara Falls' Queen Victoria Park sent plants and cuttings. Citizens of Niagara contributed seeds and a gingko tree came from a St Catharines garden. Waddell encouraged his colleagues and acquaintances to collect seeds when they saw a fine shrub or tree. In 1928 members of the St Catharines Horticultural Society supplied plants, bulbs, and cuttings for gardens at locks and bridgeheads. The St Catharines and District Game and Fish Protective Association supported the notion of the Ship Canal corridor as a game preserve, imagining a sanctuary with "ducks nesting and rearing their broods there, ring neck Pheasants, grouse and quail, unmolested on its banks and pickerel and bass in its reaches, where the fishing will be safe." The Association undertook to stock the canal and its ponds with fish and to care for the feeding and protection of game there.[13] The *St Catharines Standard* kept tabs on the project, reporting, for example, on progress of the nurseries in October 1927 and on the park concept in December 1929.

Grant, Waddell, and their supporters wanted the Forestry Project to have a certain "outreach" into the wider Niagara community. Not only tourists but also local people were to be attracted to the waterway for passive recreation. To this end park benches were set up at particular spots near the canal, such as on either side of Lock 1. Waddell tried to co-operate with Niagara historical societies, advising them on the restoration of old cemeteries and other historic sites along the waterway. He was particularly keen on the plan to stock the canal with fish and to provide shelter for endangered species such as whistling swans. These engineer/horticulturists, however, did not always find the public spotlight comfortable. Jewett, for example, later complained that "the work that has been done has naturally attracted some attention; and already we are pestered with high pressure 'Specialists,' 'landscape architects,' and town planners, – usually Americans."[14]

Parks were developed at major canal crossings, such on the east bank south of the Homer Bridge; at "Green Forest Park," near Bridge 5, east of Lock 3; on the east and west piers at Port Weller; on the reach between Port Robinson and Welland at Merritt Island; and at another man-made island at Humberstone, near Port Colborne, between the Third and the Ship Canals. A road was planned to wind back and forth across the canal from park to park. Nevertheless, because Jewett and Waddell feared having automobiles plunging into the water, they did not entirely approve of suggestions to build a parkway or boulevard, such as the Niagara Parkway, exactly parallel to the channel. They disagreed with George S. Henry (1871–1958), Ontario's Minister of Highways, who in 1927 envisaged a "great loop scenic driveway," a "canal drive" linking Port Weller and Port Colborne with the Niagara Boulevard which was then nearing completion.[15] Such a project was not achieved at this time.

WADDELL, JEWETT, AND GRANT – HORTICULTURISTS

William Howard Vincent Waddell (b. 1881), concrete inspector for Sections 1 and 2 from 1919 to 1927, was in charge of the Forestry work from 1927 until 1931. Without his efficiency and enthusiasm, the project would never have thrived. He was a former captain in the Canadian Forestry Corps in France, a man of "honesty and integrity," said his former commanding officer, "a born naturalist."[16] He had worked in Mexico and Cuba and described himself as "a natural admirer of all things out-of-doors, pertaining to nature."[17] While working on the Ship Canal he took an extension course in forestry at the University of Toronto. His commitment seems to have reinforced Jewett's and Grant's own enthusiasm for the project.

Almost as soon as Waddell was put in charge of the Forestry Branch, a representative of the Ontario Department of Agriculture said that he was "doing excellent work."[18] Nevertheless, Waddell had initial hesitations. "When we first started," he said in 1931, "I was really dubious about whether it would be worth anything or whether it would be a success or be looked upon as a favourable undertaking." He and his assistant referred to themselves as "orphans,"[19] a reflection of the unorthodox position of their "department" within the Ship Canal project, where no officially designated "departments" existed and where, although reporting to only one sectional engineer (Jewett), Waddell worked in the jurisdiction of all the others as well. Although in charge of the Forestry Branch, Jewett himself did not believe that he had authority in matters pertaining to the other canal sections. Yet both men were under pressure from Grant to speedily complete the beautification project. Perhaps the irregularities which helped to scuttle the Forestry Branch's work would never have occurred if there had been a clear line of authority and responsibility in this "department."

At all events, Waddell was inspired by the support of Jewett and Grant and was passionately committed to the Forestry work, claiming later that he and his staff happily worked overtime without any extra remuneration. Jewett had full confidence in Waddell, occasionally defending to Grant the cost of his orders of shrubbery and other plants which might seem too high. As for Grant, he said of Waddell in 1929, "I attribute the unqualified success ... [of the Forestry Branch] in the past two seasons ... very largely to the keen interest and enthusiasm of ... W.H. Waddell," adding that several provincial forestry officials had sought the latter's advice "on account of the remarkable results obtained by him." In fact Grant was so impressed with Waddell's work that he suggested to Dubuc that this "rather valuable man" be placed in a new post, "Superintendent of Forestry Work," for the next six to seven years at a higher salary. He repeated his recommendation in October 1930, warning that the Provincial Forestry Branch might want to hire him.[20] Rumours circulated that at least two American firms had offered him employment.

If Jewett began the tree planting and sodding, the beautification project was the hobby horse of Grant himself. In 1928 Waddell remembered a meeting with Grant: "A little over a year ago [April 1927] you requested my presence at your office where you talked over the possibilities of making a start at maintenance and clean-up work along the canal."[21] But Grant was interested in more than just clean-up or forestation. He was fascinated by horticulture and, understanding the nature of such seasonal work, always urged speed in the execution of Waddell's work. For example, in September 1927 Grant ordered mowers, harrows, and a wagon from Massey Harris by telegram: "RUSH ALL POSSIBLE – VERY URGENTLY REQUIRED."[22] Indeed, many of Grant's orders and requisition requests were labelled "Rush" or "Needed Immediately." Grant's constant pressure on both Waddell and Jewett may have contributed to some unorthodox procedures.

The doting patron of the Forestry project, therefore, was Alex Grant, a fact of which Jewett gently reminded the engineer in charge in February 1930, when he explained and defended Waddell's ordering of sixty-two expensive shrubs: "As this order is entirely on account of decorative work that you yourself have initiated, and as the beds are already prepared, I trust that you will see this order through at your earliest convenience."[23]

Such a jibe was unnecessary for Grant was always willing to support Waddell's requisitions. His deep interest in gardening is revealed by his correspondence with other engineers on the Ship Canal project. He insisted that they justify any of their actions that might damage natural growth or create eyesores on the canal right-of-way. In April 1926 C.W. West, sectional engineer on Section 3, felt compelled to explain to Grant that, because trees near the road crossing the Third Canal at Lock 25 at Thorold obstructed drivers' visibility, they would have to be cut down. "The park-like effect at Lock 25 would be destroyed," he lamented, but safety was the first requirement.[24] This was before the Forestry Project began, but West was probably aware of Grant's own concern for embellishing engineering work with greenery and gardens. At other times Grant's instructions to Waddell reveal his sense of asesthetics. For example, in 1929 he told him to have a knoll west of Lock 5 terraced, sodded, and planted with trees so that it "would lend itself for a small, beautiful park that would have one of the finest outlooks on the Niagara Peninsula." In early 1930 he wrote to Waddell, "Don't overlook getting your shrubbery and flowerbeds in good shape this summer, as I would like to have the grounds around these locks looking pretty during Blossom Week this spring." Even thousands of kilometres away from Niagara, Grant was thinking about beautifying the Ship Canal. In December 1928 he wrote to Waddell that he was sending him "some seeds from a laburnum tree which were picked this Fall at Westness on Rousay Island, Orkney. I saw the tree in full bloom last September. I do not know whether the tree will stand this climate or not, but you might experiment with it in any event."[25]

"IRREGULAR, IMPROPER, AND UNWARRANTED"[26]

Unfortunately, these grand plans soon fell under a cloud. In February 1931, E.H. Lancaster, a St Catharines lawyer, was appointed commissioner to investigate and report on charges of irregularities committed by Jewett and Waddell in their Forestry and Maintenance Branch work. Lancaster had been the local Conservative MP, 1900–17. Complaints against Waddell and Jewett had been filed by Lancaster's successor, another Conservative, J.D. Chaplin, who had been Minister of Trade and Commerce and who was associated with the Welland Vale Manufacturing Company of St Catharines.

Lancaster's investigation began in April 1931 with several issues on the table. The commissioner wanted to know about a private account in a St Catharines bank, opened in August 1927 with Jewett's approval. Waddell had been authorized to sell "Porter's Cottages," the contractor's abandoned barracks, and to deposit the proceeds from the sale into the account, again with Jewett's knowledge. Other deposits were made into this account from, for example, the proceeds of the sale of hay from canal lands. Although the Departmental auditor had found the accounts in order and all funds accounted for, the procedure was unusual. Furthermore, when Grant had requested photographs of progress on the Forestry work, Waddell said that he had found it necessary to buy a camera, using money from this account.[27] The use of the account for such purchases was also unusual, especially since the Ship Canal employed a full-time photographer. Cameron, the first assistant engineer, knew nothing of the account, a fact which only added to the slightly devious appearance of the proceeding.

In their defence Jewett and Waddell claimed that they had experienced too much "red tape" in trying to get requisitions approved through normal channels. "We are not supposed to get any printing or rubber stamps or anything except from the Department at Ottawa [said Jewett] and we are supposed to requisition them anywhere from three to twelve months ahead of the time required ... [but] ... we couldn't wait for those things." The St Catharines account, Jewett said, allowed them to have funds on hand to use in an emergency. For his part, however, Lancaster concluded: "I cannot find that any difficulty existed with regard to their requirements that would justify such a step being taken and even if it had, I hardly think it would be an answer to the handling of public money in such a way."[28]

Another problem which the commissioner investigated concerned specific work for which Waddell and Jewett paid certain persons from a regular account but which was work of a sort never actually done under that account's heading. For example, topsoil was purchased from a local supplier and charged to a trucking account. A plow was purchased in the same way and charged to the same account. Again, Waddell and Jewett stated that this was their way of expediting purchases for the Forestry project and overcoming bureaucratic delays. In this case, plantings had immediately to be put in the soil, which had to be prepared. "Experience led me to believe that I couldn't get the implement [the plow] through regular channels at all," explained Jewett, "or if I did it would be too late." However, Lancaster concluded that "I cannot find that any such a state of affairs existed to any degree."[29]

Despite his critical conclusions, Lancaster affirmed in his final report that neither Jewett nor Waddell had sought personal gain from their actions nor had they benefited financially. Nevertheless, in January 1931 the Minister of Railways and Canals had already directed the suspension of Jewett and Waddell without pay. As a result of Lancaster's report, submitted in April 1931, Dubuc decided to ask both Jewett and Waddell to resign because of the alleged financial irregularities. For his part, Grant did not want to lose Jewett and Waddell, noting in his diary on 15 December 1930, "I don't believe any such charges." His sympathy for Jewett was exemplified in his inviting the latter to have dinner (presumably at his home in St Catharines) with his wife Maude, Lazier, and the contractor A.W. Robertson on 19 January 1931.[30] Nevertheless, he evidently believed that he had to conform to his superior's wishes.

When Grant informed Waddell of Dubuc's order, the Forestry Project director resigned immediately, declaring that "the whole affair has been most heart-breaking to me." He asked for employment elsewhere in the Department – a request which was denied.[31] Jewett, on the other hand, flatly refused to resign. In a letter to Grant dated 24 July 1931 he briskly defended himself, mainly on the principle that Lancaster's investigation had been carried out with traditional courtroom procedures as if he were being tried for a crime. Yet he was not charged or sentenced for any misdemeanour, only asked to resign: "Am I guilty on all counts or none, or some? [Jewett asked.] What ones are they? Did I profit? ... If I profited, is not the Department condoning a felony if I am not proceeded against? Can I accept a sentence that is not as reasoned and dignified as the court proceedings above referred to? I am waiting for such a judgement ... If I resign at this stage, will not my action be construed ... as evidence of a guilty conscience?"[32]

In March 1933, after the waterway was finished, Jewett was formerly retired from the construction staff of the Ship Canal, never having resigned and never having been fired. Did Grant ever "go to bat" for these two men, whose work he had encouraged and expedited? There is no documentary evidence that he did so, although the records suggest that telephone calls were exchanged between St Catharines and Ottawa. In one of these, the engineer in charge may have asked for the reinstatement of Jewett and Waddell, because Dubuc wrote to Grant in July 1931 telling him that he could not re-employ them because of the general reduction of engineering staff taking place.[33]

Despite the obvious irregularity of Jewett and Waddell's actions, we still wonder at the motivation behind the investigation and the forced resignations. Was politics involved? Throughout most of the construction period Mackenzie King's Liberals had been in power in Ottawa. During that time the federal Conservative opposition regularly questioned appropriations for the Ship Canal work. By the winter of 1930–31 the Conservatives were back in office and both Chaplin and Lancaster were Tories. Jewett was known to be a Liberal supporter. Was the Ship Canal seen as a Liberal boondoggle? Were these Conservatives indirectly meting out "punishment" to their rivals? Or was the chance to make a patronage appointment the motive?[34] Finally, we cannot ignore the personality factor here. Did the feisty, outspoken Jewett make political enemies?

FATE OF A BEAUTY SPOT

In 1929 a Toronto newspaper relished the possibility that the Ship Canal and its park would acquire "world renown as a beauty spot and become a greater mecca for landscape lovers than it has been for connoisseurs of engineering *tours de force*."[35] Although all signs seemed propitious, unfortunately, this did not happen.

The loss of Waddell and Jewett contributed to the demise of the project but the Great Depression and the reduction of parliamentary appropriations for the entire Ship Canal also led to the work's neglect. Cutbacks to the Forestry Branch's staff and budget began in early 1931. In August of that year, Grant told West: "It is ... absolutely essential that you reduce, at the end of August, the forestry work to a minimum."[36] By 1932 planting was winding down with work limited to the maintenance of stock already planted and to the nursery areas. After that year, few references to the Branch can be found in the records.[37] Time, the Second World War, disease, and wild natural growth finally led to the near obliteration of Waddell and Jewett's work. The Port Weller greenhouse still stands, and evidence of the tree-planting project may be seen but no trace of the original flowerbeds remains. In November 1930 Grant had described to Dubuc a small park to be established at the corner of Chapel and Peter Street in Thorold, overlooking the Flight Locks but, typically, the area remained an urban desert until 2000.

HERITAGE CONSERVATION AND RECYCLING

The Forestry and Maintenance Branch's work was not the only example of the canal engineers' sensitivity to the local built and natural environment. Although many structures of the earlier waterways had to be destroyed in the process of building the new channel, some were "recycled" for use. A sense of the importance of certain other structures was also expressed by Grant and his engineers as they attempted to preserve them as historic monuments.

At Thorold the impressive Third Canal Hydro-Electric substation with its domed belvedere was refurbished and used for a while after 1932 as a storehouse. Although the Third Canal aqueduct was demolished, the Second Canal one was provided with a platform and flight of steps for use as a small boat landing. Later it was used as a swimming pool, a function it retained until the 1980s. Except for those at the Niagara Escarpment, most of the locks of the Third Canal were abandoned. Water would continue to flow through those gate-less lifts as waste from the Twin Lock 6 pondage to Lock 3's pond.

Elsewhere the historic canals became derelict or disappeared. For example, in 1934–36, the Third Canal on its diagonal route through Grantham Township was de-watered and filled in. Most of the locks here were buried with the channel itself. As for the Second Canal between Thorold and St Catharines, it had long been used as a source of water for local industries. From time to time when rumour spread that the old canal would be permanently unwatered, business opinion was outraged, with the result that part of the channel was placed in a culvert – but the locks were allowed to decay.

Public opinion saw the old waterways as dangerous eyesores and, after the completion of the Ship Canal, several campaigns were launched to have them filled in or, if still used by industry, culverted. Bridges on the Grantham Township route of the Third Canal were regarded as traffic hazards and the water of the Second Canal as a source of offensive smells. When suggestions were made to unwater the old canal from the Escarpment to St Catharines in 1929, however, local millers, finding that the water was too polluted to use, came up

230 This Colossal Project

with the idea of creating a "wonderful park drive ... all the way from Kinleith [Paper, in St Catharines] up to Thorold."[38] Unfortunately, the time was not ripe for such a concept. Nor, at the time of this writing, has it yet succeeded.

The engineers were certainly aware that their work had obliterated valuable historic sites. Because the Second Canal lifts were still in good repair in the early 1930s and certain of the wooden structures of the First Canal were still extant, Grant entertained the idea of preserving some of them as historic sites. George W. Yates, assistant deputy minister in the Department of Railways and Canals, was also interested. In August 1930 Grant sent him photographs of some of these structures, asking, "Would not this be a good opportunity for the Dept to spend a little money in the preservation of one of these old wooden locks as an historical monument of canal progress in this country. I look upon one of these old wooden locks as being to the canals of this country what Stephenson's 'Rocket' is to the railways of England."[39]

A wooden lock extant near Lock 25 of the Second Canal in Thorold would be the most likely candidate for preservation, thought Grant. Yates agreed with him and promised to speak to the deputy minister about the matter. Local authorities became interested, and in June 1931 St Catharines mayor F.C. McCordick wrote to Manion, Minister of Railways and Canals, about the Second Canal's Lock 3, near the heart of the city, suggesting it become a national historic monument. The minister seemed appreciative, promising to discuss the matter with his staff. Dubuc wrote to Third Canal superintendent L.D. Hara on the subject but there, after 1933, the matter rested.

Meanwhile, Ship Canal construction destroyed the site of the Battle of Beaverdams in the War of 1812 and, with it, community awareness of its significance. The demolition of Third Canal lock gates also proceeded. In November 1932, when a local scavenger wanted to use the gates of Lock 23 for firewood, sectional engineer West asked Grant if the lock should be preserved for its historical interest. In 1933 a lockmaster, James Phillip, also recommended keeping Lock 23 as a historic site. Today, however, the lock remains inaccessible and partly demolished. The Depression, the Second World War, and the postwar economic boom distracted Canadians from local heritage conservation with the result that the older Welland Canal locks, like the park concept, suffered severe neglect and still do.

PUBLIC INTEREST AND PUBLIC RELATIONS

On the other hand, public interest in the new Ship Canal construction was intense. As early as July 1914 Weller was taking interested local businessmen over the site. After construction got fully under way again in 1920, local people were fascinated by the project. "I have invented an aqueduct to cross the Welland," said one John Silverthorn of Port Robinson in a handwritten letter to the Minister of Railways and Canals in 1922.[40] Other people requested information, maps, and photographs, inquiries coming from as far away as France and Egypt. Certain sites were of particular interest. The engineers were constantly invited to give talks and to write papers. In August 1928, for example, Cameron urged the Steel Gates Company to finish its work at Lock 1 quickly because the site on the much-travelled Highway 8 was "becoming more and more the chief point of interest to visitors inspecting the Ship Canal work."[41]

Alex Grant himself was not loath to have the widest possible publicity for the undertaking. The Department continually employed photographers on the site, with Grant often giving explicit directions as to what they should record. In February 1928 he directed E.P. Johnson to show the departmental photographers certain ships in Port Colborne's harbour, suggesting taking shots from the Canada Furnace Company's unloader and from the top of the Maple Leaf Mill (fig. Pref.1).

Many were the groups which the engineers herded along the Ship Canal construction site in tours from 1914 to 1932. Weller began this tradition, also giving lantern-slide lectures on progress of construction to men's church groups and boys' clubs. He arranged tours for groups such as the Toronto branch of the Canadian Society of Civil Engineers in the fall of 1914 and in November 1915 a group of Australian cadets. During Grant's tenure, this practice was continued. For example, in June 1924 two hundred members of the Toledo Board of Trade were "amazed at the magnitude of the work."[42] In the twenties, the range of groups extended from the Boy Scouts of Port Dalhousie to representatives of the Lumbermen's Association (fig. 11.3). Occasionally, distinguished individuals made up these visitations, although the weather did not always co-operate, as when the governor general, the Duke of Connaught, visited the works on a cold and wet day in May 1914. The weather seems to have been better when, in July 1922, a large

11.3   On the new Ship Canal, 1931. A group of fourth formers from Ridley College's Lower School enjoy a cruise on the new waterway. The Ship Canal's engineers inaugurated the practice of public tours for both educational and promotional purposes.

delegation of the Great Lakes–St Lawrence Tidewater Association appeared, including several state governors, members of the American Senate and House of Representatives, as well as businessmen. Former prime minister Robert Borden welcomed them.

Sometimes the visits had an exotic aspect, as when in 1929 Hugh Cooper, a New York City engineer, asked Grant to take around the site "two very intelligent ... highly educated Russians of the non-communist type," one of whom spoke no English.[43] Other guests came from Japan, Manchuria, India, Sweden, New Zealand, and, of course, Britain and the US. Large groups travelled on specially outfitted cars of the construction railway. Most visitors were escorted by one or two of the sectional engineers. These guide duties may have become onerous for some engineers, to judge by Jewett's remark in the busy year 1929: "I hope there will be no 'excursions' in July."[44]

The only important permanent relic of this flurry of requests for information and visits was a series of articles printed in the British journal *Engineering*. They were written by P.J. Cowan, MBE, the journal's editor and a well-known civil engineer in Great Britain. He had worked on engineering sites in the UK and the US, as well as on railways in Egypt, and had served in the Royal Engineers. He visited the Ship Canal in 1927 and, with advice from the canal's engineers, published very detailed articles, which were reprinted in book form in 1935. The possibility of doing such articles had emerged in 1924, but was confirmed only in 1926, when Dubuc gave his approval for Grant to assist Cowan in the writing. The Englishman began the articles in February 1928 and Grant asked Jewett, West, and Johnson to proofread the drafts of one of the first articles because, as he wrote to Jewett, "many of the paragraphs could be written much better than they are, and others ... [are] entirely wrong." Cowan was disturbed by the delay in getting the corrected versions back to him, but Grant explained that much rewriting was necessary and suggested "a little literary dressing up." For his part Jewett was also critical of some of what he read.[45] Grant was particularly concerned to exclude any controversial matter from the articles and Dubuc rejected the publication of a list of men killed on the job when the book was to be published. The revisions inserted by the Ship Canal engineers delayed publication of the first articles in 1929, but in April of that year Cowan was beseeching Grant for more data for future articles. The corrections seem to have been made; thus the reprinted collection in book form stands as a reliable resource. As shown by the many references to it in the notes and illustrations in our book, Cowan's work remains a classic on Canadian canal construction and is still consulted by Seaway personnel in St Catharines.

GREAT MOMENTS

Parts of the Ship Canal were inaugurated at different times. On 16 September 1929, Lock 8 at Port Colborne was opened formally (fig. 11.4). Whereas this opening took place on "a typically bright Canadian day," conditions were different in 1930 when another opening took place. "The day was raw and cold," wrote Grant on 28 April, when, amid "a slight drizzle of rain,"[46] three hundred people turned out at Lock 1 to watch the GEORGIAN pass through (fig. 7.1). Probably many were

11.4   Port Colborne, 16 September 1929. The Canada Steamship Line's
MEAFORD at the opening of Lock 8, with the admiring public. Note the
double lock gates, protecting against a surge of water from Lake Erie.

relatives and friends of the engineers and labourers who believed that,
to quote the engineer E.P. Murphy, the event was "a great moment for
those ... who had toiled so faithfully for so many years."[47]

The official opening of the entire canal took place on 6 August 1932,
nearly two years after the waterway had actually become operational.
Fully aware of the great publicity which would pertain to the formal
opening of this monument to Canadian technological expertise, the

11.5 Thorold, Lock 7, 8 August 1932. In the depths of the Great Depression, Canada had something to celebrate: the new, ultra-modern Welland Ship Canal. The star performer at the official opening was the LEMOYNE, then the largest ship on the Great Lakes. Note the ship arrester in the foreground.

Departmental authorities arranged to have the delegates to the Imperial Economic Conference being held in Ottawa attend a function at the Twin Locks. The program included the formal opening ceremony, visits to historic sites in the Niagara-Queenston area, "as well as a stop off at St Catharines for tea."[48] The official party came to Thorold by train to perform the opening on a platform at the north end of Twin Locks 6. In attendance were Governor General the Earl

11.6 Thorold, 8 August 1932. The governor general, the Earl of Bessborough, moves a lever to raise the fender at the upper end of Lock 6. Top right, engineer in charge Alex Grant with his family; centre right, Stanley Baldwin and J.H. Thomas, British delegates to the British Empire Economic Conference; lower right, the governor general reviews the guard of honour; lower left, he greets Grant; top left, he is with the Begum, wife of Haji Abdullah Haroon of India, and their daughter.

of Bessborough, Prime Minister R.B. Bennett, Minister of Railways and Canals Robert Manion, Prime Minister Stanley Baldwin of the United Kingdom, and representatives of the British Dominions. They watched as the then-largest ship on the Great Lakes, the LEMOYNE, formally inaugurated the Ship Canal (figs 11.5 and 11.6). Meanwhile, the print media rhapsodized. The *St Catharines Standard* published a special edition on 5 August 1932. Of the completed Ship Canal, a *Maclean's* journalist wrote: "As a feat of engineering it ranks with the great engineering triumphs of modern times, in some respect surpassing anything of the kind ever built by man."[49] Allowing for the bias of justifiable Canadian pride here, we find the journalist's judgment to be fair, as our last chapter will suggest.

CHAPTER TWELVE

"Surpassing anything of the kind"

In the early nineteenth century, some romantic Americans began to find in the new technologies embodied by railways, steamships, and canals an inspiring, awesome beauty that was as stunning as that of rivers, mountains, and oceans. Works such as the Brooklyn Bridge, completed in 1883, seemed to have an almost transcendent significance for those who witnessed them.[1] Here in Canada, when the Welland Ship Canal was opened, much that was written about it expressed a similar sense of awe. In contemporary accounts, we have found little of the anxiety and ambiguity over technology that Leo Marx later found in American literature.[2] On the contrary, in 1932, a local poet, echoing what many observers felt, described the new waterway as "inspiring, grand, impressive."[3]

THE CANADIAN TECHNOLOGICAL SUBLIME

In August 1932, J.B. Carswell, an Ontario businessman, described his recent visit to the formal opening of the new Lock 1 at Port Weller, the northern terminus of the Ship Canal, when the evening breeze was beginning to cool the air (figs 11.5 and 12.1). Confronted with a huge piece of smooth-running technology – a giant, elongated water-powered machine – he evidently felt a sense of the sublime. Thousands were waiting for the LEMOYNE to arrive from the south to ceremonially inaugurate the waterway. Carswell wrote:

> Men who had spent a lifetime building the canal, – all their
> women folk and children – all the shipping men for miles around
> those who had spent their lives on the lakes earning their daily
> bread – they knew that the great event was still to come – they
> knew when and where to go to witness the real history making

12.1   Port Weller, Lock 1, 1932. Here the artist Charles Simpson (1878–1942) has reflected the sense of awe which his contemporaries felt upon seeing the great locks of the Ship Canal under construction and in operation, dwarfing the mere humans on the shore. Among the thousands who today annually watch the locks in operation, such an impression is not uncommon.

ceremony ... The day had been one of pomp and ceremony, with the prime minister of Canada and several of the Dominions, and politicians of all stripes, including visitors to the Imperial Economic Conference in Ottawa, in attendance. The proceedings were sent across the air waves throughout Canada and the United States and recorded for posterity on film. But by the evening all that had been over for some time, and yet at Port Weller there was still traffic congestion on the Lakeshore Road and a flotilla of freighters waited to pass up the waterway. What had they stopped for? Suddenly, blotting out the stars, one became conscious of a great ship slipping slowly into Lock One – a great imposing ship – twice as long as any ship that heretofore had graced the waters of Lake Ontario. The bow of S.S. Lemoyne towered away above the heads of the crowd. She seems to fill the whole length of that vast lock. Now she is at rest; the cables are fast and she commences to sink. Down – slowly down she goes; for the first time in history the Queen of the Upper Lake Freighters reaches the level of Lake Ontario; – under her hatches half a million bushels of golden wheat from the West; – the culmination of one of the world's greatest engineering achievements.

The vast crowd holds its breath ... The steel gates quickly swing open and through the opening the dark night is cut by flashing searchlights – a dozen beams of brilliant light pick out the scarlet funnel of the Lemoyne – pick out her proud burgee [flag] in front – pick out her well-known houseflag behind. Her nose starts to move, – almost imperceptibly at first, and then a shout from up on the dock – "She's off," and the next moment the night is shattered in a thousand fragments. Steam whistles from the waiting fleet in front, steam whistles from ships behind in the canal, ten thousand automobile horns, all shriek their welcome, and the great Lemoyne answers back with her lusty horn – three longs, two shorts – her Company's salute. The steel decks vibrate with a roar as she slips past.[4]

Yet despite all the modern technology that went into the construction of the Welland Ship Canal, it still relies on the force of water restrained in its weirponds to fill and empty its locks, flowing through its penstock to power the opening and closing of the lock gates and to illuminate the lake-to-lake system. It is almost as if, insofar as the Ship Canal harnesses the power of the Great Lakes, the waterway is a great man-made river, a version of Richard White's "organic machine," an intricate energy system in which human beings, machinery, and the force of nature are interdependent.[5]

The construction of this machine must rank as one of Canada's greatest accomplishments. The effort lasted eighteen years and took scores of lives. The dollar costs of the Welland Ship Canal were tremendous, even by twenty-first-century standards: $132 million. Perhaps even in these statistics a certain "sublimity" resides. Millions of tonnes of materials and millions of dollars of equipment were involved, and the builders had to contend with fiscal shortage, inadequate machinery, intractable forces of nature, and human frailty.

In overcoming these challenges, they created a gigantic piece of technology – we want to say "organism" – stretching 26 miles (41.8 km) across the Niagara Peninsula, channelling much of the water from four of the five Great Lakes and supporting the passage of huge ships through monolithic locks. "Sublime" by any standard.

THE SHIP CANAL THEN, LATER, AND NOW

Apart from its stature as a great Canadian technological accomplishment, the Welland Ship Canal was also a profoundly human success. The builders applied "blood, toil, tears, and sweat" as well as ingenuity and persistence. Its construction not only reflected changes in the nature of the country's workforce but also revealed society's developing attitudes to common labour and to employment conditions in general. Even early in its evolution, the waterway's construction presented Canada with a version of today's multicultural society. The professionalization of Canadian engineering was reflected in the Ship Canal's personnel, as was the growing sophistication of contracting practices in this country. The Welland was built in the heart of a developing and increasingly complex network of communities, highways, and railways which influenced and sometimes hindered its construction. Moreover, the waterway was constructed in conditions which reflected changes in the wider world – in North America, Europe, and beyond.

As part of the St Lawrence Seaway, the Welland Ship Canal continues to be influenced by changes in the national and international economies. Tonnage statistics rise and fall over the years as do the number of boat passages. When we wrote the first draft of this book, the Seaway Management Corporation, in response to rising tonnage figures, planned to modernize the system's locks, including those of the venerable Welland. There was even talk of expanding the Seaway to accommodate ships of the size that transit the Panama Canal. At the time of publication of this study, however, the decline of China's economy, the drop in steel prices, and smaller amounts of cargoes of grain, iron ore, and coal passing through the system have put all such plans on hold indefinitely.

On the other hand, whereas Niagara Falls, the epitome of the natural "sublime," still draws thousands ever year, now more than ever the Welland Ship Canal, as a monument to Canadian enterprise and achievement, is a focal point for tourists and recreation seekers. A walking, hiking, and cycling trail has been constructed along its banks from Port Weller to Thorold. Viewing facilities have been erected at Lock 3 in St Catharines, at Lock 7 in Thorold, and at Lock 8 in Port Colborne. The abandoned channel at Welland has become a centre for water sports, while the operating waterway attracts international and heterogeneous visitors.

On a more prosaic note, Niagara's waterway continues to fulfill its original function, remaining, as Robert Legget maintained, one of the few great man-made arteries of water commerce in the world. Reflecting its international significance, both its present commercial function and the remains of the earlier channels were the focus of an international gathering in early June 2004 when delegates from both Europe and North America attended the annual World Canals Conference held that year at Brock University in St Catharines. The meeting provided an opportunity for canal enthusiasts, managers, and scholars to discuss a wide variety of topics, including the future of the Welland, indeed of the St Lawrence Seaway as a whole. On the opening day of the conference a plaque was unveiled at the headquarters of the Niagara Section of the Seaway in recognition of the 175th anniversary of the opening of the First Welland Canal.

While the operating channel still compels public attention, its builders have not been forgotten. Many a family living in the canal corridor proudly tells tales about a grandfather or great-uncle who laboured on the construction of the Ship Canal. Local museums and libraries have regular inquiries from genealogists living near and abroad concerning contractors, engineers, and labourers who toiled on the Deep Cut or the lock sites.

The complaint is often heard that Canada lacks heroes. The history of the building of the Welland Canals disproves this view. The original concept of a navigable waterway linking lakes Erie and Ontario was the brainchild of William Hamilton Merritt of St Catharines. For many years now a statue of Merritt has overlooked Twelve Mile Creek at the site of the first two Welland Canals in St Catharines (fig. 12.2). Canada's "Father of Transportation" stands on a plinth from which protrudes the stylized prow of a ship. But it takes more than brilliant vision to transform a landscape and vivify a national economy. Hundreds of thousands of men have laboured to build Niagara's "sublime"

12.2 St Catharines, 1928. Unveiling of the monument to William Hamilton Merritt when construction of the new Ship Canal was nearly finished. Local people did not forget Canada's "Father of Transportation" without whose energy and imagination the fourth Niagara waterway would not exist (see Styran and Taylor, *This Great National Object*).

12.3 Thorold, ca. 1970. The twinned Flight Locks 4 in operation with Twin Locks 5 in the background. A "laker" is ascending and a "saltie" is descending. One-half of the CNR bridge is in the foreground. The photograph was taken from the powerhouse looking south.

waterway. Accordingly, if belatedly, in 2001, a monument was erected in Welland honouring the canals' labourers. Consisting of several statues grouped around a fountain (see *This Great National Object*, fig. 9.1), it was created by the Wainfleet sculptor Bas DeGroot. As well, a plaque fixed to a large stone stands on the grounds of the St Lawrence Seaway Management Corporation offices in St Catharines, dedicated to those killed in all construction accidents. As we write this, Niagara people are planning to create a more prominent memorial at Lock 3 to the men who died building the Welland Ship Canal, 1913–1932.

The most impressive monument in the world, however, cannot change the fact that, despite all the advances in nearly a century, the working life of the ordinary "navvy" was scarcely better in the 1920s than it had been in the 1820s and certainly not more "sublime." These men had little time or energy to admire the romantic qualities of the project on which they toiled. To those thousands of unsung heroes who worked "on the ground" this book is dedicated.

Some Welland Ship Canal Construction Engineers

Several of the engineers described below worked only under John Weller; some worked for both Weller and Grant. Their daily challenges, however, were similar.

Weller's principal assistant engineer was William Henry SULLIVAN (1871–1941). Like his superior he was an RMC graduate (1892) who served on various St Lawrence canals until 1900, including a spell under Weller on the Cornwall. He worked on bridges and railways in Prince Edward Island from 1900 to 1905 when Weller hired him as his assistant engineer on the Third Welland. When his boss was put in charge of Ship Canal construction, Sullivan replaced him as superintending engineer on the operating canal but not for long. In November 1913 Weller had him transferred to the Ship Canal, where he remained until he retired due to ill health in 1923.

For his sectional engineers Weller looked to the Trent-Severn system. C.L. HAYS (1886–1949) became engineer for Section 1, 1913–17; John James ALDRED (b. 1872), for Section 2 in 1913–14, then Section 5 in 1914–17. Aldred was followed on Section 2 by Evan Guthrie CAMERON (1886–1961), 1914–18. Cameron was born in Ontario, graduated from RMC in 1906, then attended McGill University the following year. He too had worked on the Trent from 1907 to 1912. In January 1916 he took over Section 2 on the Ship Canal, then headed up Section 3 until 1917. In 1918 he became chief engineer of the Saint John Dry Dock & Shipbuilding Company but in 1924 he was lured back to the Ship Canal as principal assistant engineer, a position he held until 1936. The following year, he transferred to the National Harbours Board, rising to the position of chief engineer in 1940 and retiring in 1951. Like Cameron, Harry McCready BALFOUR (ca. 1880–1953) hailed from Ontario, was educated at Queen's, and worked on the Trent Canal. He became engineer in charge of Section 3. In 1916 he was transferred to Section 2 and worked there until the wartime shutdown. All of these men had worked under Grant when he was superintending engineer on the Trent Canal from 1906 to 1919. Consequently, most of them knew each other – and their talents and weaknesses.

One of the key men on Weller's staff was his designing engineer, Frank E. STERNS (1879–1969) from Prince Edward Island. He graduated from McGill in 1903 and worked for a time with various private companies. From October 1907 to June 1912 he was assistant engineer on the Panama Canal, responsible for the design of lock gates and protective chain fenders. Appointed as assistant engineer on the Welland Ship Canal in July 1912, the following year he was named designing engineer, a position he held until work was suspended in 1917. He then worked for a year as a consulting engineer with Weller, designing concrete bridges and ships, and as principal assistant engineer for the Inner Harbour Navigation Canal at New Orleans. When Grant took over the Ship Canal in 1919 he soon had Sterns on his staff as designing engineer, a position he retained until being laid off in August 1933. In 1928 he won the Gzowski Medal awarded by the Engineering Institute of Canada for his paper "The Lock Gates of the Welland Ship Canal."

Among the assistant engineers were A.W.L. BUTLER (1882–1949), Eric P. MUNTZ (1892–1955) (fig. 3.6), and H.F.J. ESTRUP (1886–1966). Butler was born in Wales and educated at Manchester Technical University. Before joining the Department of Railways and Canals in 1910, he had worked in Manchester and Wales, and on the Canadian Northern Railway. He began his career on the Welland as an instrumentman on surveys for the Ship Canal in 1912. He worked as an assistant engineer for a short period, then served in the First World War. On his return he was again employed on the Ship Canal until 1935, when he moved to Oakville, Ontario, as a consulting engineer. Eric Percival Muntz, Weller's son-in-law, joined the Ship Canal staff in 1915, rejoined in May 1919 after serving overseas, but by 1921 had moved to Hamilton.

Hector Frederik Jansen ESTRUP was born in Horsens, Denmark, and emigrated to Canada in 1911. After working for a year or two on railways, in 1913 he was hired as engineer of bridges and lock gates on the Ship Canal, remaining there until work was suspended in 1917. He then became president of the British-American Shipbuilding Company until 1921, when he worked as a general entrepreneur. He continued to practise as an engineer in Florida until his death in 1966.[11]

W.B. MACDONALD (b. 1874) attended Glasgow University (1903–04), emigrated to Canada and served as designing mechanical engineer on the Ship Canal 1912–1916. In 1920 he was one of those men who left Ship Canal employment, probably because, in his case, the Department paid him only $3,600 a year, to go to Electric Metals Company, which offered him $4,200 and a promise of an early raise to $5,000. By 1930 he was president of the Detroit Practical School of Steam and Electricity.

As far as we can tell, of all of Weller's young engineers only Aldred, Butler, Estrup, and MacDonald were not Canadian-born and Canadian-educated.

Weller's description of his staff as "a fine lot" could also be applied by Grant to the men whom he attracted to the Ship Canal from 1919 on. As noted above, his principal assistant engineer was E.G. Cameron. Like him, most of the engineers on Grant's staff were Canadian. Carl W. WEST (1890–1963) was born in Ontario and educated at the University of Toronto. In 1919 he became assistant engineer on the Ship Canal and by 1925 he was senior assistant engineer. In that year he was put in charge of Sections 3 and 4 until 1932. He was acting superintendent for a time, then superintending engineer of the Ship Canal until 1947, when he was appointed director of canal services for the Department of Transport. In 1955 he became a member of the St Lawrence Seaway Authority.

Another Ontario native, Emmet Patrick MURPHY, was born in Ottawa in 1887 and graduated in civil engineering from Queen's. After extensive experience on several Canadian waterways he became senior assistant sectional engineer on Section 4 in 1921, later becoming engineer in charge of Section 8 in 1927. From 1930 to 1934 he was superintendent of operations for the southern half of the canal. Edward Preston JOHNSON, also born in Ottawa (1873), was a McGill graduate and had wide experience in railway and canal work before becoming engineer on Section 1 in 1919. In 1921 he was transferred to Sections 5, 6, and 7.

From Quebec came George KYDD, born in Montreal and yet another McGill graduate, who was engineer on Section 8, 1924–27. He had worked with Grant on the Trent as sectional engineer on the Couchiching lock, 1916–18. In 1927 he was transferred by the Department of Railways and Canals to supervise the Fort Churchill terminal of the Hudson Bay Railway.

Frederick Coburn JEWETT (1880–1951), from New Brunswick, took a degree in civil engineering at McGill and worked for private engineering firms until 1919, when he became engineer supervising Section 2 of the Ship Canal. In 1921 he took over Section 1 as well and administered both until 1930, when he was appointed acting superintendent of the northern section. After the inquiry into the Forestry Project, he was suspended in January 1931. Despite the cloud that hung over him, he later had a distinguished career during the Second World War with the Department of Transport, becoming a Commander of the British Empire in 1948.

Francis Stuart LAZIER (Section 3, 1919–25) was the lone American on Grant's engineering staff, born in Charlottesville, Virginia, but with a BSc from Queen's University in Kingston. He rose from instrumentman to sectional engineer on the Trent (1907–10), then in 1918 worked for the Hydro-Electric Power Commission in charge of a survey on the St Lawrence River. In 1919 he became engineer on Sections 3 and 4, and made the plans for the concreting plant but resigned in 1925 to work with T.A. Brown, a contractor based in Toronto, who was awarded the contract for the Ship Canal Gate Yard in 1928. In the fall of 1926 he was on the move again, starting a small steel foundry in Campbellford, on the Trent. In the following May he was working in Peterborough but later in that year was back on the Ship Canal site, employed by the contractor J.P. Porter, and by July 1929 he was acting as chief engineer for Peter Lyall & Sons.

Construction Sections and Contractors

Ultimately there were eight construction sections of the Welland Ship Canal (fig. 3.9). Section 1 extended from the breakwaters of the new Port Weller on Lake Ontario nearly 3 miles (4.8 km) south to the planned but never built Bridge 2. Section 2 was 4.5 miles (7.2 km) long. (In 1921 Sections 1 and 2 were combined.) Section 3 was a short 2 miles (3.2 km) in length but involved surmounting the Niagara Escarpment with the twinned flight locks (4–6) and the single Lock 7 – "a very expensive and arduous piece of work," wrote Grant to Dubuc (13 November 1929 [LAC, GR43, vol. 2183, file 1100.2]). Section 4 was also only 2 miles (3.2 km) long, consisting mainly of earth and rock cuts and the building of the substructures for Bridges 10, 11, and 12. Section 4A involved a small contract for certain portions of the work for Section 4 while Section 4B dealt with the problem of accommodating east-west watercourses. Section 5 lay between Allanburg and Port Robinson – the notorious Deep Cut, which had bedevilled the Welland's builders in the nineteenth century. It was 3.25 miles (5.2 km) in length. The existing channel was to be widened and deepened to 80 feet (24.4 m) with a width of 200 feet (61 m) at bottom. Section 6 extended 3¾ miles (5 km) from near Port Robinson south to Welland. Section 7 ran for 6 miles (9.65 km) on a relatively straight line south of Welland to the northern outskirts of Humberstone. The contractor would deepen and widen the Third Canal on its west side and erect the substructures for several bridges.

The exact conformation of Section 8 was decided upon only in 1922–23. It was 2 miles (3.2 km) long and included the towns of Port Colborne and Humberstone. A new cutting was to be excavated in earth and rock through the point formed by Ramey's Bend on the Third Canal, the Onondaga Escarpment, north of the site for the guard lock. The older channel would be used as a regulating weir (fig. 3.9).

SECTIONAL CONTRACTORS

1   Dominion Dredging (Port Weller Harbour, piers, Lock 1; bridges
1 and 2 substructures), 1913–17, 1919–20
J.P. Porter 1921–27 (combined with Section 2)
T.A. Brown (gate yard) 1928–30

2   Baldry, Yerburgh & Hutchinson (Locks 2 and 3, substructures
for Bridges 3, 4, and 5; a temporary bridge over the operating
canal for the Construction Railway), 1913–17, 1919–21
J.P. Porter, 1921–1927 (combined with Section 1)

3   O'Brien, Doheny, Quinlan & Robinson (flight locks, railway and
highway bridges), 1913–1917
Peter Lyall, 1922–1930
William Arrol (subcontractor: watertight embankment, concrete,
and some excavation on Section 4)

4   Peter Lyall, 1922–30 (earth and rock cuts and bridge
substructures)
G.L. Campbell and J.A. Grant (subcontractors for part of
the work)

4A   C.D. Maguire and N.K. Cameron 1914–1915 (a supply weir)

4B   J.P. Porter, 1926–31 (two culverts between the Third and the
Second Canals; a supply weir)

5   Canadian Dredging (widening and deepening the Deep Cut,
bridge substructure; filling the low land between the Second and
Third Canals with excavated material), 1913–17, 1921–26

6   Atlas Construction and E.O. Leahey (syphon culvert, earth
excavation, bridge substructure, raising and diverting a road;
removal of a stone aqueduct), 1925–32
J.P. Porter (subcontractor for most of the excavation)

7   Canadian Dredging, 1924–29

8   A.W. Robertson (excavation), 1924–29
     Sub-contractors:
     Northern Construction (dry earth, rock excavation, some
     concrete work)
     C.S Boone Dredging
     Killmer & Barber (breakwater cribs and superstructure)

Note: We have found no information regarding how many tenders
were received for the various sections, nor from which contractors. We
usually know only the names of the successful bidders – most of them
Canadian.

Construction Fatalities

What follows is the result of an ongoing project by local Niagara historians, including Arden Phair and the late Alex Ormston; at the time of this writing (2014–15), it is as yet incomplete. Readers will note what seem to be possible spelling errors which the researchers will be correcting in future publications.

Surname	Given Name(s)	City/Town/Village/ Municipality	Prov/State	Country	Year	Cause of Death	Age	Year
			Birthplace		Date of Birth		Date of Death	
Aiello	Carmine			Italy	1883c	Crushed; conveyor pulley	32	1915
Alder	Thomas	Earlestown		England	1879	Collapse Blaw-Knox form	46	1925
Anderson	George			Finland	1892	Crushed; shovel bucket	29	1921
Bagnall	Frederick	Birmingham		England	1908	Crushed by large rolling flat car	17	1926
Bayusz	Mihály	Rakamaz		Hungary	1892	Fall	36	1928
Bassett	Fernley	Wixenford, Plymstock		England	1905	Crushed; locom. crane	23	1929
Bassett	William	Blackdown, Mary Tavy, Tavistock		England	1885	Crushed; bridge ct wt, Bridge 21	43	1929
Benasho	Stana			Russia	1891c	Drowned; dumping car	23	1914
Benson	Henry	Homer	ON	Canada	1879	Fall	53	1932
Berardi	Francesco	Mangone	Calabria (regione)	Italy	1884	Drowned	46	1930
Bianco	Carlo	San Vito Chietino (comune)	Abruzzo (regione)	Italy	1898	Explosion	29	1928
Bisson	Achille	St-Cœur-de-Marie	QC	Canada	1897	Crushed and drowned by collapse of cofferdam	29	1927
Boccioletti	Luigi	Mombaroccio	Le Marches (regione)	Italy	1894	Collapse of crane and gate	34	1928

Surname	Given Name(s)	City/Town/Village/ Municipality	Prov/State	Country	Date of Birth Year	Cause of Death	Age	Date of Death Year
Bode	John			Hungary	1901	Smothered; slide of earth	27	1928
Boyle	Peter	Wigan		England	1898	Crushed under [rail]car	28	1927
Brady	Timothy			USA	1876	Run over by train	49	1925
Brennan	Samuel	Merritton	ON	Canada	1896	Chronic injuries from form collapse 13 yrs previous	38	1935
Burt	William	Guelph	ON	Canada	1877	Drowned	36	1914
Campbell	Ross	Humberstone	ON	Canada	1891	Crushed; steam shovel	34	1925
Carrig	Joseph	Kilrush		Ireland	1899c	Collapse of crane and gate	29	1928
Caseron	Attilio			Italy	1884	Struck by shovel	40	1924
Cherriere	Antoine	Hamilton	ON	Canada	1888	Drowned	34	1923
Chisholm	Alexander	Rear Long Point	NS	Canada	1897	Buried in sand	25	1922
Collini	Antonio	Silvi (comune)	Abruzzo (regione)	Italy	1912	Fall from lock wall	15	1927
Constantino	Stefano	Mutignano frazione of Pineto	Abruzzo (regione)	Italy	1895	Crushed; bank cave-in, Lock 3	30	1925
Corkum	Albert	Whitefield	NH	USA	1905	Fractured spine	25	1930
Crowe	Edwin	Port Elgin [now Saugeen Shores]	ON	Canada	1886	Crushed; stone	28	1915

De Biasi	Giovanni	Conegliano	Treviso	Italy	1880c	Electrocuted	44	1924
Dion	Léon	Sherbrooke?	QC	Canada	1895	Collapse of crane and gate	33	1928
Douglas	William	Charney Bassett, Wantage		England	1892	Caught between [railway] cars	31	1924
Dugan	Manus		PA	USA	1870	Fell in lock	53	1924
Dumoulin	Joseph	Grenville	QC	Canada	1897	Buried by slide of bank	31	1928
Dupalo	Stanko	Rujevac		Austria (now Croatia, though he is referred to as Serbian)	1885c	Fractured skull; boom	29	1914
Eliashevich	Estafy			Russia	1895c	Electrocuted; power wire	19	1915
Farris	Ginseppe	Nughedu [Nughedu San Nicolò?] (commune)	Sardinia (regione)	Italy	1891	Crushed; concrete bucket	24	1915
Fater	Janos	Pusztaszentlászló	Western Transdanubia (region)	Hungary	1904	Drowned	24	1929
Finnemore	Reginald	Stoke Newington, Hackney, London		England	1896	Drowned	22	1919
Fiore	Gineseppe			Canada	1896c	Head crushed; dump car	18	1914
Foster	Joseph	North Dorchester [Middlesex?] [source – Baptism]	ON	Canada	1873 [source – Baptism]	Fall from trestle	42	1916
Fratangelo	Luigi	Castellino del Biferno	Molise (regione)	Italy	1879	Fall	49	1928

Surname	Given Name(s)	Birthplace City/Town/Village/ Municipality	Prov/State	Country	Date of Birth Year	Cause of Death	Age	Date of Death Year
Fraracci	Rocco	Castropignano	Molise (regione)	Italy	1885	Fall from trestle	42	1928
Gardner	Richard	Selkirk	MB	Canada	1896	Crushed by train	19	1916
Gordon	William		ON	Canada	1871	Struck by construction train	53	1924
Hansler	Sheldon	North Pelham	ON	Canada	1902	Electrocuted	28	1930
Harkness	Andrew	Belfast		[Northern] Ireland	1889	Shock; fell into cold water	38	1928
Hawthorne	John	Collingwood	ON	Canada	1879	Struck by timber	54	1932
Hines	Elmer	Dunnville	ON	Canada	1908	Crushed; Bridge 14	21	1930
Horton	James		ON	Canada	1878	Crushed; falling timber	47	1926
Hutchison	William			Ireland	1880	Fell over lock wall	44	1924
Iannizzi	Rocco	Mammola	Calabria (regione)	Italy	1892	Crushed by train	33	1925
Jusko	Stefan	Raslavice	Prešov (region)	Austria	1898	Electrocuted	28	1926
Kady	Karoly	Ugod		Hungary	1890	Crushed by falling timber	38	1928
Kellett	Benjamin	Wyke or Farnley		England	1854	Bank slipped; fell	69	1924
Kennedy	David	Dunbarton		Scotland	1885	Struck by falling ice	39	1924
Koner	Mike			Austria	1869c	Buried by slide of bank	59	1928
Kopinak	Steve	MacKenzie Twp. 34	SK	Canada	1910	Smothered; gravel	18	1928

Surname	First name	Place	Region	Country	Year	Cause	Age	Year
Koran	Janos			Hungary	1891	Fall	35	1927
Kruzle	John			Italy	1899c	Drowned	26	1925
Kuchenbecker	Luther	Duluth	MN	USA	1895	Struck by snapped cable on dredge	37	1932
La Croix	Wilfred	Calumet	QC	Canada	1902	Crushed; steel form	21	1924
Larocque	Gorman	Calumet	QC	Canada	1899	Crushed; steel form	25	1924
Lengjel	Daniel			Yugoslavia	1895	Head crushed by timber	34	1929
Lethbridge	Robert	Port Hope	ON	Canada	1869	Crushed and drowned by collapse of cofferdam	57	1927
Lindsay	Thomas	Windsor Junction	NS	Canada	1865	Blasting; struck by clay	59	1924
Lynch	Charles				1890	Crushed by train	38	1928
Lynch	Elzéar	Rigaud	QC	Canada	1866	Collapse Blaw-Knox form	58	1925
Lynch	Lionel	Chute-à-Blondeau	ON	Canada	1905	Collapse Blaw-Knox form	20	1925
Macallister	Richard	Calcutta (now Kolkata)	Bengal	India	1870	Drowned	60	1930
MacDonald	David	Toronto	ON	Canada	1899	Drowned	26	1920
MacDonald	Donald			Scotland	1898c	Dynamite explosion	26	1925
Mahon	Ira	North Wakefield	QC	Canada	1879	Crushed by crane boom	48	1927
Martinelli	Giuseppe			Italy	1890c	Drowned	36	1926
Mastericola	Cornelio			Italy	1895c	Crushed; fall from train	20	1915
Mattei	Guiseppe	Civitella Roveto	Abruzzo (regione)	Italy	1895	Fall	33	1928
McArthur	James			Ireland	1866	Collapse of crane and gate	62	1928

| Surname | Given Name(s) | Birthplace | | | Date of Birth | Cause of Death | Age | Date of Death |
		City/Town/Village/ Municipality	Prov/State	Country	Year			Year
McArthur	James	Greenock		Scotland	1892	Collapse of crane and gate	36	1928
McCoy	James	Lynedoch	ON	Canada	1890	Struck by chain blocks; fall	38	1928
McDonald	Daniel	Stayner(?)	ON(?)	Canada	1873	Drowned	52	1926
McInnis	Charles	Souris	PEI	Canada	1903	Struck by falling pole	24	1928
McKinley	Archibald	Belfast		Ireland	1885	Electrocuted	44	1929
McMullen	Samuel			Scotland [not Ireland?]	1907	Collapse of crane and gate	21	1928
Monsson	Otto			Sweden	1886c	Struck by falling ice	38	1924
Montemurro	Antonio	Mangone	Calabria (regione)	Italy	1892	Electrocuted	22	1915
Moretti	Giovanni	Rocca San Giovanni	Abruzzo (regione)	Italy	1870–71c	Crushed; locomotive	43 (41 on Passgr Rec.)	1914
Morin	Edward		QC	Canada	1904c	Caught in gears on dredge	24	1928
Moronk	Ivan			Yugoslavia	1899	Struck by crow bar	24	1924
Murray	Murdo	Stornoway	(Isle of Lewis, Outer Hebrides)	Scotland	1901	Fall from derrick chain	23	1925
Nealis	Henry	Royal Road	NB	Canada	1891	Crushed and drowned by collapse of cofferdam	36	1927

NICOlOZZO	Nicola	Petrona	Calabria (regione)	Italy	1895c	Fell beneath train	20	1915
Nottingham	Fergus	Utica(?)	ON? (or QC?)	Canada	1895	Drowned	33	1929
Onyschuk	Michaël	Torskie		Ukraine	1896	Struck by falling tree	35	1932
Ostarijas	Josip	Klenovnik	Varaždin	Yugoslavia	1897c	Crushed; dump car	25	1925
Overholt	Chester		ON	Canada	1876	Collapse of crane and gate	51	1928
Pakalo	Osip			Russia	1890c	Crushed; dump car	24	1914
Paolozzi	Folco	Colle San Magno	Lazio (regione)	Italy	1883	Crushed; truck	46	1929
Patterson	John	Diocese of Clones		Ireland	1859c	Crushed; dump car	55	1914
Payne	Hudson	Goulbourn	ON	Canada	1870c	Crushed by train	45	1915
Pearce	Amos	Twp. of Grantham	ON	Canada	1892	Crushed; train	33	1926
Penteskul	Alexander		Bukowina (region)	Austria	1881c	Struck by dragline bucket	45	1926
Phillip	Charles			Hungary	1906c	Struck by train	19	1925
Pirro	Charles	Guglionesi(?)	Molise(?) (regione)	Italy	1898	Killed by drill	28	1926
Plantedi	Franceico	Mangone	Calabria (regione)	Italy	1883	Drowned	45	1927
Pollard	Thomas		NL	Canada	1895	Fall from Bridge 5	34	1929
Price	Benjamin	South Shields(?)	Durham	England	1877	Fall from [rail]car on trestle	43	1919
Procopovich	Wasily			Russia	1887	Drowned	28	1916
Radford	David			England	1880	Shafting pulley	49	1930

Surname	Given Name(s)	Birthplace			Date of Birth	Cause of Death	Date of Death	
		City/Town/Village/Municipality	Prov/State	Country	Year		Age	Year
Rantucci	Luigi	Ovindoli	Abruzzo (regione)	Italy	1865	Fall from trestle	57	1922
Robinson	George		Surrey	England	1893	Crushed; train	21	1914
Romkey	Leo	West Dublin	NS	Canada	1898	Drowned	29	1927
Ryan	Andrew	Nethergate, Dundee		Scotland	1883	Fall	47	1930
Saunders	James	Northwich		England	1890	Drowned	36	1927
Sawchuk	James			Ukraine	1906	Tractor overturned	22	1928
Seaman	John	Holbeach		England	1867	Heat prostration	54	1921
Sharpe	Robert		ON	Canada	1895	Fall from lock wall	25	1921
Simmons	John	Point Anne	ON	Canada	1876	Struck by cable	51	1928
Smalko	Theodore			Ukraine	1890c	Collapse of crane and gate	38	1928
Smith	Edward	Power Glen	ON	Canada	1902	Electrocuted	28	1930
Stackew	George			Austria	1883c	Crushed; dump car	x40	1923
Stahl	Joseph	Peoria (or St Joseph?)	IL (or MO?)	USA	1863 (or 1864?)	Fall into lock	64	1929
Stanbury	William	Palmerston	ON	Canada	1906	Drowned	22	1929
Swan	John	Arbroath		Scotland	1905	Drowned	21	1926
Szolonyik	Peter	Buj		Hungary	1901	Blow from bucket	27	1928

Surname	Given name	Place	Prov./region	Country	Year	Cause	Age	Year
	William			Russia	1890	Collapse of crane and gate	37	1928
Thibeau	William	River Bourgeois	NS	Canada	1890	Fall from tower to floor of locks	32	1922
Thomson	Robert	Low Glengannon, Larkhall.		Scotland	1908	Fall into lock	19	1928
Tice	Lloyd		ON	Canada	1904	Electrocuted	25	1930
Wachowicz	Marcin	(maybe Zaperze [Zabrze?])		Poland	1901	Struck by train	26	1927
Wacpnovick	Michael			Poland	1894c	Drowned	26	1920
Watt	Alvin	Haliburton	ON	Canada	1907	Drowned	18	1926
Watt	Harry	Haliburton	ON	Canada	1911	Drowned	21	1932
West	James				1872c	Crushed; train	43	1915
Whitwell	Lorne	Stoney Creek	ON	Canada	1895	Explosion	32	1928
Willard	A.					Drowned	n/a	1915
Wilson	Alexander	Grangemouth		Scotland	1894	Collapse of crane & gate	34	1928
Wilson	Arthur	Sheffield		England	1886c	Crushed; locomotive	28	1914
Wodilla	Janos	Výborná	Prešov (region)	Hungary [north Slovakia] aka Austria on some documents back then	1881	Struck by train	46	1926
Wylde	Elmer	Welland	ON	Canada	1906	Crushed; locomotive	20	1927

The Welland By-Pass

Thanks to the construction of the St Lawrence Seaway (completed in 1959), tonnage on the Welland Ship Canal increased radically, aided by the installation of new instruments and machinery at lockside. The use of closed-circuit television cameras, for example, expedited the control and management of vessels.[1]

Despite these changes and the deepening to Seaway size, however, even the improved Welland Ship Canal presented a partial bottleneck to "the navigation." Transit through the southern stretch of canal between Port Robinson and Port Colborne was hampered by six bridges, one of which was a railway swing crossing with a dangerous central pier which was struck by ships as many as six times in one navigation season. The other spans included the notorious vertical lift Bridge 13 in the heart of Welland and other lifts at Lincoln Street (14) and Forks Road (18). Ship captains complained about these hazards as well as the curving nature of the canal at Welland and its insufficient width. Consequently, a ship could take as long as forty-six hours to traverse the waterway. As many as fifty vessels could be seen anchored off Ports Weller or Colborne, awaiting entrance to the waterway. Some would wait for days.[2] Meanwhile the city of Welland had developed on both sides of the channel, which meant that thousands of people in cars and buses or as pedestrians had to cross the canal every day and were often delayed by the raising of bridges to allow for the increasing frequency of ship transits (fig. 10.6).

Back in Grant's day, the twinning of Locks 1, 2, 3, 7, and 8 had been considered (fig. 5.5). This concept, renewed in 1963, envisaged maintaining the same route for the waterway, yet faced the prospect of conflict with adjacent homes, farms, industries, and businesses. As well, much excavation and infilling would be needed. Because these new locks would presumably be duplicates of the existing ones, however, they would allow only more, not bigger, ships through. A completely new canal was also a consideration. A line from the mouth of Twenty Mile Creek on Lake Ontario to Willow Bay on Lake Erie, reminiscent

App. IV.1   Welland, ca. 1970, showing the route of the By-Pass, the Ship Canal, and the Welland River (Chippawa Creek). The new syphon culvert on the By-Pass is at the upper right.

of suggestions sixty years before, was under review. Two completely new harbours, however, would have to have been built and the whole effort would have been very costly. Finally, the widening or reconstruction of the present channel on the same route, with as few as four "superlocks," was on the table. In fact, to build this "Fifth Welland Canal," some land was expropriated to the east of the channel, north of the Niagara Escarpment, in 1966.

App. IV.2   South of Port Robinson, ca. 1970. Excavator working at the area of the future syphon culvert on the By-Pass.

The eventual solution to the difficulties at Welland was construction of a "by-pass" channel to the east of the city (fig. App. IV.1). Although this would not change the route north of Thorold, the engineers hoped that it would reduce transit time on the southern section by nearly an hour, improve ships' safety, and remove a daily irritant to Welland residents.

But where to build it? Three possibilities emerged. One, very close to the eastern suburbs of Welland, would have involved considerable expropriation and disruption to the life of the community. Another, much farther to the east, would have involved a direct line from Port Robinson south to Lake Erie. Because of its greater length, of course, this route would have been expensive to build, requiring a great deal of rock excavation and a new lock and harbour on the lake. Ultimately, the engineers opted for compromise, a line running from just south of Port Robinson, near Chippawa Creek, due south and then curving slightly to the west to meet the operating canal north of Lock 8

App. IV.3   Construction of the Welland By-Pass, ca. 1970, looking south, showing the new harbour and a temporary "plug" retained for railways.

at Port Colborne. Construction of this By-Pass would be less expensive and less disruptive and would eliminate the Welland bottleneck.

Between 1967 and 1973, therefore, a new channel 8.5 miles (13.6 km) long was excavated between Port Robinson and Port Colborne, with a bottom width of 350 feet (106.67 m) and a depth of 30 feet (9.14 m). In 1968–69 expropriation involved the removal of businesses such as a gasoline station and grocery store and two farms, as well as 180 private homes; 325 property owners had to be compensated.[3] As was traditional, the route was divided into sections, but the perennial challenge of maintaining east-west land traffic routes during construction required that "plugs" or dikes be left on the channel for these arteries until shortly before the water was admitted (fig. App. IV.3).

Beginning in 1967 huge machinery thundered in and out of the deepening prism east of Welland. Scrapers drawn by large tractors and massive draglines chewed away at the earth while fifty-ton trucks removed the spoil (fig. App. IV.2). The latter process created great berms on either side of the channel. In simple monetary terms, the cost of the By-Pass – $188,300,000 (over one billion in 2015 dollars) – dwarfed that of the Ship Canal. During the peak of construction, four thousand labourers were employed on the new waterway.[4]

Several of the challenges which contractors and engineers now encountered were identical to those half a century earlier. When, south of the guard gate at Thorold, 3.9 feet (1.2 m) of the reach was dredged, the work threatened to make the canal water turbid. Just as in the 1920s, local paper companies, which used unfiltered canal water in their processes, were nervous, as were municipalities, who feared pollution of domestic water supplies. Accordingly, suction dredges were used to remove carefully the silt which might have caused problems. Accumulations of silt were also found at Port Weller harbour north of Lock 1. These, too, had to be removed by dredging. Because underwater drilling and blasting were also necessary for the deepened channel 4.2 miles (6.8 km) from north of Lock 8 to Lake Erie, precautions had to be taken to prevent damage to local homes and businesses, as well as to a section of the Third Canal wall which formed part of the Ship Canal at Port Colborne.

Equipment and machinery were larger and more powerful now but, with some exceptions, resembled that of the Ship Canal construction. Notable was the employment of an underwater television camera provided by the National Research Council of Canada. At Port Colborne a diver descended to inspect timber cribs, taking this camera with him, and directed images to the engineers on land.

The Ship Canal engineers' response to the challenge of Chippawa Creek was repeated. The river was taken under the By-Pass by a new syphon culvert south of Port Robinson. Its four reinforced concrete tubes are 638 feet (194.5 m) long. When the culvert was completed in 1971, the river was once again diverted into a new bed and the old one filled in. Lyons Creek, which crosses the canal between Welland and Port Colborne, was also rerouted in several places. At one site, a pumping station was installed to take its waters under the canal. Because the huge ships that now plied the Welland could damage the banks, stone protection was laid down 8 feet (2.4 m) below and 3 feet (0.9 m) above the water line.

A large reinforced concrete dock, 1,000 feet (304.8 m) long, was constructed on the reach between the two tunnels to serve Welland's industries. Within the city itself, six bridges ceased to function: 7, 8, and 9 were moved in 1973; 13, 14, 15, 16, 17, and 18 were abandoned by the Seaway Authority and the railway companies. At the especially problematic Bridge 13, the Main Street lift span was fixed in the down position and is now considered a historic monument and a symbol of Welland. This stretch of the canal is used for recreational purposes.

Obviously, this project would involve the relocation of long-established roads and railway lines. Traditionally, tunnels under the canal and, more frequently, bridges over the waterway were built. Originally a vertical lift bridge was envisioned for the Townline Road crossing of the By-Pass south of Thorold but, as had happened in the past, the first plans, upon consideration, were altered. Ultimately no bridges would cross this new channel.[5]

Instead, three huge tunnels would direct land traffic under the By-Pass. At Thorold an extension of Highway 406 is taken under the new canal in two separate tubes each 2,396.85 feet (730.6 m) long, constructed after the new waterway was built and in operation (fig. App. IV.4). Near Welland, the East Main Street Tunnel for highway traffic (1,054.29 feet [321.3 m] long) was built in the "cut and cover" method just as in the 1880s the Grand Trunk Railway tunnel had been constructed. A cut or trench for the highway was excavated, then roofed over and covered with earth, over top of which the new canal was constructed.

To the south of Welland, the Townline Road-Rail tunnel (1,071.83 feet [326.7 m] long) was also built in the "cut-and-cover" method. It takes three sets of railway tracks as well as Highway 58A under the By-Pass. Several rail lines were rerouted to pass through this tunnel. In fact, 100 miles (160.9 km) of new railway line were built along with new freight depots and a new station. For these tunnels, altogether 50 miles (80.5 km) of roads were relocated, and telephone, sewer, gas, and hydro conduits had to be laid down. As well, Ontario Hydro constructed eight high transmission towers to take its cables across the By-Pass.[6]

These tunnels were part of a large scheme of tunnel building which was never fully accomplished. Back in the heady 1950s and '60s, when it seemed that canal traffic would continue to increase steadily, and so would surface traffic, the federal Department of Transport and the Ontario Ministry of Highways, to say nothing of the communities affected, were greatly concerned with the problems that were becoming unbearable at various locations. For St Catharines, the situation

App. IV.4   South of Thorold, ca. 1970. The Highway 58 tunnel, twin tubes replacing two bridges, was constructed over three winters, when the canal was dewatered.

at Bridge 4 (the Homer bridge) was the most critical (fig. App. IV.5) and in December 1954 the St Catharines and District Chamber of Commerce declared its intention of continuing to bring the matter to the attention of the Department of Transport. By 1955 Transport was making plans for both tunnels and high-level bridges at the most congested points. One tunnel would be at Carlton Street or Queenston Street. There were also two possible sites for a high-level bridge.

By May 1958 the provincial Ministry of Highways announced that it would spend $100 million (over $800 million in 2015 dollars), to include four high-level bridges, three of which were to cross at Welland. The fourth was to be at Bridge 4 Queenston Street (Homer). The latter, known as the Garden City or Homer Skyway, was opened to traffic

App. IV.5   Homer (near St Catharines), ca. 1950. Backed-up vehicles begin to move again after a twenty-minute wait while Bridge 4 was up for the passage of a ship. The bridge continues in operation today, but the Garden City Skyway now stands to the north (right) of the older structure.

in 1963 but was the only one built. In the same year an arrangement was made between the Seaway, which by then controlled the Welland, and the Ontario Ministry of Highways for cost-sharing of a number of tunnels and bridges, with the Seaway accepting responsibility for a two-lane tunnel in the Lock 1/Lock 2 area. By 1964 the precise lo- cation of that tunnel had become a subject of debate, with Linwell Road, the site of the "bridge that never was" and Glendale Avenue (Bridge 5) suggested as well as Carlton Street (Bridge 3). Detailed engineering plans were drawn up, and by 5 May 1964 the Seaway and the Ontario Ministry of Highways announced that they had hammered out an agreement in principle to construct a number of crossings, including the Carlton Street tunnel. In mid-summer 1965 the word from the Seaway was that the tunnel would not be finished until late 1968. However, although the Ministry of Highways sent an invoice to the Seaway for almost $750,000 and by 1969 $954,555 had been spent,[7] by late 1970 the Carlton Street tunnel was no longer under consideration – the tunnel that never was.

Associations, Commissions, Committees, and Treaties Affecting the Welland Canals

ASSOCIATIONS CONCERNED WITH THE GREAT LAKES SYSTEM (WITH DATE OF FORMATION)

1894 Deep Waterways Association (Canada)
1895 Deep Waterways Association (US)
1895 International Deep Waterways Association
1910 Lakes-to-the-Gulf Deep Waterways Association
1921 Great Lakes–Tidewater Association

COMMISSIONS AND COMMITTEES

The route, function, and usefulness of the Welland Canal have been the subject of study and debate for nearly two hundred years. Here we list those Canadian and American committees and commissions that studied the North American internal waterway system, including the role of the Welland.

1821 Select Committee on Internal Resources (Upper Canada)
1823 Committee on the Improvement of the Internal Navigation of the Province of Upper Canada
1826 Select Committee of the Upper Canada Legislature
1845 Commission of Enquiry
1870 Royal Commission on Inland Navigation
1872 Special Committee on the Enlargement and Route of the Welland Canal
1879 Commission of Enquiry
1895 Deep Waterways Commission (USA)
1896 Deep Waterways Commission (Canada)
1909 International Joint Commission
1920 Great Lakes Tidewater Commission

1924   St Lawrence Waterway Commission
1926   Interdepartmental Committee on the St Lawrence Waterway (US)
1954   Welland Canal Commission

INTERNATIONAL TREATIES AFFECTING THE WELLAND SHIP CANAL

1862   Commission on the Defence of Canada
1909   Treaty Relating to Boundary Waters
1921   St Lawrence Deep Waterway Treaty
1941   Agreement in Relation to the Utilization of the Water in the Great Lakes–St Lawrence Basin

Martyrs of Progress (Poem)

To the Workers Who Met Death on Canal Construction

It was inspiring, grand, impressive.
An event for the great to behold,
When thousands on thousands witnessed
The leviathan entrance unfold.

Long ere the approach of the hour,
From areas distant and near,
Came eager, expectant people,
To gaze from the bank, tier on tier.

The foremost voice of our country,
Through receptive air channels hurled,
Cried forth the great shipway's importance
To an audience girdling the world.

About what were some of us thinking –
We who stood on the grassy banks –
As scintillant invocations
Inspired the close-serried ranks?

We were loved ones, friends and companions
Of men crushed, or hurled, to their doom,
By the sudden snap of a tackle ...
Collapse of a defective boom –

We stood on the sward and remembered ...
Yes, we heard suave sentences flow.
But we knew – despite the orations –
To whom highest tribute should go.

There were those of the people present ...
Remembering ... stifled a sob
For the hundred and more of workers
Who went to their death "on the job."

The author was "C.A.D.T.," Clarence Arthur Dowling Thompson.
(*St Catharines Standard*, 5 August 1932, 4)

APPENDIX VII

Historiographical Essay

Publication details, when not given here, are in the Bibliography.

Little has been written on the construction of the Welland Ship (the Fourth) Canal. The only scholarly work related to this theme is John N. Jackson's *The Welland Canals and Their Communities: Engineering, Industrial, and Urban Transformation*, which has a valid, well-supported argument but contains serious weaknesses of expression and presentation. Dr Taylor reviewed this title online at H-Urban, December 1997. Although not on the construction of the original Ship Canal, Dr Jackson's *Welland and the Welland Canal: The Welland By-Pass* is useful for the subject of the title. Reliable but somewhat outdated is *The Welland Canals. A Comprehensive Guide* (1982) by Dr Jackson and Fred Addis.

A primary source for students of the technological aspects of the Ship Canal's construction is P.J. Cowan's *The Welland Ship Canal between Lake Ontario and Lake Erie 1913–1932*, not an academic work but essential to an understanding of the problems that engineers and contractors encountered. Basically a summary of Cowan's long study is "The Welland Canal" by George W. Yates in the *Canadian Geographical Journal* (1931). At the time he wrote this, he was assistant deputy minister in the Department of Railways and Canals. Another contemporary account is that of one of the canal's sectional engineers, E.P. Johnson, whose article "Canal Engineering Yesterday and Today" (1926) is limited in scope but useful for the view from "on the ground." In *The Welland Canals: Proceedings of the First Annual Niagara Peninsula History Conference* (1979), Charles H. Atkinson discusses "Aspects of Engineering of the Welland Canals," including a brief discussion of the Ship Canal's construction. Of related interest, from a nineteenth-century engineer's viewpoint, is T.C. Keefer's "The Canals of Canada," in *Transactions of the Royal Society of Canada*, Sec. III (1893), 25–30. The first stage of the Ship Canal's construction is covered by John Weller's granddaughter, Madelein Muntz, in her *John Laing Weller: The Man Who Does Things*.

Norman R. Ball's *Mind, Heart and Vision: Professional Engineering in Canada 1887–1987* offers some insight into the training and careers of Canadians supervising the construction of the waterway, as does J. Rodney Millard's *The Master Spirit of the Age: Canadian Engineers and the Politics of Professionalism 1887–1927* but with only peripheral reference to the Welland's construction.

The Ship Canal is briefly discussed in John P. Heisler's *The Canals of Canada* and in Robert F. Legget's *Canals of Canada*. Both these studies are reliable on the general history and influence of all four Welland Canals but offer little on construction of the Ship Canal. We consulted several MA theses such as that of Robert Stanley Taylor, "The Historical Development of the Four Welland Canals 1824–1933" (University of Western Ontario, 1950), but these provide no special insight into the building of the modern waterway.

Several popular works on the canals have been written, some originating in the Niagara area, such as *The Welland Canal: A History* by DeWitt Carter, or David M. Michener's *The Canals at Welland*, but are of limited interest for the construction era. Louis Blake Duff's *The Welland Ship Canal*, published in 1930, gives a sense of the national excitement surrounding the new channel.

Few works describe the working and living conditions of the labourers on the Ship Canal's construction, but some insight into their lives can be gained from Craig Heron's *The Workers' Revolt in Canada 1917–1925*, John Potestio and Antonio Pucci's *The Italian Immigrant Experience*, and Donald Avery's *Dangerous Foreigners*. On the other hand, much has been written on the nineteenth-century canal labourers elsewhere in North America. The Welland's navvies are part of the story each of these titles recounts. Useful with regard to the Second Welland Canal is Ruth Elizabeth Bleasdale's MA thesis, "Irish Labourers on the Cornwall, Welland and Williamsburg Canals in the 1840s," as is Peter Way's *Common Labour: Workers and the Digging of North American Canals 1780–1860*. A popular history is Fern Sayles's *Welland Workers Make History*. Michael Power and Paul Hutchinson illuminated a little-known incident in the Second Canal's labour history with *Goaded to Madness: The Battle of Slabtown* (St Catharines: Slabtown Press, 1999). Another popular work is J. Lawrence Runnalls's *The Irish on the Welland Canal* (St Catharines, 1973). For purposes of comparison, we could recommend Robert Passfield's *Military Paternalism, Labour and the Rideau Canal Project*, reviewed by Dr Taylor in *Ontario History* 107, no. 2 (Autumn 2014): 228–9. Obviously, these titles have little to do with the building of the twentieth-century Welland Canal but they offer an insight into how little had changed in working conditions over one hundred years.

Of related interest, applying mainly to the Third Canal while the Ship Canal was under construction, is William A. Smy's *Guarding Niagara: The Welland Canal Force 1914–1918*. An excellent book of photographs, both historic and contemporary, with maps and plans relating to the nineteenth-century canals has been published by Roger Bradshaw, *The Historic Welland Canals* (San Francisco: Blurb, 2011). Our own *The Welland Canals Corridor. Then and Now* contrasts the Ship Canal landscape with that of previous centuries (St Catharines: Looking Back Press, 2004, with photography by Thies Bogner).

Dr Styran edited a new edition of Hugh F.G. Aitken's *The Welland Canal Company: A Study in Canadian Enterprise* (St Catharines: Canadian Canal Society, 1997). As the title suggests, this has nothing to do with the Ship Canal but is an invaluable study of the financing of the First Canal. We both compiled *The "Great Swivel Link": Canada's Welland Canals*, a collection of documents for The Champlain Society (2001) that covers all four Welland Canals with necessary but brief references to construction matters. Our *This Great National Object: Building the Nineteenth-Century Welland Canals* may be useful for readers who want to contrast construction techniques and working conditions over a century.

Milestones in the Construction of the Welland Ship Canal, 1913–1932

30 August 1913: contract let for Section 1

4 October 1913: contract for Section 3

22 December 1913: contract for Section 5

31 December 1913: contract for Section 2

2 October 1914: contract for Section 4A

27 November 1916: decision taken to suspend construction for the duration of the Great War, effective at the end of the 1916 season
January 1919: contracts re-let to the original contractors after the wartime suspension

27 February 1924: contract for Section 8

30 December 1924: contract for Section 7

12 October 1926: contract for Section 6

28 July 1926: contract for Section 4B

22 November 1930: first vessel through, draft of 18 feet (5.48 m)

6 August 1932: official opening: ships with a draft of 21 feet (6.4 m)
1933: draft of ships increased to 23 feet 6 in. (7 m); in 1935 to 25 feet (7.6 m)

1954: for the St Lawrence Seaway, deepened to 27 feet (8.22 m)

GLOSSARY

ABUTMENT: a solid pier of stone or timber designed to support bridges or other similar works.

APPROACH WALLS: walls of considerable length leading up to locks, designed to protect locks and gates by allowing vessels to pull up alongside well before the lock itself.

APRON: the platform or sill at the entrance to a lock.

AQUEDUCT: a bridge with a trough filled with water to allow ships on a canal to cross over a valley or river.

BASCULE BRIDGE: a crossing with a counterweight that constantly balances a single span, which can consist of one or two parts or leaves; a drawbridge.

BASIN: the enclosed part of a dock where ships are moored to load, discharge, or be repaired.

BERM: an earthen embankment forming the side of a canal channel.

BOLLARD: a low, thick post of iron or concrete, set on the berm along a canal, to which mooring lines are secured when docking a vessel. Also used for controlling a rope or cable that is running.

BOOM (on a lock): see GATE FENDER

BREAKWATER: a structure for protecting a harbour from the force of waves.

BREAST WALL: a section of wall leading up to the gates of a lock.

BURGEE: a signal or identifying flag on a ship.

CEMENT: a fine powder of limestone and clay.

CHAMBER: see LOCK

COFFERDAM: a temporary enclosing dam built in the water and pumped dry to protect labourers while some work, such as the construction of pier foundations, is in progress.

CONCRETE: a mixture of cement, sand, aggregate, and water that hardens to a strong consistency over time.

CONDUIT WELL: a vertical tube in a lock wall extending from the filling culvert to the surface.

CRANE: a machine for lifting heavy weights, consisting of a vertical post bearing a horizontal projecting arm on which the hoisting tackle is fixed.

CRIB: a wooden or concrete frame upon which to build a wall or pier.

CULVERT: any artificial covered channel for the passage of water under a road, canal, or embankment.

DAM: a barrier of earth, wood, stone, or concrete for holding back or confining water.

DERRICK: a lifting device consisting of a post at the bottom of which is attached an arm attached by a cable to the top of the post. Like a crane, it can move freely in every direction.

DONKEY ENGINE: a locomotive for switching rolling stock in a railroad yard.

DRAFT/DRAUGHT: the depth of water that a ship needs for floating, or the depth to which a vessel is immersed when bearing a given load.

DRAGLINE: a lifting system that consists of a large bucket suspended from a boom and manoeuvred by ropes or chains to scoop up soil.

DRY DOCK: a basin or chamber with watertight gates for controlling the water level, used in the construction or repair of boats.

FLUME: a narrow channel or pipe to carry water from a canal, river, or raceway to drive a mill wheel.

GATE CHAMBER: the recess in the lock wall into which a gate may swing so that it is flush with the wall when fully opened. See also HOLLOW QUOIN

GATE FENDER: a steel wire rope with a diameter of 3.5 in (9 cm) on an 82-foot (25 m) steel boom, extending horizontally across the lock chamber at coping level to prevent the accidental ramming of a gate by a ship.

GATES: movable barriers swinging on hinges for closing the passage into a lock.

GATE YARD: a canal maintenance yard for building or repairing gates or other lock mechanisms, as at Port Weller.

GUARD GATE: a safety gate pointed towards the flow of water, to prevent flooding in case of accident or to stop the flow of water when repairs are needed. A guard gate was placed above Thorold at the beginning of the Summit Level on the Second, Third, and Fourth Canals as a safety gate to prevent flooding in the system below it.

GUARD LOCK: Lock 8 at Port Colborne that serves mainly as a guard against fluctuations in the level of Lake Erie.

HARBOUR: a sheltered area for a ship, either natural or man-made.

HARDPAN: a layer of hard, unbroken clay, usually found underneath the uppermost layer of topsoil.

HEAD GATES: the upstream gates of a canal lock.

HEADRACE: see FLUME

HOIST: a load-lifting device that uses a drum or lift-wheel around which is wound a rope or chain.

HOLLOW QUOIN: the vertical recess in the lock wall into which the end of the gate leaf fits.

INSTRUMENTMAN: on canal surveys, assisted the surveyors with research and measurement while supervising and leading the crew.

INTAKE: the point at which water is taken into a pipe or channel.

JACKKNIFE BRIDGE: a bascule bridge.

LAKER: a ship intended primarily to serve on the Great Lakes.

LEAF: a division or part of a pair of lock gates or bridge spans. See also GATES

LEVEL: see REACH

LIFT: the distance which a ship is raised from one reach to another by means of a lock.

LIGHTERING: unloading all or part of a ship's cargo to reduce its draft.

LIGHTHOUSE: a tower containing a light for guiding navigators by night or during inclement weather, erected at the entrance to a port or at a point of danger.

LOCK: an enclosure with gates at each end used in raising or lowering ships as they pass from one water level to another.

LOCKMASTER/LOCKTENDER: canal worker responsible for locking boats into a canal, opening and closing gates, and recording ship passages.

LOWER GATES: the downstream gates of a lock.

MITRE: the angle of a pair of closed lock gates, pointing towards the upper water level.

MITRE SILL: wood or stone structure along the bottom ledge at each end of a lock, shaped in a "V," pointing upstream, upon which the lock gates close.

MONOLITH: any massive structure such as a concrete lock wall.

MOORING PASSAGE: a tunnel along the interior of each lock wall connected by branch tunnels to mooring posts set into the lock wall

PIER: a structure extending from land into a canal, acting as a breakwater to provide a safe point of entry for vessels approaching the canal system. Also, any solid support for the ends of adjacent spans in a bridge.

PILINGS: heavy pointed timbers or steel beams forced into the earth to form a foundation for a wharf or building.

PINTLE: the post on which a lock gate swings.

PIVOT POST: see PINTLE

PLINTH: the support for a gate pintle.

POND: a basin of water built up behind a regulating weir.

PRISM: the cross-section of a canal channel; also used to refer to the channel itself.

QUAY: landing stage built alongside a basin or harbour for loading and unloading cargo.

QUOIN: see GATE CHAMBER or HOLLOW QUOIN

REACH: the level expanse of water between locks.

REGULATING WEIR: a dam-like structure which maintains a correct level of water in a pond and/or reach above a lock.

RODMAN: on canal surveys, transports and sets up the canal surveyors' equipment and instruments while preparing a site for surveying (i.e., laid out the stakes).

SAFETY WEIR: a weir used in conjunction with a guard gate to regulate canal water in the event of an accident.

SALTY: an ocean-going vessel, as opposed to a "laker."

SHEET PILING: walls made of steel or wood that are driven into the ground to retain earth or prevent seepage.

SILL: see MITRE SILL

SLAB: protection on the side banks of a canal.

SPEEDER: a track maintenance car, sometimes powered by a crew, more recently by a small engine.

SPILLWAY: a passageway in or around a dam to release the water in a reservoir.

SPOIL: excavated material.

STONEY SLUICES: to control water flow out of a wier, a vertical gate which moves on rollers, invented by the Irish engineer Francis Goold Morony Stoney (1837–1897).

STOP LOGS or GATES: gates placed at intervals along a waterway and usually kept open but which can be shut when required to isolate a stretch of water containing a breach of the walls, or when repairs of any kind are necessary. Originally a stack of logs kept beside a canal to form a gate or dam.

SUMMIT LEVEL: the highest level in a canal system from which no further lifts are necessary.

SURETIES: a person or persons acting as guarantors for fulfillment of a contract.

TAINTOR (OR TAINTER) VALVES: floodgates used to control water flow into a lock, invented by the American engineer Jeremiah Burnham Tainter (1836–1920). A side view of such a gate looks like a slice of pie with the curved part facing the source of water and the tip pointing downwards.

TRANSIT: the action of passing through a canal.

UNWATERING: emptying a canal of water. Necessary when inspecting or repairing lock mechanisms.

UNWATERING GATES: timber gates used to control the water when service gates are painted or repaired, or when maintenance of the concrete lock walls is necessary. They are found below Lock 1, to control Lake Ontario; below twin Locks 4 to close off the reach between Locks 3 and 4; and at both ends of Lock 8 to guard aganst Lake Erie fluctuations.

VALVE: a contrivance that opens or closes an aperture.

WEIR: a dam-like structure along a canal berm with openings for controlling the water level. Water not required for lock operation may be diverted to the weir and pond system which parallels the canal locks.

WINCH: cranking mechanism which opens or closes valves in lock gates in order to fill or empty locks.

WING WALLS: walls that are flared at an angle forming the approach to the ends of locks.

Abbreviations

AO	Archives of Ontario
CBE	Commander of the British Empire
CNR	Canadian National Railway
DOT	Department of Transport
DPW	Department of Public Works
DRC	Department of Railways and Canals
GWVA	Great War Veterans' Association
HEPC	Hydro-Electric Power Commission
LAC	Library and Archives Canada
MBE	Member of the Most Excellent Order of the British Empire
MP	Member of Parliament
MPP	Member of the Provincial Parliament
NDTLF	Niagara District Trades and Labour Federation
NMC	National Map Collection
NS&T	Niagara, St Catharines and Toronto Railway
PCHMM	Port Colborne Historical and Marine Museum
RMS	Roberta M. Styran
RRT	Robert R. Taylor
SCL	St Catharines Public Library
SCM	St Catharines Museum
SP	Sessional Papers of the Dominion of Canada
SLSMC	St Lawrence Seaway Management Corporation (Western Region)
WCR	Welland Canal Records (St Catharines Public Library)
WHM	Welland Historical Museum

NOTES

PREFACE

1 The Fourth Welland Canal was referred to as the "Ship" Canal in order to differentiate it from the Erie "Barge" Canal in New York State.
2 Richard White, *The Organic Machine*, 60.
3 Department of Railways and Canals, *A Canadian Conception. A Canadian Achievement. Opening of the Welland Ship Canal. August Sixth – Nineteen Thirty Two.*

INTRODUCTION

1 Robert F. Legget, Preface to *The Welland Canals: The Growth of Mr. Merritt's Ditch*, by Roberta M. Styran and Robert R. Taylor, vii.
2 "There being now a larger proportion (more than half) of the tonnage upon Lake Erie, unable for want of length of lock, to descend to Lake Ontario, than there was at that time." T.C. Keefer, "The Canals of Canada," *Transactions of the Royal Society of Canada*, 31.
3 Heisler, *Canals of Canada*, 143.
4 W.A. Bowden, Chief Engineer (DRC), to G.P. Graham, Minister of Railways and Canals, 16 March 1912 (SCL, MS 191, file 5371, WCR). William Arthur Bowden was Quebec-born and, like so many of Canada's engineers of that era, was educated at McGill University. His career was spent almost entirely with the Department of Railways and Canals. He became chief engineer in 1910, in which position he worked, with a break for overseas service 1918–19, until his death in 1924.
5 Corthell, *An Enlarged Water-Way*, 20.
6 This became even more of a problem in 1930 when the nearby construction of the Ship Canal's syphon culvert disturbed the current. On 21 April 1930 alone, three ships were stuck in the aqueduct or collided with its walls. E.P. Johnson to Grant, 8 May 1930 (LAC, RG 43, vol. 2163, file 714.2). See chapter 6.
7 Cowan, *The Welland Ship Canal between Lake Ontario and Lake Erie 1913–1932*, 8. Hereafter referred to as *Welland Ship Canal*.

8 Weller to DRC, 23 February 1905 (LAC, RG 43, vol. 469, #199746).
9 Report of the Chief Engineer, S.P. (no. 32) for 1925, 98–9.
10 Hara to DRC, 26 March 1930 (LAC, RG 43, vol. 1376, file 3434, pt. 3). In 1919 a ten-thousand-ton freighter, the CHARLES R. VAN HISE, too long and wide for the locks at 460 feet long with a 50-foot beam, was bisected, then each half was rolled over so that the ship passed through the locks on its side. *Illustrated London News*, 5 April 1919, 1; or "Floating a Ship on Her Side," *New York Times*, 19 January 1919, 67.
11 Quoted in a letter from J.L. Payne, Comptroller of Statistics, to Campbell, Deputy Minister of Railways and Canals, 29 May 1912 (SCL, MS 191, file 5371, WCR). The mayor of Ottawa took his city's support for this waterway to Toronto. *The Empire Club of Canada Addresses*, 7 December 1911, 86–94, speeches. empireclub.org/results?mt=text&dy=1911&fz=0.
12 If the experience of building the Welland Ship Canal is an example, building the Georgian Bay route would have taken longer than one decade. Other routes from Georgian Bay were occasionally discussed, including from there to Toronto, sometimes called the Hurontario Canal.
13 Quoted in the *St Catharines Standard*, 15 July 1914, 1.

CHAPTER ONE

1 Quoted in Styran and Taylor, *The "Great Swivel Link": Canada's Welland Canal*, 358.
2 Marvin McInnis, "Engineering Expertise and the Canadian Exploitation of the Technology of the Second Industrial Revolution," 4–5, qed.econ.queensu.ca/pub/faculty/ mcinnis/EngineeringExpertise.pdf.
3 Weller, *Annual Report for 1914–1915*, S.P. (no. 20); for 1916, 355; ibid., 335–6.
4 An estimate probably made in 1917 (SCL, MS 191, file 5371, WCR).
5 Weller to Bowden, 18 November 1916 (LAC, RG 43, vol. 2156, file 255.1).
6 Work on Section 1 was 50 per cent completed; on Section 2, 45 per cent; on Section 3, 30 per cent; on Section 5, 50 per cent. Of course, the Ship Canal construction site was not directly affected by the hostilities, but the authorities feared that the operating canal might be sabotaged and therefore arranged to have it guarded by a military force. William A. Smy, *Guarding Niagara: The Welland Canal Force 1914–1918*, www.niagarahistorical.museum/media/ 04.GuardingNiagara1914copy.pdf.
7 Bowden to J.D. Reid, Minister of Railways and Canals, 17 November 1917 (SCL, MS 191, file 5371, WCR).
8 Cameron to Weller, 7 April 1917 (LAC, RG 43, vol. 2156, file 393).
9 Weller to Bowden, 16 March 1917; 12 April (LAC, RG 43, vol. 2156, file 393).
10 In fact, even after the shutdown, some work, including certain surveys as well as soundings in Port Weller harbour, was continued on a limited scale. But the department sold nearly all the rails, ties, locomotives, and cars of the construc-

tion railway, as well as the steam hoists, locomotive cranes, and the equipment of the machine, carpenter, and blacksmith shops. The rock-crushing plant at Twin Locks 4 was almost completely dismantled at the end of 1916.

11 Grant to Bowden, 11 August 1919, and 4 November 1919 (LAC, RG 43, vol. 2162, file 660).

12 Exemplifying the emergence of Canadian engineering talent was Arthur Edouard Dubuc (born 1880 in Quebec). Educated at Laval, he worked for the Department of Public Works for many years until his war service began. In 1919 he returned to public service, this time with Railways and Canals, and was appointed chief engineer of the latter department in 1924.

13 Quoted in *Welland People's Press*, 25 May 1920, n.p.

14 Grant to Bowden, *Annual Report for 1920–1921* (LAC, RG 43, vol. 2164, file 713.3, pt. 1, 18).

15 Bowden to Grant, 17 February 1923 (LAC, RG 43, vol. 2191, file 1210).

16 Grant to Dubuc, 19 March 1926 (LAC, RG 43, vol. 2183, file 1100.3).

17 Grant to W.G. Richardson, 22 October 1926 (LAC, RG 43, vol. 2166, file 780, pt. 2). The Financial Administration Act allows the governor general, under special circumstances, to permit the government to make expenditures not authorized by Parliament.

18 Grant to Bowden, 25 November 1920 (SCL, MS 191, file 5371, WCR). The Niagara Falls hydroelectric project, begun in 1917, was completed in 1925.

19 A.M. Ellis (for Dubuc) to Industrial Brownhoist, 9 May 1930 (LAC, RG 43, vol. 2193, file 1240.3).

20 Tom Moore, president of the Dominion Federation of Labour, quoted in the *St Catharines Standard*, 11 September 1919, 1.

21 Quoted in Meighen to Reid, 25 November 1920 (SCL, MS 191, file 5372, WCR).

22 Bowden to Reid, 1 December 1920; Meighen to Reid, 25 November 1920; Reid declared that he agreed Haney has "not gone as fully into the question he discusses as its importance warrants" (Reid to Meighen, 2 December 1920). Haney, however, was not to be silenced, declaring in a further letter to Meighen that lake vessels would not get any larger in the future. Haney to Meighen, 14 December 1920 (SCL, MS 191, file 5372, WCR).

23 *Montreal Star*, 20 September 1929. Adjusted for inflation in 2015, such estimates would amount to over $1 billion and over $2 billion, respectively.

24 Dewitt Carter, "Two-Way Navigational Channels between Lakes Erie and Superior Four Times Width New Welland – Largest Steamers Will Not Navigate to Lake Ontario. New Welland Ship Canal Will Not Hold Canadian Grain Trade in Canada Until Larger Elevator Facilities Are Provided at Port Colborne" (offprint), 27 March 1928, 4.

25 J.A. Currie, 19 May 1911, Debates of the House of Commons, 1910–11, vol. 5, 9563.

26 The name of the newspaper is not available in the files (22 March 1921, LAC, RG 43, vol. 2166, file 780, pt. 1).

27 Debates of the House of Commons, vol. 1, 1926–27, 784.
28 Harold Glenn Moulton, Charles S. Morgan, and Adah L. Lee, *The St Lawrence Navigation and Power Project*, 236.
29 Paradoxically, the most sustained public criticism came from a respected citizen of Port Colborne. In a series of letters to the *Toronto Mail and Empire* in 1928, the aforementioned Dewitt Carter averred that the width of the new Ship Canal was inadequate. Two-way navigation would be impossible, he believed. Ships would collide with the breast walls of the locks and transshipment of cargoes would still be necessary. Carter to *Toronto Mail and Empire*, 27 March April 18, 8 May 1928. In an interview on 29 March, Grant had declared Carter's view "absurd" (LAC, RG 43, vol. 2169, file 813.1).
30 See Hodgetts, McCloskey, Whitaker, and Wilson, *Biography of an Institution: The Civil Service Commission of Canada, 1908–1967.*
31 Bowden to Grant, 22 December 1919 (LAC, RG 43, vol. 2157, file 450). In his diary, Grant records one such meeting on 5 June 1920.
32 Grant to Bowden (LAC, RG 43, vol. 2166, file 755).
33 Grant, *Diary*, 5 March 1924; Ross to Grant, 16 July 1924; Grant to Ross, 8 July 1924 (LAC, RG 43, vol. 2194, file 1285).

CHAPTER TWO

1 Thorold and Beaverdams Historical Society, *Thirty-Five Years Later. Supplement to Jubilee History of Thorold. Township and Town*, 35. Given the inadequacy of the Third Welland, recognized as early as the 1890s, Conlon was probably not the first to suggest an enlargement.
2 Dunnville Board of Trade to the Minister of Railways and Canals, 5 April 1911 (SCL, MS 191, file 5371, WCR).
3 The Niagara Peninsula is characterized by several small rivers which run south to north into Lake Ontario. They are numbered from the Niagara River westward. See figs 2.2 and 7.10.
4 Weller to Bowden, 18 March 1911 (SCL, MS 191, file 5371, WCR).
5 W.H. Sullivan to Bowden, 1 February 1911; Weller to Bowden, 13 July 1911 (LAC, RG 43, vol. 2153, file 90.2).
6 Weller to Bowden, 13 July 1911 (LAC, RG 43, vol. 2153, file 90.2).
7 George Graham, 30 March 1911, Debates of the House of Commons, 1910–11, vol. 4, 6397.
8 Grant, *Annual Report for 1924–25*, 17 (LAC, RG 43, vol. 2164, file 713.3).
9 MacLachlan to Grant, 25 March 1922 and 6 April 1922 (LAC, RG 43, vol. 2190, file 1187).
10 Grant to MacLachlan, 18 January 1923 (LAC, RG 43, vol. 2192, file 1231).
11 An echo from the past was heard in 1961 when one William Kirby called the attention of the mayor and council of Niagara to the *Shanly Report* of 1871, which had recommended the Lateral Cut to that community. See Styran and

Taylor, *This Great National Object*. Kirby urged – to no avail – that the project be revived. Kirby to the Mayor and Council of the town of Niagara, 31 January 1961 (SLSA 33-2-28-1, vol. 2). Speculation and concern over the Welland and its place in the Seaway occasionally still occurs. During the summer of 2002, for example, several newspaper reports concerned calls for a further enlargement of the whole Seaway connection to the Great Lakes in order to accommodate ships the same size as those which can transit the Panama Canal. Such a decision would have to take into consideration the environmental consequences as well as the enormous cost and would engender considerable discussion and debate on the route. *St Catharines Standard*, 26 and 30 August 2002.

12 J.D. Reid to Arthur Meighen (Prime Minister), 2 December 1920 (SCL, MS 191, file 5371, WCR). The dimensions were to be 829 × 80 feet (252.7 × 24.4 m) with a depth of 30 feet (9.1 m) on the sills. In what follows, we have used the past tense because some of these dimensions have changed or will change in the future.

13 See Styran and Taylor, *This Great National Object*, chapter 5.

14 [Signature illegible, probably W.A. Bowden] Memorandum, 15 March 1912 (SCL, MS 191, file 5371, WCR). In October 1931, construction staff were notified that they would be dismissed after 30 November 1931. (22 November 1930 [LAC, RG 43, vol. 2183, file 1100.1]).

15 *Welland Ship Canal*, 225.

16 *St Catharines Standard*, 5 August 1932, 4.

CHAPTER THREE

1 See Millard, *The Master Spirit of the Age*, esp. 53. Marvin McInnis has found that whereas in 1901, 2,076 engineers were employed in Canada, by 1911 the figure had risen to 5,610. Some of these were immigrant, trained abroad, but Canadian universities were "rapidly expanding" the number of their engineering graduates, and by 1925 70 per cent of engineers working here were born in Canada. "Engineering Expertise and the Canadian Exploitation of the Technology of the Second Industrial Revolution," 15–30, qed.econ.queensu.ca/pub/faculty/ mcinnis/EngineeringExpertise.pdf.

2 Quoted in *Montreal Gazette*, 9 February 1934.

3 Much of the quoted information on Weller has been taken from the biography written by his granddaughter, Madelein "Peggy" Muntz, *John Laing Weller: The Man Who Does Things*. The documents in Library and Archives of Canada occasionally show how he did not "suffer fools gladly," bearing out Millard's description of this generation of engineers as "staunch individualists, self-reliant and independently minded … ambitious, fiercely competitive" (*Master Spirit of the Age*, 86).

4 Cochrane to Treasury Board, 22 January 1912 (LAC, RG 43, vol. 1381, file 3856). Surveys and borings for the Ship Canal had begun in 1905. Report of the

Deputy Minister, Sessional Paper no. 20 for 1920, vol. 56, no. 10, 17. W.H. Sullivan took over as superintendent of the Third Canal, with L.D. Hara as his assistant.

5 Weller, *Annual Report for 1912–1913*, S.P. (no. 20-20b.) for 1914, 330.
6 Ibid.
7 *St Catharines Standard*, 3 May 1913.
8 Quoted in Muntz, *John Laing Weller*, 1.
9 Bowden to Weller, 20 November 1916 (LAC, RG 43, vol. 2155, file 255).
10 Perhaps his hard-driving nature sapped his health, for the Department of Railways and Canals records show several requests – usually granted – for sick leave. For example, in December 1910 he asked for six weeks' "leave of absence" because "Mrs. Weller has not been very well and requires Southern air, and I think it would do me good also, in any event I have to go with her." Similar requests were granted in January 1914, February 1916, and January 1917. On the latter occasion, Weller wrote to Bowden that he had "been notified by my Physician to go to a warmer climate for a month or so in order to protect my eyesight." These leaves were all taken in the winter months when construction was reduced to a minimum. Weller to Bowden, 12 December 1910; 21 January 1914; 14 February 1916; 8 January 1917 (LAC, RG 43, vol. 1381, file 3856). Grant's diaries contain no indication that the two engineers ever met officially or socially.
11 Weller, *Annual Report for 1912–1913*, S.P. (no. 20-20b.) for 1914, 330. Most of these employees were Canadian-born and -educated, which may explain their "great interest."
12 Grant, *Diary*, Friday, 27 July 1928, in Montreal on the eve of sailing to Liverpool for a three-month "holiday."
13 Jewett to J.P. Porter, 15 October 1921 (LAC, RG 43, vol. 2182, file 1100).
14 Jewett to Grant, 1 May 1929 (LAC, RG 43, vol. 2183, file 1100.1 31), August 1929 (LAC, RG 43, vol. 2183, file 1100.1).
15 *St Catharines Standard*, 5 August 1932, 2.
16 Grant to Dubuc, 13 November 1929 (LAC, RG 43, vol. 2186, file 1101.4).
17 Peter Grant was a civil engineer on the Intercolonial Railway in the Maritimes, and his grandson, another Alex (Sandy), worked on the Ship Canal for various contractors during the summers while he was studying for his degree in science (civil engineering) at McGill.
18 George Graham, 28 July 1911, Debates of the House of Commons, 1910–1911. vol. 5, 10476.
19 Grant to P.J. Cowan, 24 October 1929 (LAC, RG 4, vol. 2168, file 780.2).
20 *Engineering Journal* (1930), quoted in the *St Catharines Standard*, 5 August 1932, 6.
21 Fred Collins, a war veteran who worked as clerk and paymaster on the Ship Canal construction, quoted in the *St Catharines Standard*, 7 August 1982, 33.

Grant's diary records payments for a new "toupee" on a number of occasions, as well as the cost of having it cleaned.

22 Grant, *Diary*, Friday, 27 January 1922. Grant's journal, now in the possession of the St Catharines Museum, provides valuable insight into his professional problems and his emotional and social life, as our many quotations show.
23 Ibid., Wednesday, 4 July, and Saturday, 17 November 1928.
24 Ibid., 5 February 1924.
25 Ibid., 9 May 1927.
26 Grant to J.P. Porter, 15 January 1923 (LAC, RG 43, vol. 2183, file 1100.1).
27 Grant to Atlas Construction Co., 15 June 1926 (LAC, RG 43, vol. 2203, file 1348).
28 Grant to E.C. Shurley, 2 March 1933 (LAC, SLSMC, 63-27-9, "Stability of Canal Bank").
29 For example, as late as February 1923, Grant asked Bowden if Sections 8 and 9 were to be let as one contract or two, Weller having originally planned for two. On 21 August, when he visited Bowden in Ottawa, the latter informed him that Section 8 was to be advertised as one section. As to who made the decision, and when, we have found no record, either in official sources or in Grant's diary. (6 February 1923, LAC, RG 43, vol. 2192, file 1231.)
30 Grant, *Diary,* Sunday, 3 February 1924, in the entry recording Bowden's death at 4 a.m. that day.
31 Ibid., Tuesday, 13 May, 1919. The following day Grant, Bowden, and W.H. Sullivan (principal assistant engineer) toured Section 5:
 Walked over disposal ground from Malett's [Marlatt's] bridge to Allanburg. – Water from spoil bank is much clearer than in the canal. Drove from Allanburg to Port Robinson where we had dinner ... & then looked over work on stone & concrete protection of slope & foundation of canal bridge at P. Robinson – We then went to Niagara Falls via Welland. At the Hydro Electric office we got Rex Johnson to go over the work with us. Saw shovels 1 & 2 working in clay near the office & in forebay. Out to dumping ground & at crusher plant & lower end of forebay. Supper at Clifton Inn. Mr. Bowden left at 7.35 for Toronto. Sullivan & I motored back to St Catherines [*sic*].
32 Ibid., Saturday, 26 March 1921: "several of the office men who have been working after supper for 2 months were away today."
33 Grant to E.G. Cameron, 29 August 1927 (LAC, RG 43, vol. 2203, file 1348).
34 Grant, *Diary*, Friday, 2 September 1921.
35 Ibid., Wednesday, 24 October 1924.
36 Ibid., 18 December 1925.
37 Ibid., 17 September 1920.
38 *St Catharines Standard*, 11 August 1921, 1.
39 Grant to R.S. Peotter (Second Ward Securities Co., Milwaukee), 19 March 1922 (LAC, RG 43, vol. 2174, file 877).

40 Grant to Porter, 18 September 1922 (LAC, RG 43, vol. 2182, file 1100).
41 Grant to Dubuc, 13 November 1926 (LAC, RG 43, vol. 2208, file 1368.1).
42 Grant, *Diary*, Wednesday, 27 October 1920.
43 Grant to C.H. Edgett, 16 June 1922; Grant to Knox Bros. Ltd., 18 July 1922 (LAC, RG 43, vol. 2190, file 1173); Grant to Knox Bros. Ltd., ibid.
44 Grant to F.C. Jewett, 1 May 1924 (LAC, RG 43, vol. 2183, file 1100.2).
45 Grant to Porter, 12 May 1924 (LAC, RG 43, vol. 2183, file 1100.2).
46 Grant to Jewett, 17 October 1923 (LAC, RG 43, vol. 2183, file 1100.1).
47 Grant to Dubuc, 29 November 1930 (LAC, RG 43, vol. 2227, file 1524.1).
48 Grant, *Diary*, Monday, 4 February, Tuesday the 5th, and Tuesday the 12th, 1924. "The news does not please the heads of the Dept branches," he noted. Subsequently his salary was raised to $7,500, at which level it remained until 30 March 1928. On that date Dubuc telephoned him to say he was now to be paid $9,000, as of 1 October 1927. Grant added that "He [Dubuc] has been working for this since Feb. 1928."
49 Grant, *Diary*, Saturday, 31 March 1934.
50 After attending Weller's funeral, Grant noted that "A number of the Canal Staff were at the funeral to pay their last respects to their former superior in charge of the Canal." Grant, *Diary*, Thursday, 26 May 1932. Weller had died at his residence in Hamilton on the 24th.
51 Grant, *Diary*, Saturday, 24 March 1934. Grant left that evening for two weeks of golf at Pinehurst, North Carolina.
52 British suppliers were Drysdale & Co. of Glasgow, William Beardmore & Co., also of Glasgow, and Emerson Walker of Gateshead-on-Tyne. Canadian branches of American firms, especially Allis-Chambers and Canadian Westinghouse, supplied equipment for the giant floating crane.
53 Quoted in *Montreal Gazette*, 27 May 1924 (LAC, RG 43, vol. 2185, file 1101.2).
54 Lyall to Grant, 15 February 1924 (LAC, RG 43, vol. 2185, file 1101.2); emphasis in original.
55 *St Catharines Standard*, 1 and 2 August 1928; Grant, *Diary*, Wednesday, 15 August 1928.
56 Grant, *Diary*, 27 March 1929.
57 Porter to Lyall & Sons, 4 July 1925; Lyall's response, 6 July; Porter to Jewett, 7 July (LAC, RG 43, vol. 2183, file 1100.2).
58 Grant to A.E. Dubuc, 13 November 1929 (LAC, RG 43, vol. 2186, file 1101.4). On 27 June 1922, Peter Lyall and Sons of Montreal had been awarded the contract to complete Sections 3 and 4, including Twin Locks 4–6 and the guard gates, the project to be finished by 31 March 1926. Although the completion date was repeatedly extended, the firm went bankrupt before finishing the job. Born in Scotland in 1841, Lyall had emigrated to Canada in 1870. In Montreal, he was active as a justice of the peace, an alderman, and a member of the Board of Trade. He and his sons had also been given the contract for the Port Colborne grain elevator in 1908.

59 George Kydd to Grant, 20 March 1925, *Annual Report* for Section 8 (LAC, RG 43, vol. 2164, file 714, 9).
60 E.P. Murphy to Grant, 31 March 1930, *Annual Report 1929–30* (LAC, RG 43, vol. 2165, file 714.3, 22).
61 *Welland Ship Canal.*
62 For the specific purpose of erection of the gates, the company was formed by the Lyalls, E.S. Mattice, and J. Gardiner, who then sublet the work to Hamilton Bridge Company, Montreal Locomotive Works, Foster Wheeler of St Catharines, and McGregor-McIntyre Iron Works. We know nothing else about the latter firm, except that while it was listed by Cowan as a contractor for miscellaneous metal work, it received no official contract for work on the Ship Canal. Mattice was named manager of the company and moved temporarily from Montreal to Hamilton to supervise the work. A.W. Robertson, another Ship Canal contractor, was also involved with the company. Hamilton Bridge subcontracted for most of the structural steel work; Montreal Locomotive Works for gate machines as well as castings and forgings. Dominion Bridge Company of Montreal supplied trial machines installed at Lock 1.
63 LAC, RG 43, vol. 2219, file 1435.1. Grant met with F.G. Warburton, manager of Harland, in Alloa, on 20 August 1928, and was taken through their plant, "a small one, in cheap buildings, but where I believe they do good work. The office buildings are one story cheap affairs. The concern would rank with the D. [Dominion[Bridge Co. about 1890." Grant, *Diary*, 20 August 1928.
64 LAC, RG 43, vols 2229–40.
65 Grant to Montreal Locomotive Works, 4 June 1929 (LAC, RG 43, vol. 2219, file 1435.3).
66 *Welland Ship Canal*, 237.
67 Legget, *Canals of Canada*, 175. Actually, Legget uses these words to praise only the engineers, but we believe that the contractors exhibited similar virtues, combined, of course, with their own particular weaknesses.

CHAPTER FOUR

1 Weller, *Annual Report for 1913–1914*, 364.
2 *Welland Tribune and Telegraph*, 24 December 1925, 1; Grant, "Monthly Reports. Construction Railway 1921–31" (LAC, RG 43, vol. 2182, file 1062).
3 *Welland Ship Canal*, 37.
4 John N. Jackson mistakenly locates the rock-crushing plant at Allanburg. *The Welland Canals and Their Communities*, 280.
5 Today's Welland Canals Parkway (formerly Government Road) runs along the west side of the Ship Canal and still curves at this site, following the route of the Construction Railway, which was aligned for a right-angled crossing of the Third Canal.

6   Lampard to Grant, 6 October 1920 (LAC, RG 43, vol. 2175, file 916); Lampard to Grant, "Monthly Reports. Construction Railway 1921–31" (LAC, RG 43, vol. 2182, file 1062), 1928, and Palmer's reply of 31 October (LAC, RG 43, vol. 2210, file 1370.2).

7   Earth turned up by the graders was delivered automatically into wagons, also pulled by mules, following along beside the graders. The arrangement was technically efficient, but the motive power remained traditional. *Welland Ship Canal*, 57.

8   Atkinson (for Grant) to R.K. Palmer (Chief Engineer, Hamilton Bridge Co.), 29 October 1928, and Palmer's reply of 31 October (LAC, RG 43, vol. 2210, file 1370.2).

9   Hand (of S. Morgan Smith-Inglis Co.) to Grant, for the attention of F.E. Sterns (LAC, RG 43, vol. 2158, file 519.2).

10   M.B. Atkinson to Grant, 2 June 1930 (SLSA 28-19-1-1, vol. 1).

11   Weller, *Annual Report for 1913–14*, 353.

12   E.P. Murphy to Grant, 31 March 1930, *Annual Report for 1929–30* (LAC, RG 43, vol. 2165, file 714.3, 6); Grant, *Annual Report for 1924–25* (LAC, RG 43, vol. 2164, file 714.3, 13).

13   Grant, *Annual Report for 1929–30* (LAC, RG 43, vol. 2165, file "Annual Report," 12).

14   Legget, *The Seaway*, 9.

CHAPTER FIVE

1   30 March 1911. Debates of the House of Commons, 1910–1911, vol. 4, 6397–98 (Ottawa: MacLean, Roger). A 1911 drawing of such a lock can be seen in SCL, microfilm MS 191, Sect. G; Weller to Bowden, 8 October 1910 (SCL, MS 191, file 5371, WSC). Weller's thoughts on lock size and operation may reflect the influence the "technological imperative," the notion that the development of new technology is inevitable and essential for the well-being of society. See Francis, *The Technological Imperative in Canada*.

2   Quoted in Grant to Bowden, 15 April 1920 (LAC, RG 43, vol. 2169, file 803).

3   "Specifications for Section 1," 1 May 1913 (LAC, RG 43, vol. 1704, file 10652).

4   23 May 1919 (LAC, RG 43, vol. 2158, file 495).

5   *Welland Ship Canal*, 12.

6   Jewett to Grant, 24 March 1920 (LAC, RG 43, vol. 2169, file 803).

7   Grant to Bowden, 15 April 1920 (LAC, RG 43, vol. 2169, file 803).

8   A pencilled note on the estimated cost of lock gates reads "Change from single leaf gates to mitering gates was authorized verbally by Mr. Bowden in his office on May 5th 1920 after an all day discussion with Mr. D.W. McLachlan Mr. A.J. Grant" (5 May 1920, LAC, RG 43, vol. 2169, file 803).

9 Grant to Bowden, 13 March 1922 (LAC, RG 43, vol. 2176, file 1015). In 1928, when the canal's powerhouse was being planned, the future twinning of all locks was frequently mentioned. "Hydro-Electric Power Plant. Correspondence. 1928" (LAC, RG 43, vol. 2176, file 1017.2).

10 17 April 1920 (LAC, RG 43, vol. 2166, file 780, pt. 1).

11 Because the mooring galleries began to seem dangerous to lock personnel, they have since been filled in. In the early twenty-first century, however, the manholes leading to these passages can still be seen.

12 *St Catharines Standard*, 14 June 1924, 1 and 5.

13 Bricklayers and Masons International to F.D. Monk (DPW), 26 April 1912 (SCL, MS 191, file 5371, WCR). In 1896, canal engineer Thomas Monro had written "for the purposes of lock walls, weirs, retaining walls, and other hydraulic structures, concrete made of sound and properly tested Portland cement, good clean broken stone and sharp silicious sand, is in all respects better than the expensive masonry hitherto in vogue." *Canadian Engineer* 3, no. 12 (April 1896): 318.

14 *Welland Ship Canal*, 91.

15 Grant to Jewett, 27 June 1922 (LAC, RG 43, vol. 2182, file 1100).

16 Jewett to Cameron, 14 October 1924 (LAC, RG 43, vol. 2183, file 1100.2).

17 T.C. Cain to Grant, 27 August 1920 (LAC, RG 43, vol. 2171, file 85). See also *St Catharines Standard*, 26 August 1920, 1.

18 A.W. Robertson to Grant, 11 October 1920 (LAC, RG 43, vol. 2171, file 853).

19 Grant to Canada Cement Company, Toronto, 16 October 1922 (LAC, RG 43, vol. 2190, file 1181).

20 Grant to Watson Jack, 2 October 1920 (LAC, RG 43, vol. 2162, file 617).

21 Weller, *Annual Report for 1913–1914*, 30 June 1914, S.P. (no. 20), for 1915, vol. 50, pt. 14, 368.

22 Steel frames from which were suspended wooden forms in sections 60 feet (18.3 m) long by 50 feet (15.2 m) high, manufactured by the Blaw-Knox Company of Pittsburg.

23 Hugh L. Cooper (New York) to Grant, 16 February 1924 (LAC, RG 43, vol. 2166, file 780, pt. 1).

24 *Welland-Port Colborne Evening Tribune*, 4 November 1930, 1.

25 John S. Leitch (Collingwood Shipyards) to Grant, 19 April 1930 (LAC, RG 43, vol. 1704, file 16003.3).

26 Grant to Dubuc, 20 May 1930; Collingwood to Allis-Chambers, 25 June 1930; H.B. Smith, (President Collingwood Shipyards) to Grant, 26 June 1930 (LAC, RG 43, vol. 2172, files 872.2 and 872.3).

27 Leitch to Grant, 6 September 1930 (LAC, RG 43, vol. 1704, file 16003.2).

28 Grant to Dubuc, 29 September 1930 (LAC, RG 43, vol. 2172, file 872.2).

29 Grant to Dubuc, 10 October 1930 (LAC, RG 43, vol. 1704, file 16003.3). A day-by-day account of the voyage of the lifter from Georgian Bay across Lake

Huron and through Lake Erie can be found in LAC, RG 43, vol. 1704, file 16003.2 and RG 43, vol. 2172, file 872.2.

30 *Evening Tribune,* 4 November 1930, 1.

31 Smith to Grant, 30 December 1930 (LAC, RG 43, vol. 2173, file 872.4).

32 Grant, *Diary,* 14 November 1930.

33 Grant, 10 June 1930, *Annual Report for 1929–30* (LAC, RG 43, vol. 2165, file "Annual Report," 13).

34 Grant to Bowden, 31 March 1921, *Annual Report for 1920–1921* (LAC, RG 43, vol. 2164, file 713.3, pt. 1, 12).

35 Jewett to Grant, 18 January 1924 (LAC, RG 43, vol. 2183, file 1100.2).

36 Grant had heard complaints about delays and the quality of the job, and snapped, "I want the work done immediately ... otherwise I will do the work early next week at your own expense and cost." Grant to Peter Lyall Sons, 15 September 1927 (LAC, RG 43, vol. 2177, file 1017.1).

37 Grant to R.N. Norris (Harland, Montreal), 20 February 1929 (LAC, RG 43, vol. 2220, file 1436.3).

38 Murphy to Grant, 31 March 1930, *Annual Report for 1929–30* (LAC, RG 43, vol. 2165, file 1930, 25).

39 Slaton, *Reinforced Concrete and the Modernization of American Building*, 168.

40 *Welland Ship Canal*, 127.

41 Ibid., 174.

CHAPTER SIX

1 During winter drainage these locks may still be seen, half-submerged in a sea of mud. On the cemetery's removal, see chapter 10.

2 William Hamilton Merritt, "Account of the Welland Canal, Upper Canada," *American Journal of Science and Arts* 14 (July 1828): 164.

3 George Phillpotts, "Report on the Canal Navigation of the Canadas," *Papers on Subjects Connected with the Duties of the Corps of Royal Engineers*, vol. 5, part 6 (London, 1839), 155.

4 Weller memorandum, 10 September 1912 (SCL, MS 191, file 5371, WCR).

5 Weller, *Annual Report for 1912–1913* (S.P. no. 20-20b.) for 1914, 331.

6 *St Catharines Standard*, 12 December 1912, 1.

7 17 April 1920; see also 14 April 1920 (LAC, RG 43, vol. 2166, file 780, pt. 1).

8 John Goodwin (Mayor), 6 October 1913 (LAC, RG 43, vol. 1699, file 10993); J.C. Stevenson (Toronto) to W.A. Bowden, 16 August 1923 (LAC, RG 43, vol. 2160, file 593).

9 Grant to Bowden, 22 March 1920 (LAC, RG 43, vol. 2160, file 593.1); Bowden to McLean, 31 March 1920, ibid.; Dubuc to Grant, 15 December 1924 (LAC, RG 43, vol. 2154, file 131.2).

10 Grant, *Diary*, 6 September 1929.

11 *Welland Ship Canal*, 146.

12 Johnson to Grant, 8 June 1926; R.W. Lipsett (Dominion Marine Association) to G.A. Bell (Deputy Minister, DRC), 8 July 1926 (LAC, RG 43, vol. 2205, file 1348.3).

13 LAC, RG 43, vol. 2155, file 255.

14 He was later General Superintendent of Canals, DOT.

15 Weller to Bowden, 30 April 1917 (LAC, RG 43, vol. 2156, file 393).

16 Along with the delay in starting the stone protection work, Weller said, Bowden had neglected to make a decision on matters concerning salary, staff housing problems, and bridge superstructures. The result was "restlessness ... and discouragement" among his staff. Weller to Bowden, 30 April 1917 (LAC, RG 43, vol. 2156, file 393).

17 Weller to Bowden, 26 September 1916 (SCL, MS 191, file 5371, WCR). Unknown to Weller, the purpose of Jost's visit was to make a report to Bowden on the situation at the harbour. The engineer took Jost over the site by automobile but found his report "superficial and misleading," as might have been expected from "observations [made] from the seat of a motor car" (Weller to Bowden, 30 April 1917, LAC, RG 43, vol. 2156, file 393).

18 F.S. Lazier memorandum, 10 February 1920 (LAC, RG 43, vol. 2177, file 1017.1). On the Grand Trunk Railway tunnel, see Styran and Taylor, *This Great National Object*, chapter 7.

19 McGrath (Chair, HEPC) to DRC, 7 November 1928 (LAC, RG 43, vol. 2177, file 1017.2).

20 Bowden to Grant, 3 March 1923; Grant to Bowden, 15 January 1924 (LAC, RG 43, vol. 2176, file 1017).

21 Grant to Sterns, 20 July 1928 (LAC, RG 43, vol. vol. 2176, file 1017.2).

CHAPTER SEVEN

1 In March 1925 the Ontario Motion Picture Bureau made a silent film of the Ship Canal construction, as did Hugh Aird of the Bank of Commerce in August 1927 (LAC, RG 43, vol. 2166, file 780, pt. 2; and vol. 2171, file 840.22). These films are in the National Archives (LAC 1972 – 0105). In September 1929 Paramount News cameramen also filmed parts of the construction site. Around 1931, British Pathé filmed some of the first ships transiting the canal (http://www.britishpathe.com/record.php?id=28742).

2 For technical details on bridges, see *Welland Ship Canal*, 205ff.

3 Grant to Bowden, 9 January 1923 (LAC, RG 43, vol. 2154, file 154).

4 Dubuc to Grant, 27 April 1931 (SLSA 28-19-1-1, vol. 1).

5 *Welland Tribune and Telegraph*, 24 December 1925, 2.

6 E.P. Johnson memorandum, 12 January 1927 (LAC, RG 43, vol. 2207, file 1354.1).

7 *Welland Tribune and Telegraph*, 24 December 1925, 2.

8 By 1979 only ten of the original bridges were left crossing the Welland. Bridge 7 at Peter Street, above Lock 7, had been dismantled. Bridges 8 and 9, both south of Thorold, have also been removed. The history of the Ship Canal bridges has occasionally been dramatic. Bridge 12, at Port Robinson, was wrecked in 1974 by the STEELTON and never rebuilt. The community remains severed in two parts, connected in good weather by the ferry, which the locals call BRIDGE-IT.

9 The mayor's objections, he snorted, were "puerile and selfish in the extreme." Grant to Dubuc, 25 May 1926 (LAC, RG 43, vol. 2203, file 1347).

10 *St Catharines Standard*, 12 December 1912, 1.

11 *Welland People's Press*, 3 October 1916, 5.

12 Grant to Dubuc, 15 May 1925 (LAC, RG 43, vol. 2178, file 1018.2).

13 *St Catharines Standard*, 31 May 1927, 8.

14 H. Ibsen to J.B. McAndrews (Ship Canal structural engineer), 29 April 1924 (LAC, RG 43, vol. 2175, file 912); Joseph B. Strauss to Dubuc, 11 September 1924 (LAC, RG 43, vol. 2179, file 1018.2); Atkinson, Sterns, and Monsarrat to Dubuc, 10 October 1924 (LAC, RG 43, vol. 2179, file 1018.2).

15 Grant to Dubuc, 14 July 1925 (LAC, RG 43, vol. 2178, file 1018.3).

16 Atkinson to Dubuc, 6 December 1924 (LAC, RG 43, vol. 2180, file 1018.2).

17 Grant to Bowden, 8 December 1919 (LAC, RG 43, vol. 2157, file 478).

18 W. Chase Thomson to Graham, 8 February 1924; Thomson to Grant, 20 February 1924; Thomson to Grant; Thomson to Atkinson, 1 April 1924 (LAC, RG 43, vol. 2178, file 1018.2); in May 1925 he was writing to Dubuc on the same theme. Thomson to Dubuc, 8 May 1925 (LAC, RG 43, vol. 2178, file 1018.3). Thomson's remarks here may be an example of the new national and professional pride of Canadian engineers at this time. They had "acquired confidence, drive, and ambition," writes Millard, and, fearing a possible "foreign [i.e., American] invasion," "they began to resent being passed over in favour of Americans of equal or less ability, especially for government contracts." Millard, *Master Spirit of the Age*, 53.

19 Grant, Stern, and Atkinson to Dubuc, 15 May 1925 (LAC, RG 43, vol. 2178, file 1018.3).

20 Grant to Harrington et al., 29 April 1926 (LAC, RG 43, vol. 2200, file 1340).

21 Atkinson to Sterns, 2 July 1924 (LAC, RG 43, vol. 2179, file 1018.2).

22 3 April 1923 (LAC, RG 43, vol. 2178, file 1018.2).

23 Grant to W.I.S. Hendrie (president, Hamilton Bridge), 16 January 1928 (LAC, RG 43, vol. 2210, file 1370.2).

24 Atkinson to Cushing, 21 February 1929; Cushing to Atkinson, 22 February 1929 (LAC, RG 43, vol. 2222, file 1452.1).

25 In the small world of Canadian engineering, many of these men were former university colleagues and friends. Another example of this camaraderie can be found in a handwritten note from J.P. Mantle of the Hamilton Bridge Com-

pany to Atkinson in late February 1930, chiding the latter for his anxiety over the progress of the bridges: "Brodie – I saw today your list of *extra* [Mantle's emphasis] tools required for the machinist on Bridge 9. You overlooked providing him with a liquor cabinet and humidor for his cigars. Some time when passing a drug store please enter and ask for a good supply of Dr. Chase's nerve pills. You need them badly. J.P. Mantle" (LAC, RG 43, vol. 2225, file 1464.2).

26 Dubuc to Grant, 22 February 1927 (LAC, RG 43, vol. 2154, file 138).

27 *St Catharines Standard*, 11 August 1921, 5.

28 The process of building the bridges elsewhere was followed here. The sites for the piers were prepared by dredging; foundation piles were driven in the canal bed using a submersible steam hammer until they were under water. The tops of the piles were cut off uniformly under water using a submarine saw, mounted on a pile gantry erected over the pier site. Then a steel and timber caisson was built and floated to the site. See Nora Reid, *Main Street Bridge (Bridge 13 on the Welland Canal)*, 3.

29 Grant to Hamilton Bridge Co., 7 June 1927 (LAC, RG 43, vol. 2201, file 1342.4).

30 J.P. Mantle (vice-president in charge of sales, Hamilton Bridge Co.) to Grant, 30 January 1929 (LAC, RG 43, vol. 2218, file 1421); Grant to Dubuc, 31 January 1929 (LAC, RG 43, vol. 2218, file 1421); 11 February 1929 (LAC, RG 43, vol. 2218, file 1421); 11 and 18 February 1929 (LAC, RG 43, vol. 2214, file 1398.4).

31 Grant to Dubuc, 10 April 1929 (LAC, RG 43, vol. 2218, file 1421).

32 Grant, *Annual Report for 1927–28* (LAC, RG 43, vol. 2164, file 714.3, pt. 2, 33).

33 Atkinson (for Grant) to Hamilton Bridge Co., 28 January 1930 (LAC, RG 43, vol. 2225, file 1464.2).

34 Dubuc to Grant, 22 February 1927 (LAC, RG 43, vol. 2154, file 138).

35 Jack Cohut (secretary, Thorold South Fire Department) to "Gentlemen" [i.e., Ship Canal construction staff], 13 March 1930 (LAC, RG 43, vol. 2179, file 1018.4).

36 Atkinson (for Grant) to C.D. Henderson (Canadian Bridge Co.), 22 January 1929 (LAC, RG 43, vol. 2218, file 1421).

37 Jewett to Grant, 1 November 1929 (LAC, RG 43, vol. 2210, file 1370.3).

38 In 1905 the Lincoln Power Company received permission to erect two steel and concrete poles across the lower end of Lock 3 of the Second Canal to carry their transmission wires. Because concrete was a relatively new construction material, these poles aroused a great deal of interest, both locally and elsewhere in the engineering world. The poles were designed by Weller, then superintending engineer on the (Third) Welland Canal, with his partner, fellow engineer W.H. Sullivan, and built by their Concrete Pole Company Limited. At 150 feet (45.7 m) they were then the tallest concrete structures in the world and flanked the lock until 1971, when they were taken down.

39 SLSA 28-19-1-1, vol. 1.

CHAPTER EIGHT

1 Grant to W.V. Cope, Departmental Comptroller, 13 April 1920 (LAC, RG 43, vol. 2164, file 713.3, pt. 1); Grant to E.A. Fox (Commerce Bank, St Catharines), 30 October 1924 (LAC, RG 43, vol. 2164, file 713.3, pt. 1, vol. 2166, file 780, pt. 1).

2 By now, Ottawa bureaucracy intervened frequently in the hiring and paying of these individuals, complicating matters further.

3 *St Catharines Standard*, 20 November 1920, 1.

4 Order-in-Council, 13 December 1920 (LAC, RG 43, vol. 2176, file 1000); D.T. Rogers to Hara, 28 March 1921 (LAC, RG 43, vol. 2142, file "Feeder 1919–22").

5 D.T. Rogers to Hara, 28 March 1921 (LAC, RG 43, vol. 2142, file "Feeder 1919–22").

6 Lazier to Grant, 27 July 1921 (LAC, RG 43, vol. 2223, file 1460.2).

7 A.H. German to Grant, 28 September 1921 (LAC, RG 43, vol. 2188, file 1102).

8 L.P.E. McCleary, Mayor of Thorold, to George P. Graham, Minister of Railways and Canals, 20 January 1925 (LAC, RG 43, vol. 2185, file 1101.2).

9 Heron and Siemiatycki, "The Great War, the State and Working-Class Canada," in Craig Heron, ed., *The Workers' Revolt in Canada 1917–1925*, 20.

10 Grant to Bowden, *Annual Report for 1920–1921*. His complaints are found in LAC, RG 43, vol. 2164, file 713.3, pt. 1, 3, and 18.

11 Jewett to Grant, 1 July 1919 (LAC, RG 43, vol. 2174, file 881).

12 Evidence of this is in Grant's report to Reid on 4 September 1919. On that day, he said, all the men on Section 1 worked on the eight-hour/forty-four-hour week system but on Section 2, 48 per cent of the work was eight hours and 52 per cent, ten; on Section 3, 18.5 per cent was for eight hours and 8.5 per cent for ten; on Section 5, all the men worked ten hours (LAC, RG 43, vol. 2223, file 1460.1).

13 *Welland Ship Canal*, 10.

14 "Act for Relief of Unemployment," 22 September 1930 (21 Geo. V, Ch. 1, Canada).

15 E.P. Murphy to Grant (*Annual Report for 1931–32*), 8 April 1932 (LAC, RG 43, vol. 2163, files 714.2 and 714.3.3).

16 "Act for Preservation of Health on Public Works," 11 August, 1899, 62–63 Vict., Ch. 30, Canada; "Act Creating a Department of Labour," 19 March 1909, 8–9 Edw. VII, Ch. 22, Canada; "Act Regarding Compensation for Employees Killed or Injured while on Duty," 24 May 1918, 8–9 Geo. V, Ch. 14, Canada; "Act re Department of Health," 6 June 1919, 9–10 Geo. V, Ch. 24, Canada).

17 *Toronto Mail and Empire*, 20 November 1920.

18 Lazier to Grant, 17 September 1921 (LAC, RG 43, vol. 2174, file 879). Heat stroke, which was not uncommon in the lock pits, could be fatal because the victim's constitution could no longer keep body temperature at 37°C.

19 Grant to McCullough, 18 August 1924; McCullough to Grant, 20 August 1924 (LAC, RG 43, vol. 2162, file 622).

20 Quoted in *St Catharines Standard*, 26 August 1989, 13.
21 Young to Sullivan, 3 May 1922 (LAC, RG 43, vol. 2188, file 1102).
22 Jewett to Grant, 20 August 1919 (LAC, RG 43, vol. 2223, file 1460).
23 Jewett to Grant, 1 June 1919 (LAC, RG 43, vol. 2174, file 881).
24 A.M German (Canadian Dredging) to Grant, 22 August 1919 (LAC, RG 43, vol. 2223, file 1460.1).
25 Lazier to Grant, 6 August 1919 (LAC, RG 43, vol. 2223, file 1460).
26 Jewett's *Annual Report*, 11 June 1920 (LAC, RG 43, vol. 2164, file 713.3, pt. 1).
27 Donald Avery, *"Dangerous Foreigners": European Immigrant Workers and Labour Radicalism in Canada 1896–1932*, 70.
28 Quoted in *St Catharines Standard*, 9 August 1919, 1.
29 Grant's notes on a telegram from G.A. Bell, 9 August 1919 (LAC, RG 43, vol. 2223, file 1460).
30 *St Catharines Standard*, 3 October 1918, 1.
31 Reid to Grant, 29 August 1919; Bowden to Grant, 30 August 1919; Grant to Reid, 4 September 1919 (LAC, RG 43, vol. 2223, file 1460.1). From the usually astute Grant, this attitude seems naive.
32 Grant to Bowden, *Annual Report for 1919–1920*, 30 June 1920 (LAC, RG 43, vol. 2164, file 713.3, pt. 1).
33 Grant to H.G. Acres (of the Hydro-Electric Power Commission of Ontario), 26 July 1920 (LAC, RG 43, vol. 2223, file 1460.1).
34 "When the [NDTL] Federation leaders had settled with the Hydro-Electric Commission ... they were free to attack the Welland Ship Canal, which they promptly proceeded to do ... in a particularly virulent manner." Grant to Bowden, *Annual Report for 1919–1920*, 30 June 1920 (LAC, RG 43, vol. 2164, file 713.3, pt. 1).
35 Grant to Bowden, 24 March 1921 (LAC, RG 43, vol. 2223, file 1460.2).
36 He decried the "contractors' leniency in giving more than a fair chance to all kinds of returned soldier labor [which] set a bad example to foreigners and was generally of poor effect." Lazier to Grant, 10 February 1921 (LAC, RG 43, vol. 2174, file 880). Lazier's comments recall Millard's view that Canadian engineers' values were "elitist and anti-democratic, perhaps anti-humanitarian and authoritarian" (*Master Spirit of the Age*, 146).

CHAPTER NINE

1 *Toronto Star Weekly*, 2 June 1919, 1.
2 Several of the vertical lift bridges, notably Bridge 17 at Dain City, south of Welland, are said to have been built by members of the Mohawk First Nation from the Caughnawaga Reserve near Montreal and from a reserve east of Rochester, New York (fig. 8.3). They were employed here, the story goes, by Dominion Bridge because many of these native North Americans specialized in high-level work such as New York's skyscrapers. To date, we have found no

evidence to support this interesting matter, but see https://en.wikipedia.org/wiki/Mohawk_people.

3 J. Shaw (for Lampard, Superintendent of the construction railway), 2 October [received] 1922 (LAC, RG 43, vol. 2189, file 1168.1), and *Toronto Globe*, 22 October 1928, 1 and 5. Injured were Addick Glazzo, Paul Sezanovich, Louis Gesmick, Mike Radicik, and Rocco Gerolmo.

4 *St Catharines Standard*, 1 August 1928, 1. The American spelling, "color," was common in Canada at this time.

5 Bruno Ramirez, *The Italians in Canada*, Canadian Historical Association, Canada's Ethnic Groups, No. 14 (Saint John, New Brunswick, 1989), 6.

6 *St Catharines Standard*, 26 July 1997, 1.

7 T. Crowley (for Lazier) to Grant, 4 November 1930 (LAC, RG 43, vol. 2181, file 1035.1).

8 *St. Catharines Standard*, 23 January 1914, 1.

9 19 October 1921 (LAC, RG 43, vol. 2223, file 1460.2).

10 Grant to Lazier, 13 May 1922 (LAC, RG 43, vol. 2176, file 1000).

11 Jewett to Grant, 5 February 1921; L. Cunningham (Secretary, Great War Veterans' Association) to J.D. Chaplin, 24 January 1921; C.G. McNeil (Secretary-Treasurer, G.W.V.A.) to Bowden, 6 June 1921 (LAC, RG 43, vol. 2223, file 1460.2); McNeil "slurs" French Canadians "by insinuation," said Jewett, defending the Brodeur family of Waubashene, eight of whom were carpenters and "excellent mechanics and workers"; two had served in the war. Jewett, *Monthly Report*, 11 June 1921 (LAC, RG 43, vol. 2223, file 1460.2).

12 *Welland People's Press*, 27 June 1916, 7.

13 5,954 of these Ukrainians were interned during the war. Thompson, *Ethnic Minorities during the Two World Wars*, 4 and 7.

14 *St Catharines Standard*, 8 January 1916, 1.

15 The discrepancy is hard to explain but faulty record keeping and the contemporary attitude to manual labour are probably part of the answer. Recent research by Alex Ormston, Arden Phair, and historians associated with the St Catharines Museum has revealed several omissions. Our Appendix III has the most recent tally.

16 McCombe to Grant, 31 March 1925; Grant to Dubuc, 1 April 1926 (LAC, RG 43, file 713.3, pt. 1); Grant to Dubuc, 1 April 1927 (LAC, RG 43, vol. 2164, file 713.3 – 1925).

17 McCombe to Grant, 10 April 1930 (LAC, RG 43, vol. 2165, file 714.3.3).

18 McCombe to Grant, *Annual Report for 1927–1928* (LAC, RG 43, vol. 2164, file 714.3, pt. 2, 36).

19 Grant, *Annual Report for 1929–30* (LAC, RG 43, vol. 2165, "Annual Report," 53). In 1928–29 Grant wrote that workers "were exposed to greater risks of injury, owing to their being required to work in more dangerous positions arising from the completion of principal structures on the Canal" (LAC, RG 43, vol. 2164, file 714.3, pt. 2, 61).

20 *St Catharines Standard*, 18 November 1924, 1.

21 *St Catharines Standard*, 6 February 1928, 1 and 3.

22 Grant, *Annual Report for 1926–1927* (LAC, RG 43, vol. 2164, file 714.3, pt. 2, 35).

23 *Toronto Globe*, 22 October 1928, 1.

24 *St Catharines Standard*, 1 August 1928, 1. Niagara's clay could be as hard as stone or almost maliciously adhesive. When the body of Joseph Dumoulin, killed in a 1928 landslide, was taken to the undertaker's, it was "so caked in clay that it was necessary to use a hose to clean it, so tenaciously did the clay stick." *Toronto Globe*, 22 October 1928, 1 and 5.

25 *St Catharines Standard*, 1 August 1928, 1.

26 Grant to Dubuc, 17 January 1933 (LAC, RG 43, vol. 2168, file 780.4); Dubuc to Grant, 2 March 1933 (LAC, RG 43, vol. 2168, file 780.2). At the time of this writing, a movement is afoot in Niagara to erect a more prominent memorial to those killed in the Fourth Canal's construction (e.g., *St Catharines Standard*, 19 August, 5 and 12 September 2015. The plans can be seen in the *Standard*, 6 August 2015). During the canal's construction, the families of the dead men did not receive many benefits. Moreover, according to one report, the on-site bosses "scolded" the survivors of a fatal disaster, urging them to get back to work and to forget about the incident. Bob Bratina, whose grandfather was a canal labourer, was present at the accident scene (*Globe and Mail*, 19 July 2013, A10).

27 Lazier to Grant, 31 July 1919 (LAC, RG 43, vol. 2174, file 879); Jewett to Grant, 1 September 1920 (LAC, RG 43, file 881).

28 *Toronto Mail and Empire*, 20 November 1920.

29 McCombe, *Canal Hospital Report for 1925–1926* (LAC, RG 43, vol. 2164, file 714.3 – 1925, 2); J.J. Heagerty to Porter, 25 September 1924 (LAC, RG 43, vol. 2197, file 1303); Heagerty to Dr. D.A. Clark (Assistant Deputy Minister, Department of Health, Ottawa), 2 May 1925 (LAC, RG 43, vol. 1286, file 174).

30 Cameron to Lampard, 17 October 1924 (LAC, RG 43, vol. 2197, file 1303).

31 *St Catharines Standard*, 8 January 1916, 1.

32 Jewett to Grant, 1 November 1920 (LAC, RG 43, vol. 2174, file 881); Porter to Grant, 21 August 1923 (LAC, RG 43, vol. 2182, file 1100). The tenants were evicted.

33 *Toronto Globe*, 31 May 1922, 4; the *Globe* took up the veterans' cause again later that month (*Toronto Globe*, 25 May 1922).

34 Lazier to Grant, 31 March 1920 (LAC, RG 43, vol. 2171, file 846).

35 Kydd to Grant, 19 May 1924 (LAC, RG 43, vol. 2194, file 1287.1).

36 Grant to Johnson, 15 December 1921 (LAC, RG 43, vol. 2188, file 1102).

37 Grant to W.V. Cope, 8 November 1920 (LAC, RG 43, vol. 2173, file 876).

38 Grant to G.A. Bell, 4 August 1921 (LAC, RG 43, vol. 2165, file 747).

39 Lazier to Grant, 31 March 1920 (LAC, RG 43, vol. 2171, file 846).

40 Earlier, an Ontario statute of 25 March 1886 provided compensation for injury sustained on the job (49 Vict., Ch. 28); the later act was passed on 1 May 1914:

"Act to provide Compensation to Workmen for Injuries sustained and Industrial Diseases contracted in the course of their Employment," Ontario, 4 George V. Ch. 2 (this act set up the Workmen's Compensation Board); 24 May 1918, "An Act to provide Compensation where Employees of His Majesty are killed or suffer injuries while performing their duties," Canada, 8–9 Geo. V. Ch. 15.

41 An inventory of 1932 includes an automobile, a horse, a cow, a supply of hay and oats, and one Union Jack (3 May 1932, "Inventory of Equipment, etc. at Construction Hospital," LAC, RG 43, vol. 2162, file 622).

42 Grant to John W.S. McCullough (Chief Officer, Ontario Board of Health), 18 August 1924 (LAC, RG 43, vol. 2162, file 622).

43 J.J. Heagerty (Department of Health) to Dr. D.A. Clark (Assistant Deputy Minister, Department of Health, Ottawa), 2 May 1925 (LAC, RG 43, vol. 1286, file 174).

44 Boulter to Jewett, 9 September 1922; Jewett to Boulter, 12 September 1922; Boulter to Grant, 14 September 1922; Grant to Boulter, 15 September 1922 (LAC, RG 43, vol. 2162, file 622).

45 Dr J.C. Ball to Grant, 5 February 1932 (LAC, RG 43, vol. 2162, file 622).

46 White, *Organic Machine*, 64.

CHAPTER TEN

1 Quoted in *St Catharines Standard*, 12 December 1912, 1.

2 Mr and Mrs Francis B. Grundy to Grant, 10 December 1927 (LAC, RG 43, vol. 2196, file 1287.8).

3 Weller to Battle & Martin, 8 June 1916 (LAC, RG 43, vol. 2155, file 255).

4 Grant, *Diary*, 8 December 1927.

5 Grant to Dubuc, 19 January 1927 (LAC, RG 43, vol. 2197, file 1301).

6 W.G. Reive (Welland Board of Health) to Grant, 29 June 1927 (LAC, RG 43, vol. 2203, file 1348).

7 Weller, *Annual Report for 1914–1915*, S.P. (no. 20.), for 1916, 349.

8 *St Catharines Standard*, 19 June 1930, 1.

9 J.F. and D.D. Gross (Solicitors for Humberstone) to Sectional Engineer G. Kydd, 17 September 1925 (LAC, RG 43, vol. 2194, file 287.1).

10 Grant, *Diary*, 23 August 1930.

11 *Welland Telegraph*, 9 December 1913, 1.

12 Bowden to Grant, 22 June 1920 (LAC, RG 43, vol. 2158, file 402).

13 Cameron to Grant, 25 November 1926 (LAC, RG 43, vol. 2198, file 1332.1).

14 G.H. Pettit (M.P.) to V.I. Smart (Deputy Minister, Department of Railways and Canals), 17 November 1933 (LAC, RG 4, vol. 2212, file 1383.2).

15 Dubuc to Hara, 3 April 1928 (LAC, RG 43, vol. 2205, file 1349.1.2); Grant to Hara, 5 April 1928 (LAC, RG 43, vol. 2207, file 1352.3).

CHAPTER ELEVEN

1 Lt.-Col. R.R. Rogers to Dubuc, 31 October 1930 (LAC, RG 43, vol. 1378, file 3540).
2 MacTaggart, *Three Years in Canada*, 161.
3 In 1932 railings were already installed on the west walls of Lock 1, 2, and 3 "to keep tourists away from mooring lines." Grant, *Diary*, 2 September 1932.
4 *Toronto Star Weekly*, 22 June 1929, 1. The journalist expresses the contradiction that Leo Marx described in his *The Machine in the Garden*. Americans – and Canadians too, by inference – could be inspired by the sublimity of the railway while simultaneously lamenting its ravaging of a pastoral landscape. The writer saw Niagara as a garden partly destroyed by the intrusion by remarkable locks and man-made channels. Similarly, representatives of the St Catharines and District Game and Fish Protective Association approved of plans to make the Ship Canal "a beauty spot, instead of an ugly scar as the old one was." O.E. Tallman and H.P. Nicholson to V.I. Smart, 23 May 1930 (LAC, RG 43, vol. 2227, file 1519); Report of the "Commission of Inquiry Concerning F.C. Jewett," 13 April 1931 (LAC, RG 43, vol. 1785, file 117) (henceforth "Concerning F.C. Jewett").
5 *St Catharines Standard*, 5 August 1932, 6.
6 Jewett to Grant, 31 May 1928 (LAC, RG 43, vol. 2183, file 1100.1).
7 *Toronto Star Weekly*, 22 June 1929.
8 Jewett, "Memorandum re Reforestation and General Maintenance Sections Nos. 1 & 2, Welland Ship Canal," 31 March 1927 (LAC, RG 43, vol. 2159, file 548 "1927"); Jewett to Grant, 31 March 1928 (LAC, RG 43, vol. 2164, file 714.3, pt. 2, 12); Waddell to Grant, 29 April 1928 (LAC, RG 43, vol. 2159, file 548, "1928"). According to Rodney Millard, Canadian engineers had long felt the need for greater public recognition of their multiple talents. (*Master Spirit of the Age*, 95.) To a degree, the Forestry Project was a result of this mood.
9 Waddell to Grant, 29 April 1928 (LAC, RG 43, vol. 2159, file 548, "1928").
10 Waddell to E.G. Cameron, 10 October 1928 (LAC, RG 43, vol. 2159, file 528, "1928").
11 The variety of trees was astonishing. Chinese elm came from Colorado. White, black, laurel leaf, golden, Wisconsin weeping, Regal, Basket, and shining willows were planted. The poplars included Carolina, Bolleano, Saskatchewan poplar, North West poplar, Russian, Norway, and Eugenei. Nut trees, such as hickory, walnut, chestnut, Japanese heart nut, butternut (native, hybrid, and Japanese) were planted as well as hornbeams, gum trees, tulip, witchhazel, cherry, mulberry, basswood, locust, and conifers (*Welland Ship Canal*, 233). In early 1928, for example, the Ontario Forester recorded that, at Jewett's request, thousands of seedlings had been sent to the canal site from the province's nurseries: 80,000 Carolina poplar, 20,000 white spruce, 30,000 white ash,

and 10,000 white cedar. Orders for seedlings of red cedar, Douglas fir, Sitka spruce, and western hemlock were placed in British Columbia. A.H. Richardson to Grant, 24 April 1928 (LAC, RG 43, vol. 2159, file 548).

12 Waddell to Grant, 15 January 1931 (LAC, RG 43, vol. 2159, file 649.2). The variety of flowering shrubs alone is impressive: clematis, japonica, cotoneaster, euonymus, forsythia, hydrangea, spirea, etc.

13 O.E. Tallman and H.P. Nicholson to V.I. Smart, 23 May 1930 (LAC, RG 43, vol. 2227, file 1519). The unwatering of the locks in winter for repairs would destroy any fish in the canal. Ultimately, steps were taken to prevent hunting and fishing along the waterway because the engineers feared hunters and fishermen would damage the banks.

14 "Concerning F.C. Jewett," 13 April 1931 (LAC, RG 43, vol. 1785, file 121).

15 *St Catharines Standard*, 30 September 1927, 1.

16 Lt.-Col. R.R. Rogers to Dubuc, 31 October 1930 (LAC, RG 43, vol. 1378, file 3540).

17 "Concerning F.C. Jewett," 13 April 1931 (LAC, RG 43, vol. 2159, files 86 and 87).

18 James A. Neilson to Grant, 25 August 1927 (LAC, RG 43, vol. 2159, file 548).

19 Waddell also remarked that "it is quite true in 1927, that we felt a little bit leery about asking for things ... We had to feel our way carefully" (LAC, RG 43, vol. 2159, files 86 and 87, 122).

20 Grant to Dubuc, 27 March 1929 and 30 October 1930 (LAC, RG 43, vol. 1378, file 3540).

21 Waddell to Grant, 29 April 1928 (LAC, RG 43, vol. 2159, file 548, "1928").

22 Grant to Massey Harris, 8 September 1927 (LAC, RG 43, vol. 2159, file 548, "1927"); Waddell to Grant, 29 April 1928 (LAC, RG 43, vol. 2159, file 548, "1928," 3).

23 Jewett to Grant, 11 February 1930 (LAC, RG 43, vol. 2159, file 549.2).

24 West to Grant, 20 April 1926 (LAC, RG 43, vol. 2185, file 1101.2).

25 Grant to Waddell, 12 April 1929, 24 February 1930 (LAC, RG 43, vol. 2159, files 548 and 549.2); Grant to Waddell, 28 December 1928 (LAC, RG 43, vol. 2159, file 548).

26 A description of aspects of Jewett's and Waddell's work on the Forestry Project, "Concerning F.C. Jewett," 13 April 1931, 7 (LAC, RG 43, vol. 1785).

27 "We also do our own photographic work," said Waddell in 1930. Waddell's "Description of Work by Employee," November 1930 (LAC, RG 43, vol. 1378, file 3540).

28 "Concerning F.C. Jewett," 13 April 1931 (LAC, RG 43, vol. 1785, file 119).

29 "Concerning F.C. Jewett," 7; Waddell to Dubuc, 24 July 1931 (LAC, RG 43, vol. 1378, file 3540).

30 Grant, *Diary*, 15 December 1930, 19 January 1931.

31 Waddell was bitter during the investigation. "There is lots I could say," he said to Lancaster, "but I think it will be better not said" ("Concerning F.C. Jewett," 115).

32 Jewett to Dubuc, 15 January 1931 (LAC, RG 43, vol. 1378, file 3540); "Concerning F.C. Jewett," 7.

33 Dubuc to Grant, 14 July 1931 (LAC, RG 43, vol. 2227, file 1530). In fact Jewett
went on to oversee harbour construction in Saint John and Montreal for the
National Harbours Board and in 1938 he was appointed chief engineer for
Gander Airport in Newfoundland. In 1943 he was made Chief of Wartime
Construction, especially airfields, by the Department of Transport. In that
position he was responsible for the airport at Goose Bay, Labrador. After the
war he opened a consulting practice in Ottawa and in 1948 was made a CBE
(Civil Section).

34 C.W. West, formerly sectional engineer on Section 3, replaced Jewett, while
R.E. Yates, instrumentman on Sections 3 and 4 who had previously been employed by J.D. Chaplin, replaced Waddell. We know nothing about the latter's
subsequent career.

35 *Toronto Star Weekly*, 22 June 1929, 1.

36 Grant to West, 10 August 1931 (LAC, RG 43, vol. 2216, file 1405.3).

37 Canal buffs with imagination and some knowledge of the Forestry Project can
today see the results of Waddell's and Jewett's work at several sites. Trees still
stand along the banks of the waterway and on the Port Weller embankments.
Near the latter site, Malcolmson Park is now thickly forested. As late as the
1990s a Japanese plum tree was still blooming at Bridge 5 in St. Catharines,
while lilacs could be found in Allanburg on the west bank of the canal. In a
grove north of Allanburg on east side of canal, three rows of trees suggest
deliberate planting. On Welland's Merritt Island, some old stands of orderly
plantings may also date back to Waddell's project.

38 "First Steps Taken towards Unwatering Old Canal from Thorold to Lock 3 in
City," *St Catharines Standard*, 12 March 1929, 1.

39 Grant to Yates, 16 August 1930 (LAC, RG 43, vol. 2167, file 780.3).

40 John Silverthorn to W.C. Kennedy, 17 July 1922 (SCL, MS 191, file 5371, WCR).
In 1921 he had already offered his plan to Grant. John Silverthorn to Grant, 6
October 1921 (LAC, RG 43, vol. 2160, file 593).

41 Cameron to Steel Gates Company, 16 August 1928 (LAC, RG 43, vol. 2211, file
1379.2).

42 *St Catharines Standard*, 9 June 1924, 1.

43 Cooper to Grant, 16 October 1929 (LAC, RG 43, vol. 2171, file 840.27).

44 Jewett to Grant, 2 July 1929 (LAC, RG 43, vol. 2183, file 1100.1).

45 Grant to Jewett, 15 November 1928; Grant to Cowan, 18 December 1928; Jewett
to Grant, 7 December 1928 (LAC, RG 43, vol. 2167, file 780.2).

46 Grant to Cowan, 28 April 1930 (LAC, RG 43, vol. 2167, file 780.2).

47 Murphy to Grant, 30 April 1930 (LAC, RG 43, vol. 2195, file 1287.1.3).

48 "Tomorrow's Program," *St Catharines Standard*, 5 August 1932, 17.

49 W.A. Irwin in *Maclean's* magazine, reported in the *St Catharines Standard*, 5
August 1932, 18.

CHAPTER TWELVE

1 Nye, *The American Technological Sublime.*
2 Marx, *The Machine in the Garden*, passim.
3 Clarence Arthur Dowling Thompson, "Martyrs of Progress," *St Catharines Standard*, 5 August 1932, 4. See full text in Appendix VI.
4 J.B. Carswell to A.J. Grant, 14 September 1932 (LAC, RG 43, vol. 2225, file 1503). Carswell was managing director of the Burlington Steel Company of Hamilton, Ontario. His description is reminiscent of the landing of the spaceship in Steven Spielberg's 1977 film *Close Encounters of the Third Kind* when the earthlings marvel at the advanced and sublime beauty of the aliens' technology.
5 For White, the Columbia River is both "a natural space and a social space" (*The Organic Machine*, 112) in which men and elemental forces co-operate. John N. Jackson came close to this concept in his *The Welland Canal and Its Communities* but does not develop it.

APPENDIX IV

1 Legget, *The Seaway*, 54.
2 By the 1960s and late '70s, $65 million worth of innovations had been introduced, increasing the canal's capacity by 35 per cent and reducing transit time (Legget, *The Seaway*, 5).
3 St Lawrence Seaway Authority, *The Welland By-Pass*, 4.
4 Jackson, *Welland and the Welland Canal: The Welland Canal By-Pass*, 88–9.
5 Before construction of the By-Pass was decided upon, the problematic Bridge 13 on Main Street in Welland was to have been replaced by a tunnel.
6 St Lawrence Seaway Authority, *The Welland By-Pass*, 7 and 9.
7 Ibid., 12.

BIBLIOGRAPHY

ARCHIVAL SOURCES

Archives of Ontario (Toronto)
Department of Railways and Canals (Library and Archives Canada, Ottawa)
Diary of Alexander J. Grant (St Catharines Museum)
Engineering Institute of Canada (Library and Archives Canada, Ottawa)
St Lawrence Seaway Management Corporation, Niagara Region (St Catharines)
Welland Canal Records (James A. Gibson Library, Brock University, St Catharines)
Welland Canal Records (St Catharines Museum)

SECONDARY SOURCES

Andreae, Christopher. *Lines of Country: An Atlas of Railway and Waterway History in Canada*. Erin, ON: Boston Mills Press, 1997.

Angus, James T. *A Respectable Ditch: A History of the Trent-Severn Waterway, 1833–1920*. Montreal and Kingston: McGill-Queen's University Press, 1988.

Avery, Donald. *"Dangerous Foreigners": European Immigrant Workers and Labour Radicalism in Canada, 1896–1932*. Toronto: McClelland and Stewart, 1979.

Ball, Norman R. *"Mind, Heart and Vision": Professional Engineering in Canada 1887–1987*. Ottawa: National Museum of Science and Technology, National Museums of Canada, in co-operation with the Engineering Centennial Board, 1987.

Battle, David. "Plans for a New Welland Canal." *Canadian Engineer* (June 1909): 744–5.

Baxter, R.R., ed. *Documents on the St. Lawrence Seaway*. New York: Praeger, 1961.

Bishop, Olga B., et al. *Bibliography of Ontario History, 1867–1976*. Toronto: University of Toronto Press, 1980.

Bond, Ray Corry. *Peninsula Village: The Story of Chippawa*. Chippawa, 1964.

Bothwell, Robert. *A Short History of Ontario*. Edmonton: Hurtig, 1986.

Burtniak, John, and Wesley B. Turner, eds. *The Welland Canals: Proceedings of the First Annual Niagara Peninsula History Conference*. St Catharines: Brock University, 1979.

Canada. *Debates of the House of Commons*. Ottawa: Dawson, 1904 and later years.

– Department of Railways and Canals. *Welland Ship Canal (under construction). Also Brief Historic Reference to Past and Present Wellands*. Ottawa: Thomas Mulvey, 1920.

– Department of Railways and Canals. *Welland Ship Canal, Sections Nos. 3 & 4*. Specifications for the re-letting of the work to be done in connection with the completion of the construction of Section No. 3 and the entire construction of Section No. 4, including Nos. 4, 5, 6 and 7 Guard Gates. Ottawa: F.A. Acland, 1921.

– Department of Railways and Canals. Office of the Chief Engineer. *Album of Welland Canal Photographs*, 11 July 1922.

– Department of Railways and Canals. *Welland Ship Canal. Office of the Engineer in Charge. Album of Plans and Photographs, May 1923–August 1924*.

– Department of Railways and Canals. *A Canadian Conception. A Canadian Achievement. Opening of the Welland Ship Canal. August Sixth – Nineteen Thirty Two*. Ottawa, King's Printer, 1932.

– Department of Railways and Canals. *Welland Ship Canal, 1934*. Published by the Authority of the Hon. R.J. Manion, MP, Minister of Railways and Canals. Ottawa: Patenaude, 1934.

Canadian Westinghouse Company Limited. *Interesting Facts about the Welland Ship Canal*. Hamilton: Canadian Westinghouse Company Limited. Bulletin H-7016, n.d.

Carrigan, D. Owen, ed. *Canadian Party Platforms*. Toronto, 1968.

Carter, Dewitt. "Relative Sizes and Capacities of Our Canals Reflected in Trend of Traffic." *Ontario Historical Society, Papers and Records* 23 (1926): 19–27.

– *The Welland Canal: A History*. Port Colborne, ON: Helen Carter, 1960.

Chevrier, Lionel. *The St. Lawrence Seaway*. Toronto, 1959.

Christensen, Carl J., Anthomy Di Giacomo, and Joseph E. Pohorly. *History of Engineering in Niagara*. St Catharines: Lincoln Graphics (for the Niagara Peninsula Branch, Engineering Institute of Canada), 1976.

Corthell, E.L. *An Enlarged Water-Way between the Great Lakes and the Atlantic Seaboard*. Montreal: Lovell, 1891 (Canadian Society of Civil Engineers. Excerpt from the Transactions of the Society, vol. 5, Session 1891).

Cowan, P.J. *The Welland Ship Canal between Lake Ontario and Lake Erie, 1913–1932*. London: Offices of *Engineering*, 1935.

Cruikshank, E.A. *The History of the County of Welland*. Belleville, ON: Mika, 1972.

Detroit, Michigan. Board of Commerce. *The Fourth Welland Ship Canal: History and Engineering Detail*. Detroit: Board of Commerce, 1931. [The Board's Cruise of Inspection, 18–22 June 1931.]

Duff, Louis Blake, ed. *The Welland Ship Canal*. St Catharines: n.p., 1930.

Easterbrook, W.T., and Hugh G.J. Aitken. *Canadian Economic History*. Toronto: University of Toronto Press, 1956.

Evans, W. Sanford. *The St. Lawrence Deep Waterway in Relation to Grain Traffic*. Winnipeg, 1922/23.

Francis, R. Douglas. *The Technological Imperative in Canada. An Intellectual History*. Vancouver: UBC Press, 2009.

Gentilcore, R. Louis, and C. Grant Head. *Ontario's History in Maps*. Toronto: University of Toronto Press, 1984.

Gilham, E.B. *The Welland Canal Mission*. St Catharines, 1981.

Glazebrook, G.P. de T. *A History of Transportation in Canada*. 2 vols. 2nd ed. Toronto: Ryerson, 1938.

Greenwald, Michelle, et al. *The Welland Canals. Historical Resource Analysis and Preservation*. Alternatives. Ontario Ministry of Culture and Recreation. Historical Planning and Research. Heritage Branch Conservation Division, 1977.

Harvie, Fred. *Town of Thorold Centennial, 1850–1950* [1950?].

Heisler, John P. *Canals of Canada*. Ottawa: Canada. Department of Indian Affairs and Northern Development, 1973 (Canadian Historic Sites: Occasional Papers in Archaeology and History, No. 8).

Heron, Craig, ed. *The Workers' Revolt in Canada 1917–1925*. Toronto: University of Toronto Press, 1998.

Hill, Henry W. "Historical Sketch of Niagara Ship Canal Projects." *Buffalo Historical Society Publications* 22 (1918): 201–66.

Hills, T.L. *The St. Lawrence Seaway*. London: Methuen, 1959.

Hodgetts, J.E., William McCloskey, Reginald Whitaker, and V. Seymour Wilson. *Biography of an Institution: The Civil Service Commission of Canada 1908–1967*. Montreal and Kingston: McGill-Queen's University Press, 1972.

Innis, Harold, and Arthur Lower, eds. *Select Documents in Canadian Economic History 1783–1885*. Toronto: University of Toronto Press, 1933.

Jackson, John N. *Welland and the Welland Canal: The Welland Canal By-Pass*. Belleville, ON: Mika, 1975.

– *The Welland Canals and Their Communities*. Toronto: University of Toronto Press, 1997.

Jackman, W.T. "The Economic Development of Canada 1867–1921: Communications." *Cambridge History of the British Empire: Canada and Newfoundland*. Vol. 6, 581–3. New York: Macmillan, 1929.

Jacobs, David, and Anthony E. Neville. *Bridges, Canals and Tunnels*. New York: Van Nostrand, 1968.

Johnson, E.P. "Canal Engineering Yesterday and Today." *Ontario Historical Society. Papers and Records,* 13, (1926): 365–9.

Keefer, T.C. "The Canals of Canada," *Transactions of the Royal Society of Canada,* Sec. III (1893), 25–50.

Langbein, Walter B. "Our Grand Canal." *Civil Engineering* (October 1988): 75–8.

Legget, Robert F. *Canals of Canada.* Vancouver: Douglas, David and Charles, 1976.

– *The Seaway. In Commemoration of the Seaway and the 150th Anniversary of the First Welland Canal.* Toronto: Clarke Irwin, 1979.

Lewis, William L. *Aqueduct, Merrittsville and Welland. A History of the City of Welland,* vol. 2: *The Continuing Years.* Welland, ON: A.M.W. Publications, 2000.

Mabee, Carleton. *The Seaway Story.* New York: Macmillan, 1961.

Macfarlane, Daniel. *Negotiating a River: Canada, the US, and the Creation of the St. Lawrence Seaway.* Vancouver: UBC Press, 2014.

MacTaggart, John. *Three Years in Canada.* London: Colburn, 1829.

Martine, Gloria. "The Role of the Welland Canal in Industrial Location." BA thesis, University of Toronto, 1961.

Marx, Leo. *The Machine in the Garden. Technology and the Pastoral Ideal in America.* New York: Oxford University Press, 1964.

McGeorge, W.G. *Report on the Welland and Feeder Canals.* Chatham, ON, 1947.

McInnis, Marvin. "Engineering Expertise and the Canadian Exploitation of the Technology of the Second Industrial Revolution." qed.econ.queensu.ca/pub/faculty/mcinnis/EngineeringExpertise.pdf.

Meaney, Carl Frank Patrick. *The Welland Canal and Canadian Development.* MA thesis, McMaster University, 1980.

Michael, Betti(?). *Township of Thorold, 1793–1967: Centennial Project of the Township of Thorold.* Toronto: Armath Associates, 1967.

Michener, David M. *The Canals at Welland.* Welland: Rotary Club of Welland, 1973.

Millard, J. Rodney. *The Master Spirit of the Age. Canadian Engineers and the Politics of Professionalism 1887–1922.* Toronto: University of Toronto Press, 1988.

Morison, Elting E. *From Know-How to Nowhere: The Development of American Technology.* New York: Basic Books, 1975.

Moulton, Harold Glenn, Charles S. Morgan, and Adah L. Lee. *The St. Lawrence Navigation and Power Project.* Washington: Brookings Institution, 1929.

Muntz, Madelein. *John Laing Weller: The Man Who Does Things.* St Catharines: Vanwell, 2007.

Niagara Regional Chamber of Commerce. *101 Reasons Why Ontario Should Support the All-Canadian Welland Canal and the St. Lawrence Seaway.* St Catharines, April 1975.

– *An Economic Survey for the Regional Municipality of Niagara Showing Local Impact of the Welland Canal and the St. Lawrence Seaway Operations.* St Catharines, 1977.

Nye, David E. *The American Technological Sublime*, Cambridge, MA: MIT Press, 1994.

Ontario. Ministry of Highways. *The Thorold Tunnel.* Toronto, 1966.

Osborne, Brian S., and Donald Swainson. *The Sault Ste. Marie Canal. A Chapter in the History of Great Lakes Transport.* Ottawa: Studies in Archaeology, Architecture and History, National Historic Parks and Sites Branch, Parks Canada/Environment Canada, 1986.

Owen, David. *The Manchester Ship Canal.* Manchester: Manchester University Press, 1983.

Owram, Doug. *Buildings for Canadians: A History of the Department of Public Works, 1840–1960.* Ottawa: Public Works Canada, 1979.

Parks Canada and Ontario Ministry of Culture and Recreation and Ministry of Natural Resources. *Welland Canals Concept Plan: A Canada-Ontario Study.* n.p., n.d.

Passfield, Robert W. *Technology in Transition: The 'Soo' Ship Canal, 1889–1985.* Ottawa: National Historic Parks and Sites, Canadian Parks Service. Studies in Archaeology, Architecture and History, 1989.

Pennanen, Gary. "Battle of the Titans: Mitchell Hepburn, Mackenzie King, Franklin Roosevelt, and the St Lawrence Seaway." *Ontario History* 89, no. 1 (March 1997): 1–21.

Port Arthur, Ontario. Board of Trade. *The Welland Canal or Georgian Bay Canal – Which?* Port Arthur: Board of Trade, 1913.

Potestio, John, and Antonio Pucci, eds. *The Italian Immigrant Experience.* Thunder Bay, ON: Canadian Historical Association, 1988.

Power Authority of the State of New York. *Paralleling the Welland Canal and Effects on the Niagara Power Project.* 30 January 1958.

Project Planning Associates Limited. *Third Welland Canal Regional Park: Master Development Plan.* Toronto, 1964.

Provincial Great Lakes/Seaway Task Force. *The Great Lakes/Seaway: Setting a Course for the '80s.* 1981.

Ramirez, Bruno. *The Italians in Canada.* Canadian Historical Association, Canada's Ethnic Groups, No. 14. Saint John, NB, 1989.

Rannie, W.F. "When Jordan Might Have Been 'Lock 1' on the Welland Canal." In W.F. Rannie, *Lost Childhoods: 'Home' Children From Abroad and Other Stories about Lincoln*, 107–12. Lincoln, ON, 1991.

Reade, R.C. "Dolling Up Our Big Canal." *Toronto Star Weekly,* 22 June 1929, General Section, 1.

Reid, Nora. *Main Street Bridge* (Bridge 13 on the Welland Canal). Report prepared for the Welland Local Architecture Conservation Advisory Committee, January 1993.

Rice, W.B. *The History of the County of Welland*. Edited by John Burtniak. Belleville, ON, 1972.

St Catharines, Ontario and the Welland Ship Canal: The Open Door to Canadian and British Empire Markets. St Catharines: Commercial Press, 1933.

St Lawrence Seaway Authority. *Drainage Control, Welland Channel Relocation*, 1968.

– *Road-Rail Networks*. 1968.

– *The Welland By-Pass*. 1973.

– *Welland Channel Relocation 1967–1972*. 1973.

Sayles, Fern A. *Welland Workers Make History*. Welland, 1963.

Sinclair, Bruce. "Canadian Technology: British Traditions and American Influences." *Technology and Culture* (1979): 108–23.

Slaton, Amy E. *Reinforced Concrete and the Modernization of American Building, 1900–1930*. Baltimore: Johns Hopkins University Press, 2001.

Smy, William A. *Guarding Niagara: The Welland Canal Force 1914–1918*. www.niagarahistorical.museum/media/04.GuardingNiagara1914copy.pdf.

Stephens, George Washington. *The St Lawrence Waterway Project*. Montreal, 1929.

Styran, Roberta M., and Robert R. Taylor. "The Welland Canal: Creator of a Landscape." *Ontario History* 72, no. 4 (December 1980): 210–29.

– (with John N. Jackson). *The Welland Canals: The Growth of Mr. Merritt's Ditch*. Erin, ON: Boston Mills Press, 1988.

– *Mr. Merritt's Ditch: A Welland Canals Album*. Toronto: Boston Mills Press/Stoddart, 1992.

– eds. *The "Great Swivel Link": Canada's Welland Canal*. Toronto: University of Toronto Press for The Champlain Society, 2001.

– (with Thies Bogner). *The Welland Canals Corridor: Then and Now*. St Catharines: Looking Back Press, 2004.

– *This Great National Object: Building the Nineteenth-Century Welland Canals*. Montreal and Kingston: McGill-Queen's University Press, 2012.

Sussman, Gennifer. *The St Lawrence Seaway: Canada-U.S. Prospects*. Ottawa: National Planning Association, 1978.

Taylor, Robert R. "Merritton, Ontario: The Rise and Decline of an Industrial Corridor, ca. 1845–1939." *Scientia Canadensis. Journal of the History of Canadian Science, Technology and Medicine* 14, nos. 1–2 (1990): 90–130.

– ed. *Voices from the Great Ditch. The Historic Welland Canals in Pictures, Prose, Poems, and Songs*. St Catharines: Blarney Stone, 2004.

Taylor, Robert Stanley. "The Historical Development of the Four Welland Canals, 1824–1933." MA thesis, University of Western Ontario, 1950.

Thompson, John Herd. *Ethnic Minorities during the Two World Wars*. Vol. 19. Ottawa: Canadian Historical Association, 1991.

Thorold and Beaverdams Historical Society. *Thirty-Five Years Later. Supplement to Jubilee History of Thorold. Township and Town. Covering the Eventful Period 1897 to 1932*. Thorold: Thorold Post, 1932.

Thorold Township. Board of Trade. *The Township of Thorold: Advantages of Thorold Township for Industrial Purposes*. Thorold, n.d.

– *The Township of Thorold, 1793–1967*. Thorold, 1967.

Toronto Board of Trade. *The Deepening of the Welland Canal. Its Importance to Canada*. Toronto, 1910.

Watson, J.W. "The Changing Industrial Pattern of the Niagara Peninsula." *Ontario History* 37 (1945): 49–58.

Way, Peter. *Common Labour: Workers and the Digging of North American Canals 1780–1860*. Cambridge: Cambridge University Press, 1993.

Welland Ship Canal. *Souvenir Views*. Various dates.

White, Randall. *Ontario 1610–1985. A Political and Economic History*. Toronto: Dundurn, 1985.

White, Richard. *The Organic Machine*. New York: Hill and Wang, 1995.

Yates, George W. "The Welland Canal." *Canadian Geographical Journal* 2 (1931): 23–37.

Young, N.R.P. "The Economic and Social Development of Welland, 1905–1939." MA thesis, University of Guelph, 1975.

INDEX

An italic *f* following a page reference indicates the presence of an illustration.

The following abbreviations are used in the index:

CNR – Canadian National Railway
DPW – Department of Public Works
DRC – Department of Railways and Canals
FWC – First Welland Canal
SWC – Second Welland Canal
TWC – Third Welland Canal
WBP – Welland By-Pass
WSC – Welland Ship Canal

process, 49; crossings of, 131; culverts, 115–16; Deep Cut, 106–7, 216; embankment sodding, 216; financing of, 277; landslides on, 67; location and route, xxii*f*, 98*f*, 108*f*; locks, 25, 30, 72*f*; manual labour on, 168; remains of, 230; stone construction, 80; water from Grand River for, 107; wooden construction, 109, 230

First World War: Canadian Forestry Corps, 223; construction halt during, xxvii, 5–7, 36, 50, 85, 122, 195, 278; inflation following, 162–3; interned "enemy aliens," 182; labour shortages during, xxvii, 5, 7, 169, 182; strikes during, 169; veterans employed on WSC, xxvii, 8, 170, 181–2, 301n36, 302n11; Vimy Memorial, xx; xenophobia during, 181

fish and fishing, 221, 222, 306n13

flight locks. *See* twinned flight locks

flooding: of agricultural land, 200, 202–3; at Beaverdams, 118; caused by contractors, 205; for Chippawa Creek dam (proposed), 107; from construction damage, 202–5; deliberate inundation, 202–3, 215; with heavy rain, 67; with Lake Erie storms, 115, 120; at Lock 1, 95; at Lock 8, 95, 120; at Rock Cut, 67; at syphon culvert, 114. *See also* water management

Fonthill (ON), 20, 150*f*, 19*f*, 221

Forestry and Maintenance Branch (Forestry Project), 216–28; ambiguous position of, 223–4; bird and game sanctuaries (proposed), 220, 222; charges and investigation of, 14, 225–8, 248; Grant's support for, 28, 48, 218, 222, 223–8; greenhouse and garden, 219*f*, 221, 228; nurseries, 218*f*, 220, 221; political issues with, 226, 228; public interest and support for, 222; public park context of, 216–17, 305n8; shrub and tree varieties, 220, 221, 305–6nn11–12, 307n37; surviving results of, 307n37; suspension of (1931), 10

Foster Wheeler (St Catharines), 53, 293n62

Four Mile Creek, 19*f*

Fourth Welland Canal. *See* Welland Ship Canal

Frid Construction, 137

FUNDY (dipper dredge), 61, 173*f*

Gardiner, J. (contractor, partner of Lyall), 55, 293n62

gate leaves. *See* lock gates

gate lifters: cranes and derricks for, 85, 94; diagram, 92*f*; photograph, 91*f*; pontoon lifter, 53, 54, 91–5; for TWC, 90–1

gates of locks. *See* lock gates

gate yard (Port Weller), 60–1*f*, 94, 248

geological features and challenges: with bridge construction, 151–2; with excavations, 65–8; with lock foundations, 83–4, 95–6; with Port Weller construction, 125; with syphon culvert construction, 112–15. *See also* Niagara Escarpment; Onondaga Escarpment

GEORGIAN (laker), 100, 132*f*, 233

Georgian Bay canal route (proposed), xxvi–xxvii, 13, 17, 20, 286n12

German, A.M. (contractor), 161

German, W.M. (MP for Welland), 169

Germany: Kiel Canal, 4; revolutionary events, 172

GLENCASSIE (laker), xxiii

Gowan, Nassau W., and Gowan safety horns, 25, 75

grading machines, 62, 65

Graham, George P., xxv, 20, 41, 73

Grain Produce Association (Winnipeg), xxv

Grand Coulee Dam (Columbia River), xvi, 199, 308n5

Grand River, xxii*f*, 19*f*, 20, 21, 107, 126

Grand Trunk Railway: canal cargoes transported by, xxiv; disused tunnel for, 127; diversion at Twin Locks 4, 6, 133; and Georgian Bay Canal (proposed), xxvi; station gardens, 217; tunnel for, 267; and WSC route, 21, 23, 63, 117f

Grant, Alexander James (Alex)
– biographical details: career and personality, 32, 40–9; at construction sites, 44, 291n31; diaries, xvii, xviii*f*, 32, 291n22; friendships, 43–4; on his-

- Highway 8: canal construction around, 153, 231; canal crossing at Homer (Bridge 4), 131, 143*f*, 144, 151*f*
- Highway 20, 132, 133
- Highway 58, 267, 268*f*
- Highway 406, 267
historical sites, 229–30
Hobart, Lord Robert (British Secretary for War and the Colonies), 68
Homer (ON): engineers' office at, 40; ground instability and landslides at, 67, 171; location, 18*f*, 51*f*; Medical Service hospital at, 183, 196, 198; park at, 222. *See also* Bridge 4
Hoover, Herbert, 82
Horgan, Jack, 46, 56
horses: for ambulances, 198; compared to automobile traffic, 132, 133; for construction work, 64, 126; for surveyors, 161*f*; for visits to construction sites, 33, 44
Horton Steel (Welland), 53
hospitals. *See* Medical Service
Hudson Bay Railway, 247
Humberstone: blasting operations near, 206, 207, 210; Bridge 19 in, 81*f*; bridges requested for, 153; field hospital at, 183, 196, 198, 206; flooding at, 203–4, 205; location, xxii*f*; man-made island at, 222; weir at, 26, 28, 39; wells and water works for, 210
hunting and game: sanctuaries along canal (proposed), 221, 222, 306n13
"Hunt's Hollow," 22
Hurontario Canal, 286n12
Hutchinson, Paul, 276
hydro. *See* electric power and hydroelectricity
Hydro-Electric Power Commission (HEPC) and Queenston-Chippawa Hydro-Electric Canal (Queenston Hydro project), 9, 161, 163, 171–2, 174, 248

immigrants, 179–83; accidents and fatalities among, 179–80, 252–61; employed as labourers, 170*f*, 171–3, 177, 178, 301n36; language barriers with, 159, 170, 187; medical care for, 197; prejudice against, 11, 168, 179, 180–3, 190; strike

actions and political radicalism, 171–3, 177, 178, 181, 182–3
Imperial Economic Conference (Ottawa, 1932), xx, 29, 235, 238
Industrial Brownhoist (Cleveland), 10
Industrial Workers of the World (IWW), 181
industry and industrial development: construction-related problems, 211–12; Second Industrial Revolution, 4, 58, 64; water sources for, 207, 211, 229; and WBP, 266. *See also specific companies and corporations*
Ingersoll-Rand submarine drill, 63
Inner Harbour Navigation Canal (New Orleans), 246
instrumentmen, 5, 10, 246, 248, 307n34
Intercolonial Railway (Maritimes), 31, 290n17
Interdepartmental Committee on the St Lawrence Waterway (US, 1926), 272
Interlake Tissue, 211
International Deep Waterways Association, 270
International Joint Commission (1909), 69, 271
International Nickel Company of Canada, 120, 163, 212
International Waterways Association, 69
Isthmian (Panama) Canal Commission, 36
Italian immigrants, 7, 168, 170*f*, 180, 182, 187

jackhammers, 205
Jackson, John N., 275, 293n4, 308n5
JAMES WHALEN (tug), 94
Jarrett, James W., xv
Jewett, Frederick Coburn: career, 247–8, 307n33; on concrete quality, 84; on construction debris, 218; and P.J. Cowan, 232, 233; and Forestry Project, 14, 218–20, 222–4, 225–8, 305n11, 307n37; and Grant, 39–40, 47, 48, 75, 86; on labourers, 45, 163, 182, 190–1, 192, 302n11; on labour unrest, 171, 173; on Medical Service speeder, 198; "museum of defective parts," 65; and J.P. Porter, 55, 96–7; replaced by C.W. West, 307n34; responsibility for

250; embankments at, 67; length, 249;
location, 51*f*, 208*f*; mules used on, 66;
peatbeds at, 66; staff accommodation
near, 194
Section 7: contractors for, 250; delay for
Welland filtration plant, 210; length,
249; location, 51*f*, 208*f*; road and railway crossings in, 132; slides at, 67; staff
accommodation near, 194
Section 8: contractors for, 56, 251; excavation of, 55–6; flooding at, 67; heavy
clay at, 66, 67; length, 249; location,
51*f*; road and railway crossings in, 132;
Rock Cut, 66, 67, 210; Section 9 amalgamated with, 58, 291n30; staff accommodation near, 194
Select Committee of the Upper Canada
Legislature (1826), 271
Select Committee on Internal Resources
(1821), 271
Selkirk (ON), 19*f*, 20
sewage disposal systems, 107, 197–8, 209
shale, 62, 63, 84, 87, 95–6, 113
Shanly Report (1871), 288n11
Shaver's Ravine, xxii*f*
sheet piling, 23, 114, 152
ship arresters (lock gate fenders), 25–6,
235*f*
Ship Canal Gate Yard, 60–1*f*, 94, 248
Ship Canal Health Board, 168, 191–2, 197,
209
Ship Canal Medical Service. *See* Medical
Service
Ship Canal staff: Civil Service
Commission requirements, 14–15;
Grant's relationship with, 194–5; offices
and accommodation for, 40, 102, 193–5;
wages for, 10–11, 166, 195; and wartime
construction halt, 5–7; white-collar
workers, 160, 192–5
shipping collisions, xxi–xxv, 25–6, 114,
125, 212, 262
ships: clearance under lift bridges, 141;
dismantled for passage through TWC,
xxiv; lakers, 243*f*; safety measures to
protect, 23–6; salties, 12, 243*f*; sizes of,
xxiii, 72*f*, 125–6; tugboats, 63, 71, 91,
95*f*, 124*f*, 131; on TWC (*see under* Third
Welland Canal)

– specific vessels: CHARLES R. VAN
HISE (freighter), 286n10; ERICSON
(laker), 134; GEORGIAN (laker), 100,
132*f*, 233; GLENCASSIE (laker), xxiii;
HIAWATHA (laker), xxiii, 26; JAMES
WHALEN (tug), 94; JOHN MANLEY
(tug), 29, 101; LEMOYNE (laker), 235*f*,
236, 237, 239; MEAFORD (laker), 29,
101, 234*f*; MUSCALLONGE (tug), 94;
PIONEER (concrete scow), 34; STEEL-
TON (laker), 298n8; TADOUSSAC
(laker), 149*f*
shovels, steam shovels, 61, 62, 129*f*
Shriner's Creek and Culvert, 116, 117*f*,
118, 168
SHUNIAH (suction/hydraulic dredge), 61
Shurley, E.C. (contractor), 44
Silverthorne, John, 231, 307n40
Simpson, Charles: Port Weller, Lock 1
(1932), 238*f*
single-leaf rolling gates, xvii–xviii, 73–4,
75, 76
Six Mile Creek, 19*f*
Sixteen Mile Creek, 19*f*
skilled labour (tradesmen): hours and
wages for, 163–5; structural iron and
steel workers, 154–5, 301–2n2; working
conditions, 159
Slaton, Amy, 102
smallpox, 168
Smart, H.B. (CNR engineer), 141
Smith, H.B. (pres. of Collingwood
Shipyard), 94
Smith-Inglis (S. Morgan Smith-Inglis
Co.), 65
Smy, William A., 277
Soulanges Canal (Quebec), 5, 31, 41, 43
Special Committee on the Enlargement
and Route of the Welland Canal (1872),
271
speeder cars, 64, 196, 198
Spielberg, Steven, 308n4
staff. *See* Ship Canal staff
Stanbury, William, 186
Standard Underground Cable
(Hamilton), 137
statues. *See* commemorations and
monuments
Statute of Westminster (1931), xx